A Crisis of Identity
ISRAEL AND ZIONISM

To Rosetta

DAN V. SEGRE

A Crisis of Identity

ISRAEL AND ZIONISM

Oxford New York Toronto Melbourne
OXFORD UNIVERSITY PRESS
1980

Oxford University Press, Walton Street, Oxford OX2 6DP

Oxford London Glasgow
New York Toronto Melbourne Wellington
Kuala Lumpur Singapore Hong Kong Tokyo
Delhi Bombay Calcutta Madras Karachi
Nairobi Dar es Salaam Cape Town

© *Dan V. Segre 1980*

British Library Cataloguing in Publication Data

Segre, D V

A crisis of identity.
1. Israel — Social conditions 2. Zionism
I. Title
309.1'5694'05   HN660.A8   79-41789
ISBN 0-19-215862-7

Printed in the United States of America

Contents

Introduction

In 1882 a book which was to make history appeared in Odessa. It was called *Auto-emancipation*. It was written in conditions of such a lack of emancipation that its author, Leon Pinsker (1821–91), a Jewish law student (who turned to medicine because of the difficulty for a Jew in becoming a lawyer in the Tsarist Russia of the time), thought it wise—in order to make an impact on his fellow Jews, who prayed in Hebrew, spoke in Yiddish, dealt with the authorities in Russian, and some of whom sang Sabbath hymns to the tune of the Marseillaise—to publish his book anonymously in German. *Auto-emancipation* became a milestone in the development of modern, secular Jewish political nationalism—Zionism. Indeed, it deserved study because it summarized the two conflicting trends—assimilation and anti-Semitism—which were shaking nineteenth-century Jewry in Eastern Europe, where almost the totality of Jews continued to live in a distinct, traditional, religious-national way. To fight against both trends a radical solution was needed through the acquisition of a Jewish homeland. Pinsker did not know at first whether it should be in Palestine or elsewhere (he thought in the Americas); a national Jewish Congress should decide on the proper location. Yet before his death Pinsker came to the conclusion that *Eretz Israel*—the Land of Israel—should remain a spiritual rather than a political centre for the Jews. Pinsker felt that necessary as Jewish self-emancipation was for the revival and survival of the Jews, the process could not be achieved just by international recognition of the Jewish right to an independent state nor by the creation of the state itself. This could only touch upon certain aspects of the Jewish question but not solve the question as a whole. Almost a century after the publication of Pinsker's book, and thirty years after the establishment of the State of Israel, the Jewish question has not been solved and new problems, no less unique in their complexity and essence than the old Jewish ones, have been created. Zionism itself remains an unfinished revolution. As in Camus' Sisyphus story, the destiny of the Jews seems to be not 'to roll the rock' but to give a warning to the rolling—to the tragedy of human life. In this sense, Zionism has added a new challenge to the old one of traditional Judaism: how to defend both the right to be like the others and at the same time the duty to remain different. If the achievement of the first right is undoubtedly the result of exemplary efforts of self-emancipation, the difficulties which the Israeli encounters in trying to define himself point to the existence of a crisis of identity which cannot be attributed to the complicated internal situation or to severe external pressures. The crisis has deep historical causes, a central one being that emancipation, through imitation of the West, has been politically successful but morally self-defeating.

How much has this emancipation been a means to an end and how much has it turned into an end in itself? To what extent has emancipation turned into self-colonization? To what degree have the efforts to create the outer forms of political freedom dried up the sources of spiritual and cultural independence?

If the case of Jewish political renaissance were unique in our times, Zionism might perhaps have been a less controversial phenomenon. But since the Jewish national revival is taking place alongside—its start, indeed, preceded—that of a whole colonized humanity, its particularism had become provocative for both old and new nations.

Seen in this light, it becomes easier to understand why Israel, Zionism, and the Palestinian problem have occupied the centre of the international scene almost since the end of the Second World War, to an extent out of all proportion to the territorial, demographic, economic, and even religious-ideological dimensions of the conflict itself. The surprising fact in all the political debates concerning the Middle East is not that the same arguments are repeated over and over again with few variations, despite the radical changes which have taken place in the international situation: it is that the debates have spread territorially and ideologically to cover countries and peoples which have little connection with the issues themselves: whatever the international influence of Israel, there is no logical justification for Russian propaganda condemning the Chinese for being Zionist fellow travellers.

The blowing-up of events connected with the Holy Land beyond all proportion is not, of course, historically speaking, a new phenomenon. If no excavation of ancient sites has ever created such an international furor as did the archaeological work carried out on the walls of Jerusalem, the Crimean War, which altered the political situation in Europe and in the Ottoman Empire, was sparked by a lesser event: the theft of a silver star from the crypt of the Church of the Nativity in Bethlehem. And if one wants to look for older cases of momentous events originating from the same geographical spot, one can ask why, among the tens of thousands of people crucified by the Romans all over their Empire, only the crucifixion of a Jew, in Jerusalem, changed the history of mankind.

The analysis of the 'Jewish question' in Israel is the central theme of this book. In chapter 2 it will be argued that the problem is not new, since there has always been a strong tendency within the Jewish people to 'throw off the yoke of the Law', to assimilate to the non-Jewish world, and to break away from Jewish particularism. Since the emancipation of the eighteenth century, the assimilation trend has been accompanied by a rapid decline in traditional Jewish culture and authority. Zionism found itself presiding not only over a political, military, and ideological struggle for national independence, but also over a process of growing alienation from that traditional culture upon which depended the consolidation of modern Jewish national identity.

Since development and alienation are the two common faces in the life of most of the new states of the world, an attempt has been made in chapter 3 to relate the Jewish/Israeli experience to that of African societies, where the search for national identity and the clash between tradition and modernity have created psychological and social situations similar, at least in certain aspects, to those prevailing in Israel.

With these background historical and sociological experiences in mind, chapter 4 tries to answer the question whether Jewish traditional culture (apart from religion) still retains enough consistency and originality to make it relevant to the life of a modern polity.

The situation of cultural alienation willingly accepted by the Jews, termed *self-colonization*, is the subject matter of the three chapters that follow. They will discuss how this alienation from tradition stands at the heart of the major contemporary crises of Israeli society: the crises of leadership, ideology, institutionalization, identity, and legitimacy.

This book does not deal with any metapolitical aspect of the Palestine question, nor does it speculate on the work of any 'invisible hand' running Middle Eastern affairs in some special way. It tries to look at the complex sociopolitical and ideological clusters of problems called Zionism and Israel from two angles, both strongly affected by personal experience. The first is the point of view of a person—myself—who, as an assimilated, non-Zionist Jew, has searched and not without difficulty found in traditional Judaism reasons for identification with a Jewish past and an Israeli present. The second point of view is that of a student of political development, with some experience in the process of decolonization in Africa, who has been impressed by the similarities between the impact of Westernization on Third World societies and on contemporary Israel.

This book had been nearly completed when the May 1977 elections put an end to the thirty years' rule of the Social Democrats and brought into power a right-wing coalition—the Likud—headed by Mr Menahem Begin. It was a major change which seemed to confirm many of the points argued in this study, and a natural consequence of that confused trend of cultural decolonization through a revival of political religious traditionalism which takes place in many countries of the Third World. A Postscript has thus been added, to show how the main thesis of this work fits into the recent events. It may give some indication of how the Israeli political society might develop in the future.

My treatment of the subject matter of this book is, therefore, a personal one and I make no attempt to conceal it. Much of any merit which it may possess must be attributed to the patience, perseverance, and erudition of members of the Seminar on Jewish Political Thought who, under the guidance of Rabbi Adin Steinsaltz, studied and discussed many of the central questions raised in this work. I am indebted to the Van Leer Jerusalem Foundation for having made it possible for this Seminar to continue for over four years. My friends and colleagues, Joseph Agassi, Gabriel Ben-Dor, Eli Ginzberg, Mark Karp, Hillel Levine and Yael Ishai, have generously contributed intelligent advice, encouragement, and useful suggestions at various stages of the preparation of the book. I owe them deep gratitude, which I must share with Devorah Bar-Zemer and Sheila Moser, who patiently edited many drafts of this manuscript, and with Lisa Kaufman, for her assistance in researching.

Another version of the substance of chapter 3 appears in *Comparative Studies in Sociology and History* (Ann Arbor: University of Michigan), Jan. 1980, vol. 22, no. 1.

Jerusalem 1978

CHAPTER 1

Zionism as a National Movement

This book tries to look at an old question from a new angle: why do the Jews, who appear to possess such great adaptive ability to the societies in which they live, remain so different from them? This question has turned into a major international problem since the return of the Jews to the active scene of contemporary history, through the rebirth of an independent Jewish polity. Like every other national state, this polity has a distinct personality of its own; sovereignty, after all, also recognizes the right to be different. Yet no one would deny the fact that the State of Israel is a very particular case. The interest it continuously raises in world opinion is not due only to the intensity and the centrality of its struggle with the Arabs. There is a strange element in Israeli internal and external politics which one is tempted to call metapolitical a uniqueness of fate which French writer Paul Giniewski stressed when he pointed out that the State of the Jews was rapidly becoming the 'Jew' among the States.

Some new light can be shed on the old problem of the uniqueness of the Jews, as a polity, if the manifold facets of Zionism and of its outcome, the State of Israel, are compared not only with .the multiple facets of Western national ideologies and political societies but also with those of the new states of the so-called Third World, and more specifically of Africa. On the one hand, it is felt that the very quick transition of the Jewish people from a closed traditional society to an open secular state presents many problems that have more in common with those of the non-European developing countries than with the experiences of European societies. On the other hand, the search for identity of a nation which seemed to have renounced its own ancient civilization in order to galvanize its energies and re-create political independence through an effort of ideological and social imitation of foreign models, is a process which demands close examination of the conscious and unconscious impact of Jewish political tradition on the Zionist movement and on the Israeli state.

The first comparison—that between Israel and the African states—has sometimes been superficially made by Third World admirers of the Zionist movement and by Israeli publicists, but never by students of Zionist or Israeli politics. The second comparison, between the impact of Jewish and

Western political traditions on Zionism and Israel, has never been attempted for the simple reason that most students of Judaism have denied, or taken little notice of, the existence of a specific Jewish political thought and its relevance to modern politics.

This type of analysis—that is, comparing Zionism with other national movements in the West and in the Third World, and comparing the impacts of old indigenous and new foreign political traditions on a new polity—raises two major methodological problems. The first is the appropriateness of using the same terms to indicate processes which, though belonging to an identical category of sociological events, developed in totally different historical frameworks. To what extent, for instance, do words like colonization, tradition, modernization, assimilation, decolonization have meaningful application to different historical experiences such as Zionism and, say, Ghanaian nationalism? The fact that both Jews and African intellectuals may express, and possibly feel, similar hopes and frustrations when facing problems of political independence and the difficulties of prolonged social and cultural struggles, does not necessarily mean that Jews, Africans, or Asians are influenced in a similar way by foreign domination and by assimilation to the same alien cultures. Yet what seems evident when comparing Jewish contemporary political experience with that of the nations of the Third World (so evident, in fact, that the comparison is seldom suggested) does not seem to apply to the relationship between the Jews and the West. The European-American model is taken almost for granted in any analysis of the Zionist and Israeli experience, with little consideration for the fact that Jewish emancipation in the West is a relatively new phenomenon for a people who lived in great cultural and social seclusion for almost eighteen centuries. Similarly, it is often forgotten that the majority of the Israeli population is made up of people who originate from Islamic countries, where the process of Westernization was later and more indirect. Nevertheless, in spite of the obvious lack of precision in applying terms such as colonization, assimilation, or decolonization to Israel as well as to the peoples of the Third World, the comparison of modern Jewish political experiences with those of non-European societies helps to underline interesting similarities and to stress the fact that Zionism stands somewhere between Western and non-Western modern national experiences and possesses a much greater originality than is usually thought.

The second major problem constantly faced in this study, and which may not have been fully overcome, is how to avoid an indiscriminate mix of ideology and history. This, of course, is the problem of all social historians, and their presentation of events lies more in the field of arts than in that of science, because of the subjective, and always to some extent arbitrary, choice made in the collection of documentary evidence to support their interpretation of history. Where Zionism and Israel are concerned, the choices are often more arbitrary because of the difficulty in following and evaluating properly the influence of ideas to which their members have been exposed and which have seeped through a thick palimpsest of Jewish history, disconnected by time lags and geographical dispersion while at the same time connected by the unity of the Jewish people. This unity, which is at the foundation of Jewish identity, is not easy to explain, at least according to non-Jewish sociological and political models. Attempts to interpret Jewish history are endangered by the temptation to use historical and ideological material too freely.

Rational theories and explanations for the contradictory reactions of the Jews to the multiple stimuli to which they were exposed during the nineteenth and twentieth centuries can and should be constructed on the basis of a careful study of documents, comparative ideology, economic data and so on. But how does a dramatic paradoxical personality like Theodor Herzl fit into the rational pattern of events? He was a man completely ignorant of Judaism who by sheer intuition became one of its truest prophets; he was a totally assimilated Jew who, because of his assimilation and his detachment from Jewish realities, could create a theoretical world of hopes which eventually—and against all political logic—succeeded in transforming individual dejection into collective power. Herzl was the incarnation of a Jewish ideal which was totally alien to his upbringing, environment, taste, education, and even to his lifelong profession: journalism. Explanations of Herzl's case (and Zionism is full of them) can hardly be given by professional historians or sociologists. Menahem Ussishkin, a stubborn opponent and Herzl's very opposite in temperament, education, and sociological background, came nearer to understanding the Herzlian phenomenon than many students of Zionism. After his first, rather unpleasant, meeting with the founder of Zionism in Vienna, he said: 'His greatest deficiency will be his most useful asset. He does not know the first thing about Jews. Therefore he believes that there are only external difficulties to Zionism, not internal ones. We shall not open his eyes, so that his faith remains potent.'[1] This seems to be 'non-ideology' grafted directly on to 'non-historical' expediency. But this is also what forged Zionism and Israel and caused its success in one of history's most bizarre and quixotic adventures. Some freedom in mixing history with ideology should thus be allowed to bring into clearer focus the manifold causes and unconventional processes which make the history of modern Israel so paradoxical and so full of surprises for the Jews, their admirers, and their much more numerous enemies.

Of all nineteenth- and twentieth-century national movements, Zionism has remained the most controversial. Like most things pertaining to Jews and Judaism, it looks unique, and to many people abnormal, because it differs from the accepted patterns of national identity. At the time of its birth and for many decades afterwards, there was no national precedent for a claim to sovereignty and political unity by a group of people, dispersed literally over five continents; speaking different languages and more or less assimilated to different cultures; deprived for centuries of a common territory and of what appeared at least from the outside to be a common authority; everywhere held in conditions of inequality for social, religious, or political reasons. Despite its abnormalcy and lack of military, economic, or diplomatic power, Zionism realized its aim: the creation of an independent State for the Jews in their ancestral land. This was done in less time than it took the Italian, Arab, or African nationalisms to realize their political dreams. In the wake of its success Zionism caused great antagonisms which already seem more firm than those created by Germanism, Slavism, Arabism, or any contemporary ideological or political movement.

The length and pugnacity of the Jewish national conflict can be explained through the unorthodox character of Jewish nationalism and its estrangement from acceptable models. In the case of the Jews, the prototype of the 'stranger-people' among the nations added to the fear and suspicions of its enemies, and even to those of the Jews.[2] However, if one regards Zionism as a collective expression of the will of a dispersed nation to recover its ancestral land, no other national movement is its superior in coherence, perseverance, antiquity, and idealism.

The Jewish historian Simon Dubnow is perhaps the strongest interpreter of this form of landless spiritual nationalism. He distinguishes between three types of nationalism: tribal, politico-territorial, and—the highest form of all—cultural-historical or spiritual.[3] To him, Jewish nationalism is the nearest to this last and most developed form. Jews are the clearest expression in history of a nation based primarily and exclusively on spiritual ideas. 'We have many examples in history of nations that have disappeared from the scene after they had lost their land and become dispersed among the nations. We find only one instance, however, of a people that has survived for thousands of years despite dispersion and loss of homeland. This unique people is the people of Israel.' The survival of the Jewish nation is not a miracle: it is the product of Jewish historical development, which in the course of 2,000 years has converted the Jewish people from just a nation into 'the very essence of nationhood', that is, the highest form of nationalism.

Even though Dubnow's arguments are not acceptable to a modern rationalist, much of the debate on the aims and virtues of contemporary Jewish nationalism still revolves around the dichotomy between its 'very essence of nationhood' and 'lower' forms of nationalism of the politico-territorial or even tribal type. The passions and the confusion which have accompanied the idea of the Jewish return to the Land of Canaan—the ancestral home of the Jewish people—must, therefore, make it imperative that the term 'Zionism' be clarified from the outset.

If one accepts as valid the long definition of Zionism given by the Israeli delegate to the United Nations, the description of the Jewish national movement is a dramatized summary of Jewish history.[4] 'Zionism', said Ambassador Joseph Tekoah,

is the love of Zion; it is the liberation movement of the Jewish people, its search for freedom and equality with the other nations of the world. . . . When the Jews, exiled from their land in the seventh century before the Christian era, sat on the shores of the rivers of Babylon crying, but also praying and trying to recover their country, that was already Zionism. . . . When they became the last people in the whole Mediterranean basin to resist the Roman Empire and to fight for their independence, that was again Zionism. . . . When, under a succession of foreign conquests of their land they tried again and again to recover their sovereignty at least over a small part of their country, that, too, was Zionism. When volunteers from Palestine and other countries joined together to create the Jewish units in World War I, aiding the Allied armies to break the yoke of the Ottoman power, that was Zionism. . . . When they created the Jewish Brigade in the Second World War to fight against Hitler while the Arab leaders supported him, that was Zionism. When they moved towards the gas chambers murmuring with tenderness the name of Jerusalem with their lips, that also was Zionism. When the Jews fought against British colonialism, it was again and always Zionism. Zionism is one of the oldest anti-imperialist movements of the world.

Zionism in this case becomes the political expression of Judaism as a whole, a claim romantically and religiously appealing but hard to defend historically. It has little to do, in any case, with that particular secular nationalist Jewish movement—political Zionism—which Theodor Herzl[5] prophetically founded in 1897, and which, through the establishment of the State of Israel half a century later, also created the first community of Jews officially dissociated from the idea that the Jews are a people distinguished from others by their special relationship with God.

The clash between the two conceptions of Zionism, secular and non-secular (the term 'religious' is a misleading one since Judaism is a collective way of life and not only a relationship between God and man), dates back to the emergence of modern Jewish nationalism itself. It should not be surprising, therefore, that despite their daily prayers for the return of the Jews to their ancestral land, most Jewish traditionalists opposed the Herzlian programme. For a long time so did most of the liberal, wealthy Jews of Western Europe—those who believed in the solution of the Jewish problem through European socialism and communism, assimilation, and even—as in the case of Italian Jews—through the Fascist revolution. This is not the place to retrace the history of Zionism and of its enemies, Jewish and Gentile: a large literature exists on the subject.[6] The point to be made is that the dissociation of Zionism (conceived as a national movement of a nineteenth-

century type) from Judaism (conceived as a religion in the Western sense)
has been, from the early days of the Jewish national movement, the cause
of a dangerous over-simplification of the very complex revolutionary process of Jewish decolonization in the last century; of the revival of one of
the oldest and richest, though apparently defunct, civilizations; and of the
unexpected return of the Jewish factor into world history. Such a momentous event, heightened by the double drama of the Jewish holocaust in
politically dwindling Europe and the military and ideological confrontation between Israel and the Arab and Communist world, was bound to
create much confusion about the aims and nature of Zionism. This confusion exists not because it is intentionally promoted by Israel's enemies: it
is to a large extent the product of the conflicting views which the Jews
themselves hold on the nature of Zionism and Judaism. Some continue to
see in Zionism solely the content of the Basle Programme laid down by
Theodor Herzl at the First Zionist Congress in 1897, namely a political
movement for ameliorating the lot of persecuted Jews. Others, as the Israeli
representative's speech at the UN shows, see in Zionism the permanent
political expression of Judaism. And yet others, as witnessed by contemporary rabbinical liturgy, believe the creation of the State of Israel to be
'the beginning of the commencement' of the messianic salvation of Israel.
Many also hoped—at least until very recently—that Zionism could realize
a model 'just society', in which the socialist heroism of a modern Spartacus would combine with the Jewish wisdom of the ancient prophets to
create a new 'chosen' people capable of realizing both the utopias of the
Gentile societies in which the Jews suffered as second-class citizens, and
their own messianic dreams.

   But Judaism as an idea and a living reality is something very different
from these stereotyped conceptions which, without exception, reflect a
process which fits Cooley's sociological theory of the 'looking-glass self',
that is, the shaping of self-images according to the perception of how other
people see us.[7] For the modern Jew, to conceive Judaism solely in 'religious' terms or as a moral code, in accordance with ideas prevailing in
Western secular societies about religion and morals (namely a system of
beliefs or values practised by individuals according to their personal taste
or accepted social conventions with little or no relation to politics or
national ideologies), is an expression of a state of cultural dependence
common to a people subjected to colonial rule. At the same time, for
those to whom Judaism—whether practised or not—remains the only possible legitimation for the return of the Jews to their ancestral land and for
the creation of a state of their own in the middle of the Arab world, Jewish
tradition in its rabbinical form has not been able to evolve sufficiently to
face the challenges of modernity and of contemporary social and political
ideology.

The result has been a confused and paradoxical situation of self-justification through the looking-glasses of others, which has not stood up to the challenge of rational criticism and has prodded atheist Jews into supporting talmudic legislation because of its importance for the national identity of the Zionist state, and orthodox Jews into challenging the right of existence of the Jewish State itself. Small wonder that contradictions like these are easily exploited by Israel's enemies to accuse it of political hypocrisy and ideological false pretences.

Things become clearer if we remember that Zionism, in spite of its European origins and historical affinities with other non-Jewish national movements, is no more and no less than the attempt to translate the ideal unity of the Jewish people into a real unity centred in the soil of the land of Israel. Zionism is founded primarily on the fact of the existence of a group of individuals whose common tradition entitles them to be called a people, and secondly on the fact that this group of persons possesses common ideals and an outlook on life which are unique and never fully shared by the rest of the world. These are fundamental facts which were not created by anti-Semitism, although the life of the Jews since the Emancipation, more than in any other period, has been influenced by external conditions.

Zionism has helped to infuse vitality into Jewish national life. To live Judaism and only Judaism without the Jewish homeland is to live a partial and restricted life. To go beyond that restricted life without a homeland is to accept and eventually yield to assimilation.[8] The dissociation of Zionism from Judaism was the inevitable historical result of the emancipation of the Jews in Western society and of the process of their cultural assimilation to the West (and to a lesser extent in the Islamic countries, where no clearcut separation between religion and state yet exists). Through assimilation they also accepted as valid many stereotyped and negative views held by the Gentiles and the Jews, fruit of an ignorance of Jewish culture, values, history, and social development, which the emancipated Jew now increasingly shared with his Gentile compatriot. Jewish indiscriminate acceptance of non-Jewish images of the Jews made them less resistant to the two aspects which, in different conditions and at different levels of perception, have been central to the experience of both emancipated Jew and secular Zionist. One is the irrational opposition of the anti-Semite and anti-Zionist to what appeared to be a rational solution to the old Jewish question: assimilation of the individual Jew into the non-Jewish society and acceptance of the secular national state of the Jews into the family of nations. The second is the increasing cultural dependence of the Jewish society on alien sources and values, and the much greater cultural contribution of the best Jewish minds and hearts to the causes of the Gentile societies than to their own. The result has been that a people admired in the past for its extraordinary ability to develop an original, rich civilization of its own, is today faced with a cultural sterility that leads to one of the highest percentages of brain-drain in the history of any people.

So much has been written about anti-Semitism and about the tragic process which transformed the failure of Western society to absorb the emancipated Jew into a destructive hate against him as a member of a 'foreign' minority, that there is no need here to return to the subject. Less is known about the complex, and more recent, process which has transferred the same irrational hate for the Jew, as the prototype of the enemy, from the individual Jew to the Jewish Zionist polity. The French philosopher Jankelevicz sees in this transfer of hate an example of the metamorphosis of human libido in permanent search of new symbolic expression. To him, anti-Zionism is today what anti-Semitism was yesterday for the Jew-hater, but with one important difference: it provides the anti-Semite with a motive for the 'duty', not just the 'right', to persecute the Jews in their Israeli incarnation, in the name of world revolution, anticolonialism and anti-imperialism.[9]

Let us turn now to the second negative experience of the emancipated Jew, which Zionism, as a secularized national movement, has had to face from the start: ideological dependence upon alien culture, the steriliza-tion of its own, and the massive switch of Jewish brains from fields of interest and research connected with Judaism to those of the Gentile world. (These well-known and well-documented phenomena of nineteenth- and twentieth-century Jewish society are present in all colonial, non-European societies as well.) If the colonial status of European Jewry can be contested, the similarity of trends among modern Jews in the Diaspora and in Israel cannot be ignored as indicators of a 'colonial' psychological and cultural situation which exists despite the integration of the Jews in Western society and the spirited political and economic development of the Jewish state. To speak of the cultural colonization of the Jewish people and of the Israeli society may also sound surprising in view of the fact that only rarely were the Jews forced to change their traditional way of life and to abandon their own culture. It was they who wholeheartedly threw themselves into the arms of European culture and accepted as a great blessing, first emancipation and then the westernization which fol-lowed.

In this sense the case of the Jews is very different from that of the nations of Africa and Asia who were subject to colonial conquest. This Jewish acceptance of foreign social and cultural values makes it more dif-ficult to distinguish between assimilation and colonization. However, a deeper look into the history of the colonization of non-European societies reveals a similar difficulty in distinguishing between colonization and assi-milation. A whole school of economic historians have shown, for instance, that the 'devil theory' of imperialism is not substantiated by facts.[10] This approach maintains that in the fields of culture and ideology the colonized nations have drawn heavily upon the alien intellectual sources of the metropolitan conquerors. Oppression, be it colonialism or anti-Semitism, always helps to increase the desire of the inferior group to assimilate into the superior one, and particularly when the inferior group believes that through this assimilation it can best learn how to break the artificial barriers of discrimination which the stronger impose upon the weaker. In every colonial situation, therefore, there is a stage at which the élites of the conquered society consider that self-alienation is an indispensable step towards achieving self-determination, and that the imitation of the conqueror will eventually reveal the secret of his strength and ultimately lead to freedom. One must stress the fact that in spite of the totally different conditions in which Jewish and Third World nationalism developed, there are similarities between the two, and these throw light on aspects of their development which would be inexplicable if measured only against models of European nationalism. One should not be surprised, therefore, if in spite of great cultural and geographical differences, the history of Jewish and African societies is full of examples of extraordinary similarities of political behaviour.* Some of these will be discussed in chapter 3.

Clearly colonization is a very complex process, in which the will of the stronger to be different and remain apart is always accompanied by the desire of the weaker to emulate him and to close the gaps. The reason is to be found not only in the psychological dilemma of the love/hate relationship which characterizes the victim/victimizer situation but in the very nature of Europe's colonization of the world, an historical phenomenon which 'was neither a chain of crimes nor a chain of beneficence: it was the birth of a modern world itself'.[13] In consequence, dependent peoples, including the Jews, demanded—despite all ideological resistance—more and not less Europeanization. It is, after all, one of the characteristics of the modern world that all groups with any kind of common political self-consciousness tend to be politically independent, even if their 'nationhood' is an accident of very recent history, as witnessed by the case of the islands of Seychelles.

*For instance, after Theodor Herzl had convened the First Zionist Congress in Basle in 1897, he was attacked by the Rabbinical Council of Germany, a body of well-established Jewish *évolués* despite their attachment to religious tradition. They recalled, *inter alia*, that 'Judaism obliges its adherents to serve the Fatherland to which they belong'.[11] Blaise Diagne, a typical French African *évolué* and the first black deputy from Senegal to sit in the Paris parliament, declared after the second Pan-African Congress of 1922 in London (the first ever to ask for equal rights for blacks and whites) that 'we French blacks want to remain French, France having given us every liberty and mingled us without reservation with her own European children'.[12]

Jewish nationalism, indeed, remained inexplicable for a long time to many Western ideologists, with tragic effects for the Jews. How, after all, would it have been possible to apply to them the dictum 'mankind instinctively takes refuge in language as the badge of nationalism'[14] when they had no common spoken language? This was one of the reasons for the inability of Stalin to regard the Jews as one of the many nations of the USSR. For the former Commissar for Soviet Nationalities, 'there is no nation which at one and the same time speaks several languages'.[15] But the advanced interpretation of nationalism of a Jew and Zionist student of nationalism such as Hans Kohn hardly fits the development of modern Jewish political revival. He believed, for instance, that national political revivals are likely to be preceded by a revival and reformation of basic religious principles and general outlook of the rising nation.[16] With the Jews, nationalism was rather the outcome of the decadence of Jewish religion, while Jewish reformism, which followed the emancipation of the Jews in Europe, was one of Zionism's fiercest enemies.

Yet despite these and many other elements differentiating Zionism from other nationalisms, neither the movement for Jewish independence nor its result, Israeli society, could avoid the effects of westernization similar to those experienced by other colonized societies. The most prominent common symptom was the development of a self-image drawn from the negative images developed by the West of both the Jews and other colonial peoples. In this particular sense it seems legitimate to apply the term colonial to the cultural situation of the modern Jew in Israel and to underline in such terms those fields within the Israeli society which particularly resemble the most colonized aspects of non-European societies: decay of traditional systems of education and values, psychological alienation, excessive self-criticism, exaggerated admiration for the imported culture. The cultural colonization of the modern Jew, in the Diaspora and in Israel, has expressed itself more than elsewhere by a greater, more spontaneous and successful, ability to imitate the alien environment. This represents a truly revolutionary break with the Jewish past, when the traditional culture and system of education were so strong that Jews were unwilling, despite persecution or economic and social incentives, to change their own way of life for that of the Gentile societies in which they lived.

However, in view of the different political and social conditions obtaining for Jews in the Diaspora and in Israel, one must also underline the process of Jewish assimilation. In the Diaspora, Jewish particularism has remained linked to religion, and in its absence, either to expressions of solidarity with the State of Israel or to social and intellectual ferment which has brought Jews to the forefront of almost every field of activity. But even Jewish orthodoxy, with few exceptions, has made great efforts to adapt itself to the ways of the Gentile world. Diaspora Jewry neither desires nor attempts to 'decolonize' itself, even while some serious effort is made to preserve its Jewish identity, Jewish language, and traditional Jewish values.

The situation in Israel is different and more complicated. On the one hand, the emergence of the Jewish State did not stop the process of assimilation by the Israeli Jew to alien cultures but only transferred this process from the level of the individual to the collective. The trend to create for the Jews 'a state like any other state' has been accompanied by the desire to create in Israel a society of Jews like any other society—which leads to serious identity problems, if Jews are to remain Jews. On the other hand, the very fact of the physical return of large numbers of Jews to their ancestral land, the revival of the language of the Bible as a day-to-day idiom, the rapid development of centres of traditional learning—from 'religious' elementary schools to 'religious' universities, from traditional *kibbutzim* to *Yeshivot Hesder* (lit. Adapted Rabbinical Academies), élite fighting units of talmudic scholars—has in many ways brought the Israelis back to the sources of their own civilization. No less important for the crystallization of a Jewish consciousness in Israel has been the uninterrupted state of war in which the State has been living since its creation, its forced political solitude. Lastly the anti-Semitic libido has been transferred from the individual Jew to the State of the Jews and to the political movement that created that State, Zionism. These external pressures have combined to strengthen the sense of national unity of the Israeli Jew and intensify the search for a common denominator which could only be found in that cultural tradition which had kept the Jewish people alive and united through the centuries.

In so far as the growing feeling of a Jewish identity is expressed in a variety of ways in the Israeli society, side by side with the equally growing desire of the majority of Israelis to continue to live according to the moral, social, and economic ideals of the Western world, it has been largely responsible for the misinterpretation of many aspects of the behaviour of the Jewish State in international life and in its internal politics, as well as for the false images of Israel often projected.

It is a fact that Jewish nationalism is at the same time similar to and different from other national movements. Israeli Marxism appears heretical to Communism and yet is so close to the ideals of the October Revolution that Israel could be said to be the only successful menshevik experiment in the world. Judaism offers no clear division between religion and secularism, notwithstanding the extreme positions taken by both secularist and religious Jews in favour of the two opposing views of man's destiny. All these facts are a source of permanent surprise for the non-Jew who often loses his bearings when confronted by the manifold aspects of the Jewish problem.

In the past, the strangeness of the Jew, his religious particularism, his refusal to act, dress, speak, or eat 'like the others' was one of the roots of anti-Semitism. The Jew was 'the enemy' because he was 'different'. Hitler based his whole campaign of hate against the Jews on man's primordial fear of the unknown. Today, part of the psychological hostility felt towards the State of Israel by Arabs and non-Arabs alike comes as much from its difference as from its uniqueness. These are made more unacceptable by the political and ideological environment in which the State of Israel was created, by the Zionist claim to be the second oldest (after the Egyptians) of any Middle Eastern people, combined with a strange declaration of 'normalcy' through the acceptance of Western ways of life, ideology, and institutions. This ambivalence is in itself a source of suspicion and hostility. Compare, for instance, the reaction of a non-Jew to the Indian and Israeli ways of life. A tourist in India may or may not understand the symbolic significance of a sacred cow. Yet when his car is stopped by one of these animals in the street he will wait more or less patiently till the road is cleared without feeling offended or cheated by the Indian custom. The same traveller to Israel will probably react in a similar way when confronted by an Orthodox Jew with long side-locks, dressed in his black caftan, who refuses to allow him to drive through his neighbourhood on the Sabbath. He may think that such behaviour is an expression of anachronistic fanaticism but he will not feel offended or cheated by it. But in a good tourist hotel that same traveller will feel at first exactly as he would in any first-class hotel in Europe or America, faced with exactly the same type of organizational system, administrative behaviour, technological facilities and problems. And he will expect similar treatment. This impression will be strengthened by the fact that most Israelis he meets in the hotel, on the street, or in the cafés dress, speak, and behave like Westerners. But if our traveller asks for milk in his black coffee after his steak dinner, he is told that he cannot have it because his request goes against a biblical dietary law which does not permit 'cooking a calf in its mother's milk'. To make the situation more confusing, few Israelis (most of whom accept the strange milk-in-coffee prohibition as a matter of course) will be able to give him an acceptable explanation. Either they cannot explain the logic of the traditional rule, or they feel ashamed to justify it. Most would resort to a political explanation based on the government's need to maintain the status quo between the secular and the religious parties.

To the foreign traveller, explanations of this type are not convincing and could, in fact, often be irritating, since he might feel himself cheated by what appears to him—and to many Israelis—to be a double standard of behaviour. The trivial example of the milk-in-the-after-dinner-coffee may possibly belong to the same category of social phenomena produced by the clash between tradition and modernity which in India obliges the driver to stop for a sacred cow. But the outcome is very different, inasmuch as the relationship between past and present in Israel seems to strengthen that 'abnormality', that uniqueness of the Jewish case which arouses suspicion because of its inability to explain itself to the outside world or to fit into the social models of the Gentile societies.

The situation is embarrassing for many Israelis. There exists a permanent demand by secularist movements in Israel for a clear separation between state and religion as well as for legislation which would allow individuals 'officially' to discard their Jewish nationality in favour of a less complicated Israeli one.[17] However, because of the lack of political support for these movements among the public, coalition governments, with one or two exceptions, have always included religious parties who place demands on daily state practices in return for supporting government defence and foreign policy. This fact, plus the great passions aroused by court decisions attempting to define Jewish identity in the country and in the Diaspora, are clear indications of the consensus existing among Jews in favour of perpetuating many irrational aspects of the coexistence of tradition and modernity in Israel. It is not the result of hypocrisy, although hypocrisy and politics certainly thrive on it. It is the expression of a deep-rooted desire, even among the most secularist Jews, to avoid a frontal clash between Jewish tradition and assimilation, a clash which could destroy the Jewish basis on which Israel founds its complex national consciousness. The uneasy and delicate balance maintained between tradition and change is to be seen not only as the outcome of the inability to choose, but also as an indication of the efforts employed by modern Israel to cope with the dilemmas of collective national tradition and collective trends towards assimilation. The Zionist/Israeli struggle for the right to be equal and the right to be different is inevitably confusing for the outsider, particularly if he is not North American. But in spite of its sometimes negative and startling appearances, it does represent a very sincere effort by the Israelis to defend their Jewish identity. In this sense it seems legitimate to apply to this struggle the term 'cultural decolonization'. Here again, the paradoxical aspects of the behaviour of the Israeli society can be better understood if they are regarded from a non-Western angle; for instance, from the point of view of African societies which—though in a very different historical and sociological context—have to face problems of national identity similar to those of modern Jews.

CHAPTER 2

The Anguish of the Jewish Victory

A comparison of Israel's situation in 1948 and in 1978 reveals two out-standing facts: an increase in the State's power and material resources, and a decrease in its self-confidence.

In 1948 the Arab armies were situated in Jaffa, in the old and new Jewish quarters of Jerusalem and of Haifa; Tiberias and Safed were isolated; to the besieged Israelis Beersheba was no more than a distant point on the map, miles away to the rear of the Egyptian army. Israel had no air force to match that of the Arabs, no artillery, no armour. Its military industry produced primitive hand grenades and Sten guns but not nearly enough ammunition to supply them. Its economic resources were practically nil: some $15 million in exports, mainly oranges; the new state had to import even nails, had no fleet, no administrative infrastructure, no energy re-sources, not enough water for agriculture, no allies in Europe, no friends in Asia, and no special political sympathy in the diplomatic circles of the USA. When the invasion of the five Arab armies had been beaten off, the 'invasion' of hundreds of thousands of Jewish refugees began. There were no houses ready for them, no jobs, not enough food, no schools, no trans-port. There was only hope, not necessarily by the world at large which expected the new state to fall apart at any moment. 'Give up the Negev desert, which in any case Israel will never be able to defend, in exchange for Arab understanding', was the advice the US Secretary of State, J. F. Dulles, gave to Israel after a 24-hour visit to Tel Aviv in 1952.[1] Dulles is no more and Israel has considerably expanded the areas under her con-trol. Her army remains the strongest in the Middle East; her economy has turned from a backward colonial one into a highly industrialized one. The peace treaty with Egypt has legitimized, at least in the eyes of the largest Arab state, the Jewish right to build a state of their own in Palestine.

To anyone who looks back at the State of Israel a quarter of a century ago, its human, political, military, and economic achievements should seem miraculous. And yet never has Israeli society been so full of self-doubt: of its destiny, of its very right to exist as a sovereign nation; never has the world looked more hostile to the Jewish State or have its enemies —Arabs, Communists, Leftists, Rightists—been more determined to see the 'legend of Jewish farmers and workers' exploded. In a world where no one dreams of asking Soviet Russia to relinquish her European military conquests, her Asiatic colonial empire, her discriminatory restriction of internal travel; in which no one thinks it realistic to ask the Turks to get out of Cyprus or the Iraqis to stop oppressing the Kurds—the chorus of accusations against Israeli colonialism, imperialism, racism, and theocracy has become a permanent feature of international diplomacy. The 600,000 Palestinian Arab refugees residing in neighbouring countries, who have since doubled in number through demographic increase and the 1967 war, together with the million living and economically thriving in the Israeli-occupied West Bank, have come to be equated with the six million Jews murdered by the Nazis. One Arab casualty in a demonstration in Jerusalem attracts more attention in the world media than a thousand dead in Lebanon. Never has the Israeli State felt more isolated, more misunderstood, politically and economically more dependent on foreign goodwill, than at a moment when it alone, perhaps, among the developing, non-oil-producing nations of the world, is neither suffering from a crucial energy crisis nor yet feeling the pinch of unemployment. Nor does it fear the danger of another Arab attack. It does not have to cope with widespread social unrest like Italy, with civil disrupters like Ireland, with political instability like the Arab countries, with famine like Africa, or with an ideological crisis like the Communist world. And yet the image of the State of Israel in the late seventies is one which can be summarized in one word: uncertainty.

The Israeli author-engineer Joseph Duriel says Israel is in trouble because it is a system which has run amok: it has lost its sense of direction (like a ship whose skipper has failed to chart a course); it is breaking down because of the fatigue of its components (like an aeroplane with metal fatigue). It is a system overburdened, like an electrical grid, by tension without appropriate 'transformers', that is, appropriate leadership and institutions.[2]

This mechanistic and simplistic analysis can be placed at one end of the spectrum of criticism—the socio-technological. At the opposite end another type of criticism, the religio-political, stands in sharp contrast, as summarized in a letter sent to the Hebrew daily *Ha'aretz* by Professor Yishayahu Leibowitz.[3] The well-known biologist, philosopher, and talmudic scholar of the Hebrew University of Jerusalem wrote:

The character of Israeli society and of its statehood have been decided by the fact that 3 million human beings of Jewish origin define themselves in Israel as a new people without history and without tradition, without ideology or values. All this is lacking because this people is made up of Jews who in their great majority (or at least in their élites) break the link with the essential content of the historic Jewish people, namely with Judaism. . . . It is not a Jewish people which builds a state for itself, but a state which builds a people for itself. Therefore the only collective national content, the only collective value, is the State. . . . The national content does not express itself except as patriotic nationalism which becomes the 'religion' of this (new) people. . . . Israeli society, detached from Judaism, cannot fill its own national framework except with content taken from the West. . . . But Western culture cannot appear in the Israeli context except as an imitation, often as a caricature of itself. It does not show the best but the worst aspects of Western culture, such as the permanent search for the pleasures of an ever-rising standard of self-fulfilling material life; such as an extremist form of humanism, paralysed in its social sensitivity, bestialized by entertainment, sport, eroticism and pornography; such as a fanatic enthusiasm and reverence for military heroism.

In between these two types of mechanistic and idealistic criticism, many other aspects of the Israeli malaise are analysed in an atmosphere of self-denunciation which has almost become an intellectual fashion. Zionism, for instance, is described as a national movement similar to that of neo-Hellenism in modern Greece. Zionism is a movement born in a situation of exile. Ridiculed by the new generation, it has turned into a kind of Freudian unconscious revolt against its own spiritual 'father'—traditional Judaism. Israel, like Don Quixote, is intentionally dividing itself: while on the one hand it believes itself still to be the 'People of the Book', of social justice, a nation of special qualities, on the other it passionately desires to break away from its past. This has produced a process of cultural alienation and spiritual self-castration, more dangerous for the Jews than for other new nations. Jews are Jews only because of the idea of Judaism, not because of collective residence in a particular land. Thus, the breakaway from their own culture endangers the very source of the nationhood which Zionism should have preserved, defended, and developed. In similar vein, a socialist theorist like Eliezer Livneh claims that Zionism was a national-secular ideology, upheld by 'men who were brainwashed by the *Haskalah* (Enlightenment) and Western assimilation'.[4] In the eyes of its visionaries and founders, it was seen simply as one of the many national movements of Eastern Europe, and the future Jewish society in the Land of Israel was pictured as a branch of secular European society. Zionism has also been characterized by its ambition to solve the Jewish problem, which was understood mainly as the problem of the disintegration of ghetto life and of the tensions—mainly socio-economic—which such disintegration produced among the Gentiles. It was not a movement aimed at the revival of Jewish civilization.

As a result, with the obliteration of European Jewry the state created by Zionism became, in a sense, a state without a nation, since the majority of the surviving Diaspora Jews, for whom the ghetto problem had been solved through assimilation, no longer felt any impulse to emigrate from the Diaspora to the Land of Israel. 'Zionism lost its roots. Its complete degeneration was the fruit of historic logic', concludes Livneh, and as a result the modern secular national movement for Jewish political independence dried up from both the theoretical and moral points of view. Israel is in danger of turning into a Levantine province, imitating either demonstratively or quietly the 'good life' of America, and unable to reach the hearts of the élites of Western Jewry.

To the Israeli historian Jacob L. Talmon[5] the principal characteristic of Zionism was the combination of the two most potent and most history-minded of modern ideologies—nationalism and socialism. Both were to lead Israel into ideological bankruptcy; both helped to transplant into the victorious Israel of 1967 and the morally and militarily shaken country of 1973 the equally self-defeating myths of religious nationalism and egalitarian socialism which identified Israel with ethnic expansionism and Western imperialism. Thus Zionism produced in Israel a trend of polarization towards 'a type of Integro-Nationalism' on the one hand, and towards 'a decline of Zionist faith and self-criticism verging on nihilism' on the other.

Critics of Zionism, especially those opposed to it from a traditional Jewish point of view, may perhaps be exaggerating the seriousness of the Zionist predicament, but they are right to warn Israelis against the dangers of a modern, permissive way of life. Their criticism could equally well be directed against any form of contemporary capitalist or communist consumer society, but it is more relevant for a Jewish consumer society because Judaism by definition means opposition to and revulsion against all types of idolatry, certainly against those, old and new, which symbolize and exalt material needs over spiritual values. In a modern, materialistic world, in which the fascination of the body, especially in its erotic expression, has become a central focus of interest and accepted as a fountainhead of creativity, Judaism finds itself confronted from within and from without by that very lack of spirituality against which it has fought throughout its existence and by which it has been conditioned—by reaction—from generation to generation. The central question of Zionism and Israel, the 'new Jewish Question', is turning from the problem of physical survival to that of spiritual survival, and of the ability to resist the pressures of the new, pagan world.

The very biblical, prophetic type of criticism used by people like Professor Leibowitz to proclaim the mortal dangers faced by Israel remind us that the problem is not a new one in the long history of the Jews. On the contrary, it is the *permanently recurring problem* of Judaism. The Hebrew people faced it at the time of Moses, when they had to choose between the 'flesh pots of Egypt' and the wilderness of freedom; when, as a group of conquering tribes, they entered the prosperous and civilized land of Canaan and soon found themselves torn between their allegiance to the stern moral code of behaviour accepted in the Sinai and the far less exacting local customs. The dilemma of assimilation versus self-assertion was faced in the old biblical states of Judaea and Israel; at the time of the scribe Ezra, who insisted that those returned from Babylon divorce their indigenous wives as a precondition for the re-establishment of the Jewish commonwealth,[6] and again more dramatically during the Maccabean period.

The phenomenon is thus as old as Jewish history. Even before the Jews became 'a people', at a time when they were still—according to the Bible— members of one family, we find the dilemma of self-consciousness versus assimilation symbolized in the personalities of the Patriarchs. Abraham is the revolutionary aristocrat, who breaks his ties with the past and chooses new ways of life and a new faith for himself, his descendants, and the whole of humanity. He is the austere nonconformist who—according to the talmudic legend—when he decided to break with his pagan past, 'looked around to see how people were dressed, and then adopted clothing which was totally different from the others'.[7] Yet even at the time of the Patriarchs the call for Jewish aloofness was not always heard. Abraham's great-grandson, Joseph, despite his many personal virtues, and the fact that he did wilfully choose exile, already becomes the archetype of the assimilated and conformist Jew. Married to an Egyptian princess, he changes his name and hesitates to return to his native land. Like so many contemporary Diaspora Jews, he provides his 'tribe' with food, shelter, and protective political influence at a time of material stress, but at the price of assimilation and growing involvement in an alien culture and way of life.

The basic model of the Jewish question—élitist nativism versus populist cosmopolitanism—seems to repeat itself over and over again and does not change with time or geography. The story becomes better documented as the Jews advance into history—when, for instance, they are brought into the Hellenistic sphere by the Macedonian conquest of the Middle East (332 BCE). For about two centuries Judaea played the uncomfortable role of the apple of discord between the Hellenistic dynasties of Syria and Egypt, first as a Syrian-Macedonian province and later (165–63 BCE) as a more or less independent Maccabean state. Throughout this period a considerable section of the Jews, and certainly the upper class, came under the spell of the 'beauty of Japhet'. They accepted and promoted assimilation in language, social manners, political reasoning and so on, to such an extent that the expression 'stretching of the prepuce' (relating to the plastic surgery undergone by Jews to hide their circumcision in order to take part in athletic games) became a *terminus technicus* in the Talmud indicating the trend of cultural conformism and assimilation, and indeed a process of cultural self-colonization of the Jews *vis-à-vis* the Hellenistic world. Dubnow notes that in the case of Hellenism, the conflict was sharpened under the increasingly Hellenized Maccabean dynasty by the dualism represented by the clash between the national religious and the national political trend. 'Sooner or later one of the two elements, the priestly or the secular, [was] bound to prevail over the other and crush it. In the Judaean realm, with its profound religious trend, the priestly element gained the ascendancy and political ruin ensued.' He also recalls that when the Pharisees revolted against the warlike policies of the great Jewish king Alexander Yannai, they did so not because they rejected the idea of a Jewish State but because the Maccabean state had become so different from the one they had dreamt of when it was first established. Has Judaea battled against the Syrian yoke, they asked, for a quarter of a century sacrificed its material goods and the blood of its best sons, only in order to become, after achieving independence, a warrior state after the fashion of its pagan neighbours? The question has a familiar ring in modern Israel.[8]

In the time of the Maccabees the internal tension between assimilation and cultural self-sufficiency was not eased by the existence of a prosperous Hellenized Jewish Diaspora, dispersed over the Greek—and later Roman—Empire. This Diaspora adopted Hellenized customs and culture to the point where it could no longer pray in its own national language—hence the need for the Septuagintal translation of the Bible into Greek.

Living in the midst of a non-Jewish population, the Jews had to face not only the hostility of their neighbours but their own inner conflict, often greater than that faced by the martyrs of Jerusalem, when at least good and evil were clearly opposed to one another. Their problem indeed was that of the modern Diaspora Jew, called upon to choose between traditionalism and modernism, orthodoxy and liberalism. The efforts of the philosopher, Philo of Alexandria, to harmonize the 'claim of the God of Israel with the claim of intellectual culture, an opposition which exists not only between man and man but within man himself', was of little help to the Jews. So little, indeed, that it was left to the Christian Church to salvage his works and raise him almost to the rank of a Doctor of the Church. The Jewish Rabbis all over the world preferred to go back to their original Hebrew scriptures.

The love/hate relation to Judaism of Gentiles is equally old. When the Greeks first met the Jews they were surprised but certainly not repelled by their 'oddity'. In the early period of the Macedonian conquest of the Middle East two of Aristotle's disciples, Clearchus and Theophrastus, who according to a current though doubtful historical tradition are considered to be the first Greek writers to mention the Jews, described them as a community of 'philosophers' living according to a system of life befitting the idea of public stability and order which the Greek cities had dreamt about but never achieved. 'They spend their time', wrote Theophrastus, 'conversing on divine matters and observing the stars at night, calling upon the Divinity the while as they do so.' Hecataeus of Abdera, a Greek historical writer and a contemporary of Theophrastus, described the community in

Jerusalem, its symbolic symmetry and its punctual discipline, with the twelve tribes corresponding to the twelve months of the year, its youth trained as in Sparta, to courage and endurance.[9]

Once the Jews stopped being an odd, secluded people, however, and started to live in increasing numbers among the Greeks in the Diaspora, things changed very quickly. Their exclusiveness and assumption of religious superiority began to mean trouble and to give rise (initially in Alexandria in all probability) to what has been known—since the beginning of the nineteenth century—as anti-Semitism. The historian Y. F. Baer writes that it was an inevitable consequence of the Jews' exalted consciousness of religious superiority and of their mission among the nations, a consciousness all the more infuriating because it exists in a nation totally without power.[10]

Anti-Semitism moved from the Greek to the Roman world, first in literary form (as the apologetic work by Josephus Flavius—*Against Apion* —shows), and soon turned into physical violence, which erupted first in Alexandria in the year 38 CE and then in other places, usually coinciding with the great Jewish wars against the Romans.

Yet the anti-Semitism of the pagan world remained, on the whole, linked to the resentment felt by the Greek city populations towards a people who refused to share in their social interests and amusements. One of the reasons it remained relatively tolerant of the Jews was that the Hellenistic rulers needed and appreciated the Jew's devotion and military qualities. This was not the case with the Christians: the successors to the Roman Empire, the Christian Empire, had no faith in or political need of one of the bravest and most rebellious of its subject nations. As a religion which sprang from Judaism and in fact aimed at supplanting it, Christianity could not admit any compromise. Jews had to be turned into a symbol of perversity and shame, first because of their religion, then because of their 'race', and now because of their very special type of nationalism, Zionism.[11]

The persecutions to which Jews were subjected, first in the Greek, then in the Roman, and finally in the Christian society, had a vital effect on the inner life of the Jewish people, an effect far more important than any of their past political or military successes. In those long periods of crisis certain qualities shone out—uncompromising fidelity to an ideal, endurance raised to the pitch of utter self-absorption, a passionate clinging to purity —which none of the riches of Hellenistic, Roman, or Western culture could buy. These persecutions fed and developed the Messianic idea of *Redemption (Ge'ulah)* as well as the concept of the positive role of *Exile (Galut)* seen as an indispensable counterpart to Messianic redemption and as a means of disseminating Jewish ideals throughout the nations. The persecutions also served to galvanize the already developed tendency towards universal religious education. Study became not an activity reserved for an élite but the 'national profession' of the Jews, because if 'the Galut retains nothing of the divine status except the Torah (the Mosaic Law), then the energy of the community must be devoted first of all to the study of the Torah'.[12]

But there were other reasons, ingrained in both Jewish and Gentile (Christian or Islamic) society which for a long time reinforced an exclusiveness which was not only the result of persecution.[13] Jewish, Christian, and Muslim societies were all based on religion which made separation a reciprocal duty. Persecution made this separation also a source of suffering for the Jew, but it did not shake his inner conviction that he was different and should remain so. There were, of course, many Jews who could not bear such suffering, and throughout the Middle Ages, more particularly after the expulsion from Spain at the end of the fifteenth century (in the wake of which it is believed that over a million Jews were converted to Christianity), there was a continuous process of defection even if, in some cases, the national consciousness was not totally lost. But such conversions remained a matter of individual, not collective, choice, and in the case of Spain and Portugal these converts soon became, in their own eyes and in the eyes of the Gentiles, a separate group with its own social and behavioural distinctions.

Despite all this, as the sociologist Jacob Katz points out, the decisive turning point in the national history of modern Judaism occurred only around the first half of the nineteenth century, when its individual members transferred their social goals to the context of the surrounding non-Jewish milieu. Here again we find a clash between aloofness and assimilation, but in totally new conditions because for the first time since the exodus from Egypt the Jews entered a situation of being a culturally colonized minority.

Studies of colonial societies have shown that economic changes are not sufficient (Marxist theories notwithstanding) to produce radical and collective changes of social gratification. Thus the current explanation that the emergence of the free market and of the modern national state left no place for 'caste' or communal autonomy is not sufficient to explain the radical change which took place in the Jewish nation. The rejection of the ghetto life and the secularization of the Jewish community was much more than a loss of religious faith: it was a revolution, considering that the Jewish people were socially structured and emotionally educated as a very large family. Since the paterfamilias was God himself, the secularization of the Jewish people was also an act of symbolic patricide. In this sense, the process of secularization of the Jewish nation, of which political Zionism was part and parcel, was not very different from the one undergone by revolutionary France, although there was no Zionist leader who would be prepared to claim, like Robespierre, that the King should die so that the new republic could live. Jewish assimilation was thus a process of collective revolutionary conversion. But collective conversions cannot take place unless they follow the conversion of that élite which, independent of its political or economic weight, has the power to elicit imitation from the masses.[14] It would therefore have been impossible for the Jews to switch their values, their individual and collective traditional goals, and their cultural ambitions so completely as to leave empty the framework of a millenarian, national, and aristocratic culture in order to assimilate a relatively new, populistic, Western, democratic way of life, without a process of eager acceptance of foreign colonization by the Jewish élites. In other words, rather than being forced out of their traditional culture, the Jews of Europe, unlike those of the Muslim world, were led out of their intellectual and social 'fetters' by their own 'revolutionary' leaders, who came to value foreign life and culture more than their own national ones.

Professor Katz does not describe this process of self-alienation as a process of self-colonization: he uses the provocative concept of *neutral society* to explain the break-up of the traditional Jewish élite and the emergence of new competitors.[15] In his later works he qualifies and modifies the original sense of this neutrality. But his original definition serves the purpose of underlining that particular intellectual and social process in which natural law, nationalist philosophy, and utilitarian ethics combined to plant a utopian picture of the new, perfect world. This had great appeal to the minds of the new enlightened Jewish intelligentsia, the *Maskilim*, which was beginning to coalesce in Western, Central, and Eastern Europe, with a time lag of about thirty to fifty years compared with its Gentile counterpart. A typical feature of the period of rationalism in France and of *Aufklärung* in Germany, notes Katz, was that the rationalists were swept into theorizing on matters which they were unable to bring into concrete existence. But the rationalists who identified themselves with the vision of the marvellous new world of the future formed a distinct social unit. The social stratum of the intelligentsia was presumed to be above and beyond all classes, a 'spiritual élite', which was a by-product of the rise of the independent commonalty but which attracted persons from every stratum. Since the rationalist creed in theory (though never in practice, as Maurras's distinction between the *'pays légal'* and the *'pays réel'* exemplified so well a century later) recognized no class or religious divisions, the exclusion of Jews from membership in this new intellectual social group would have been contradictory. While the encounter between Jews and non-Jews was—like apostasy—by no means a novelty, the new sociological basis of the rationalist enlightened group, which allowed the transplantation of the Jew into a non-Jewish milieu without necessarily requiring his conversion, was something quite new. It certainly created problems, as shown by Napoleon's demand to the Paris *Sanhedrin* to decide, once and for all, whether the Jews were a nation of their own or Frenchmen with a particular religious belief. In other cases the matter took a more inquisitional turn, as for instance in the case of Lavater's public challenge to Moses Mendelssohn, the outstanding representative of the new Jewish enlightened society in the latter part of the eighteenth century, to admit or refute the truth of Christianity. Appeals of this sort, however, missed the point, 'for the essence of the rationalists' social achievement lay precisely in their creation of a neutral basis above religious differences'.[16] Enlightened Jewish intellectuals like Moses Mendelssohn believed that it might be possible for a Jew to live in two worlds at the same time. They were to be proved wrong by subsequent events, but at the time their intellectual flaw was not immediately evident either to them or to the liberal and nationalist Gentile world. Unlike the past, when the Jews had to declare themselves whenever forced to make a choice between their own beliefs and those of the Gentiles, the new Jewish intellectuals were now offered an apparently easier alternative by the enlightened rationalists. It was not a 'neutral' alternative, since even more than apostasy it led them to the renunciation of their own culture and eventually of their national/religious patrimony. Nevertheless, it helped them to abandon their own tradition without suffering feelings of betrayal. What is more, they believed they could join a new social group which, thanks to its theory of the positive nucleus common to all religions, was entitled to discredit the claim to uniqueness of each religion.

This new, secular, rationalist meeting-ground between Jewish and non-Jewish society accelerated the process of assimilation of individual Jews into Gentile society as never before, leading them in many cases to straightforward conversion to Christianity. But it did something more deadly to Judaism: it created a 'foreign' élite from within. This élite, as in the case of the *évolues* in African colonial societies, laid strong and successful claims to Jewish leadership and led an open intellectual revolt against the traditional rabbinical leadership which had for centuries been the main repository of authority and the source of legitimation in Judaism. The quarrel sapped the unity of a community whose identity had already been gravely endangered by physical dispersion and by the rise of centralized national states which had no sympathy for Jewish autonomies. The loss of interest by the Jews in their own culture and tradition brought about, in less than two or three generations, a cultural decay of traditional Judaism, except for those aspects—morality, equality, justice, and of course nationalism—which fitted into the Gentile framework of rationalist, and later of romantic-nationalist, ideas. It was a very rapid process of deculturation which can be measured by the decadence of the Hebrew language in countries where Jews were more exposed to assimilation, such as Italy or France, and marked by the loss of prestige of certain fundamental linguistic symbols even among those Jews who continued to be fully dedicated to Judaism. In 1810, for instance, *Sulamith*, the leading German-Jewish periodical, changed its subtitle to *Israelit* to mark the difference between an Israelite and a Jew. Later on the Israelite nation became the Mosaic confession, and by 1830 *Me'assef*, the Hebrew journal established by Mendelssohn's pupils, had ceased to appear.[17] This was partly due to lack of interest, but above all to ignorance of the Hebrew language which had become restricted to a ritual and was known by only a few scholars. It was an inevitable and natural consequence of picturing 'the future of the Jewish society on the basis of their identification with the values of the neutral society'. In doing so, the members of the new emancipated élite felt themselves to be true innovators and pioneers. From the 1780s onwards, 'the *maskilim* emerged as a group with a clear-cut social-ideological character, laying claim to the leadership of the society as a whole, just like any other society'.[18]

This leadership was not interested in the preservation of Jewish identity but in changing it. For the most convinced assimilationists the change should and could be total, namely the transformation of the Jew into a non-Jew. Many, among them members of some of the leading Jewish families at the time (Heine himself and the children of Moses Mendelssohn), were baptized. But even among those who remained formally attached to their religion there was a growing conviction that modern Judaism should be recognized at best as an intermediate stage towards Christianity. The process of self-colonization in culture went hand-in-hand with the process of self-colonization in nationhood. Gabriel Riesser, one of the most eloquent advocates of emancipation in mid-nineteenth-century Germany, declared that a Jew who preferred a non-existent state and nation (Israel) to Germany ought to be put under police protection, not because his views were dangerous but because he was obviously insane.[19]

The process, of course, was neither simple nor rapid. Nor was it easily perceived, in its ultimate tragic and revolutionary implications (the Holocaust on the one hand, and the birth of an independent Jewish State on the other), either by Jews or Gentiles, despite the warnings heard in the orthodox and secular Jewish camps against emancipation, assimilation, and Zionism.[20] The forces favouring change, within and without the Jewish community, were too strong to be neutralized. They were part and parcel of the great transformation of that European society in which most of the Jews lived[21] and their impact was felt without exception by the Jews, though unevenly because of their geographical, social, and historical differences in the Diaspora. One should, however, be very careful when trying to sort out the connections between the multiple causes and effects of emancipation. The path of Jewish assimilation and national revival was tortuous, made up of advances and setbacks, of frustrated hopes and unexpected achievements. Nevertheless, the various stimuli to which Jews have been exposed since the end of the eighteenth century, and which eventually contributed both to the loss and to the revival of their national consciousness, belong to a few clear categories.

The first main pressure from the outside was the rise, in the eighteenth century, of absolutist, enlightened regimes, pursuing mercantilistic policies in the economic sphere and centralistic ones in the political and administrative spheres. It is difficult to describe their action upon the Jews as 'colonization', since they affected all groups under their control, disrupting without distinction the social, political, and traditional structure of the *ancien régime* and of the remnants of feudalism. Yet their impact on the Jewish communities was particularly destructive, and similar to that exercised by the Western metropolis on colonial, coloured dependencies, because of the particularly weak position of the Israelite Diaspora.

Furthermore, in the nineteenth century the majority of the Ashkenazi Jews lived in Poland, Galicia, and Russia. They were almost completely isolated within themselves, living in compact, mainly urban, Jewish communities. In these declining, self-governing communities, voluntary organizations (known as *Hevrot*) proliferated. Ridden by bitter religious polemics, destitute, deprived like the rest of the population of political rights, these Jews of Eastern Europe lived in a situation of seclusion from the rest of the world. Another large group of Jews, the Sephardim, lived in the lands of Islam, equally secluded from the outside world, economically not always better off, and politically even more dependent on the local rulers. Both groups, writes Chimen Abramsky, lived in the twilight of a slowly disintegrating medieval world.[22] Although a third smaller group, the Jews of Western Europe, lived in quite different conditions, politically tolerated and economically relatively well off, it can be said that the whole of the Jewish society before the French Revolution was characterized by its 'basic autonomous self-governing institutions in a hierarchical order, based on a kind of alliance between the wealthy and the learned Jews, who were frequently linked by marriage. Legally the Jews can be compared to a medieval corporation.'

Such institutions could not stand up to the intrusion of the modern state. The *Toleranzpatent* of Emperor Joseph II of Austria (1782) was a landmark in the history of Jewish emancipation because it made important concessions, retained old restrictions while drastically weakening Jewish autonomy through direct and forceful state intervention in Jewish communal affairs. In this sense the French Revolution only increased an already established pattern of Jewish cultural dependence which the Jews could not resist. When the partisans of Jewish emancipation proclaimed that, 'to the Jews as a nation we give nothing, to the Jews as individuals everything', at the Paris National Assembly,[23] they were expressing a pious wish for individual equality some time in the future and a firm intention to do away with the Jews as an organized collectivity now. The pressure was felt all the more strongly because, as was the case later with the colonized nations of the Third World, Europe exercised an intoxicating attraction upon the weak nations subjected to her influence. The West, in the nineteenth century, seemed invincible in its power, its political organization, its technology, and above all its supreme feeling of self-confidence.

The pressures from within the Jewish communities were equally strong. First, there was the slow but profound change in the conception of the Exile. From the very beginning, the Exile has probably been one of the main distinguishing features of the Jewish nation. The history of the Jews symbolically begins with the self-exile of its founder, Abraham, from the land of Ur, and continues with the forcible exile of another biblical patriarch, Joseph, sold into captivity by his brothers. In the wake of the destruction of the Jewish polity, the Exile assumes a metaphysical value in the eyes of the Jews, just as its counterpart, the Return, melts into a metaphysical conception of the Redemption. David Vital, in a brilliant study of the origins of Zionism, places the concepts of *Exile, Return,* and *Redemption* at the starting-point of that movement.[24] He recalls correctly how the feeling of the decay of Judaism in the exile of the nineteenth century became a forceful conviction for both the orthodox and the secularized Israelites. The orthodox (he cites Rabbi Akiva Schlesinger of Pressburg (1832–1922) as a typical example) argued that it had become impossible to reconcile an ancient culture with the new, bright, immensely attractive general culture, oriented towards the satisfaction of day-to-day material needs. To him, the Land of the ancestors began to have not only mystical appeal but was looked upon as the ultimate refuge. The secular Jew, like socialist Moses Hess, became convinced that assimilation which consisted in 'giving up our Jewish culture and denying our own race' would not succeed because the Jewishness from which the Jews could not run away in the eyes of the Gentiles was the major obstacle to their desperately sought-after 'inner' emancipation. Finally, even among the most alienated, converted Jews, such as Benjamin Disraeli, who had succeeded in penetrating into the highest echelons of the Gentile society, the memories of their Hebrew origins, fertilized by the romantic climate of their age, kindled reveries of ancient glories which suited the prevailing mood of Gentile liberal and aristocratic nationalism.

All these trends predated Zionism and were fertile ground for its development inasmuch as they contributed, each in their own way, to transforming the idea of the Return and of *Eretz Israel* from the vision of a land of chiliastic attributes into an instrument for social and political change. It was only natural that through this less theological and more mundane view of the Land, some of those Jews who had become removed from the Jewish tradition became increasingly interested in the historical, geographical, and mythological rather than mystical apsects of Palestine.

Concomitant with this transformation of the Jewish approach to the Land of Return and Redemption, there were new modernizing tendencies in traditional Judaism itself. They played an unwitting but important part in the process of the cultural and social alienation of the Jew inasmuch as they legitimized from within the first steps towards emanicpation.

As in any other compact traditional religious community, there existed in Judaism transformative capacities capable of promoting 'the development of new motivations, activities and institutions, not encompassed in the original impulses and views'.[25] The talmudic scholar Nahman Krochmal (1785-1840) was one of the founders of that science of Judaism soon to be turned into the main intellectual instrument of the assimilationists for proving that the destiny of the Jews, as a separate unique phenomenon, had come to an end; Jewish ideals and values had been accepted by Western society. Krochmal believed, like every other orthodox Jew, in the eternity of the Jewish people, in contrast to the transitory fate of other nations, thanks to the special relation existing between the absolute Being and the Jews. But in spite of this he proclaimed that the people of Israel did not transcend history: their eternity was assured by a continuous renewal of national life.[26] Krochmal reconciled progress and religion by insisting upon the separate domain of divine knowledge, qualitatively and quantitatively superior to human knowledge, making room for the expansion of human enquiry in an age of progress when the knowledge of nature was increasing at an accelerated pace. In this way he became a legitimizer of change within the traditional Jewish society, as well as a forerunner of the modern nationalist-Zionist philosophy of history.

Nahman Krochmal was one of many. The Yale sociologist Hillel Levine, in his biographical study of Menahem Mendel Lefin,[27] claimed that the process of modernization within traditional Jewish society prepared the way from within for radical changes in the Jewish way of life and thought, changes which very soon began to seek their legitimation from without, against Jewish tradition. Emancipation therefore brought with it not only a transformation in the legal (if not the real) status of the Jew, but a rapid fluctuation in the inner relationships of the Hebrew nation. This was something new and disconcerting, since in the past Judaism had experienced fluctuations almost exclusively in its relations with the Gentile nations, in the form of expulsion and oppression. This time it had no strength or will to defend itself against the revolution from without and within. The biblical definition of the Hebrew people, 'It is a people that shall dwell alone and shall not be reckoned among the nations',[28] suddenly lost its significance: the people no longer wanted to dwell alone, no longer liked the Jewish tent, were no longer prepared to wait for the Messiah. The phenomenon was without precedent in the history of the Jews. The great nineteenth-century German-Jewish historian, Heinrich Graetz, called it 'mass conversion'. Numerically it involved at least 20 or 30 per cent of the people; culturally and spiritually it left no Jew untouched.

With a few notable exceptions,[29] Zionists belonged to this 'converted' group. Theodor Herzl, founder of the movement, was the very prototype of the assimilated Jew, who recovered his Jewish consciousness through a transposition of non-Jewish national ideals to the Jews.

Yet the Jewish 'Risorgimento' took a long time to emerge into a more or less coherent movement. Its roots went deep into the Jewish tradition of redemption, but the spark was certainly the shock of the brutal persecution in Russia between 1881 and 1884. These pogroms seem like child's play today when compared with any single day of the Holocaust, on which an average of 25,000 Jews were methodically killed by the Nazis. At the time, however, the pogroms shocked the conscience of the civilized world and put an end to the dreams of those Russian Jews who still believed in a liberalization of Tzarist Jewish policy. Zionism was not the invention or the creation of a single man or a single group of men. Vital notes that half a generation was to pass before it acquired a preponderant leader and something like a clear formulation of aims. Its adherents, the groups and circles of *Ḥovevei Zion* (Lovers of Zion), emerged spontaneously in many localities of Eastern Europe. The establishment of the first settlement of farmers in Palestine took place before the document which can be regarded as the movement's first manifesto was published. Zionism started as an immediate response of individuals to a situation which had come to be regarded as intolerable.[30] The story is well known and this is not the place to retell it. What should be remembered is that from the outset its rationalization was based far more on a denunciation of the situation and faults of the victim than on a denunciation of the persecutor. *Auto-emancipation*,[31] the pamphlet published by Yehuda Leib Pinsker (1821–91) and considered the first manifesto of Zionism, is a social analysis, a prescription for action, a cry of rage, but above all 'a slashing attack on Jewish feebleness, timidity, and apologetics and on the Jews' deeply ingrained habit of seeking not only the sources of their pain outside Jewry but the cure to it as well'.[32] It was a strong denunciation of the Emancipation but also of the traditional Jewish establishment which offered no alternative to it. 'When we are ill-used. robbed, plundered and dishonoured, we dare not defend ourselves and, worse still, we take it almost as a matter of course. When our face is slapped, we soothe our burning cheek with cold water. . . . When we are turned out of the house which we ourselves built, we beg humbly for mercy, and when we fail to reach the heart of our oppressor we move on in search of another exile. . . . We have sunk so low that we become almost jubilant when, as in the West, a small fraction of our people is put on an equal footing with non-Jews.'[33]

Pinsker's solution is a territorial one: not yet Palestine, but just a land. This trend was to be picked up and given new political direction by Theodor Herzl, and strongly opposed by Ahad Ha'Am (Asher Zvi Ginzberg, 1856-1927), who believed that the Jews were not yet fit for the Return.[34] For the latter, Zionism—in the pre-Herzlian version of the *Hovevei Zion* and even more in the political approach of Herzl—was bound to fail because the material obstacles standing in the way of the Jewish national enterprise were so great that a morally and physically weak people could not overcome them. The 'concentration of the spirit' must therefore precede the concentration of the people. Yet whichever way we look at Zionism—the disorganized romantic efforts of the *Hovevei Zion*, the critical 'spiritual centre' approach of Ahad Ha'Am, or the practical political one of Theodor Herzl—we find that the search for a solution to the Jewish question was neither an effort to reconstruct the Jewish identity in terms of the Jewish past and traditions nor an opposition to assimilation. It primarily answered the need to escape persecution and was the result of the failure to integrate into the nineteenth-century Gentile society. For Theodor Herzl in particular the answer to anti-Semitism was the physical removal of the Jews from the lands of persecution to the Land which, apart from its historical ties with the Jewish people, had the advantage of 'appearing' to be empty of an indigenous population and so destitute that nobody seemed to care about it. Herzl was the first to turn anti Semitism into a positive force for Jewish national revival. Those Jews who could not assimilate should look for freedom among themselves. But it also represented freedom from their traditions, their cultural heritage, and, what is more, from that very particular Jewish way of life which had perpetuated Jewish existence for non-Jews or for those Jews who no longer wanted to live as Jews. Political Zionism was not emigration-cum-Judaism, but a form of European nationalism-cum-emigration from the European centres of anti-Semitism. The 'new solution to an old question' proposed by Herzl in his prophetic booklet *The Jewish State* was obviously too simplistic to be able to encompass the complexity of the national question, not to speak of the inevitable political consequences of its realization. As a reaction to the unbearable *consequences* of the Jewish condition in Europe (persecution, individual and collective degradation, cultural and economic restrictions, etc.), it increased rather than decreased the *causes* which made the Jewish question so critical in modern political society. These causes were the uniqueness of the Jewish people, the universal impact of their civilizing ideas, the refusal of the Jews—including even some of the most assimilated—to divest themselves of their Jewish identity, and the inability of the Jewish national consciousness to exist apart from its religious-cultural-national content.

The new secular European-inspired national liberation movement of the

Jews preferred not to deal with these causes. And because of this inten-
tional avoidance of the crux of the problem, Herzl was able to give the
Jewish people his greatest contribution: the establishment, with the First
Zionist Congress in Basle in 1897, of the precedent and the principle of
unity. He brought together 'romanticists and pragmatists, orthodox and
secularists, socialists and bourgeois, easterners and westerners, men whose
minds and language were barely influenced by the non-Jewish world and
those who were largely products of it, and, above all, those whose primary
concern was with the condition of the Jews as opposed to those, like Aḥad
Ha-'Am, whose eyes were on the crisis of Judaism'.[35] Sooner or later these
different beliefs, conditions, and personalities had to clash among themselves over the very reason which brought them together in the land of
their ancestors. The physical return of the Jews to Eretz Israel could not in
itself satisfy the spiritual and cultural needs of the people, while their re-
entry into world society as a nation implied 'that the time had come for a
vastly long historical process to be brought to an end or, at the very least,
sharply redirected. What would then replace the known patterns of Jewish
life? . . . Was the Jewish State intended to be an end in itself, a Utopia . . .
through which life was to be transformed? Or was it to be primarily and
more mundanely the means by which national political power, of the advantages of which the Jews had been deprived for twenty centuries, was to
be restored?'[36]

It was to be expected that the question, the Jewish question of Israel,
would explode in all its intensity with the establishment of the State.
Against all logic, however, it did not: for three main reasons. The first was
the Arab hostility, which created in the new and fragmented Israeli society
a strong reflex of unity for survival. The second was the astonishment of
the Israelis, old settlers and newcomers alike, at the reappearance of Jewish political sovereignty, a dream searched for for so long that when it
materialized, all 'men were like dreamers', in the words of the Psalmist.
The third reason was Ben-Gurion, who not only acted as midwife to the
State but imposed on all parties, much against their will, the historic decision of not deciding on any essential problems of the State: not on a constitution, not on the national borders, not on the ideological character of
the State. This policy of non-decision-making was dictated as much by
national wisdom as by party interest: only by not deciding could *Mapai*, a
social-democratic party with 34 per cent of the seats in parliament, act
as a national party. But it was an attitude which saved Israel from grave
internal dissension in the first very difficult years of her existence.

The extent of the military victory over the Arabs in 1967 changed all
this. It relieved the State from the Arab menace of physical destruction;
the conquest of populous Arab areas obliged Israel to define itself in relation to its enemies: what it meant to be 'Jewish' or Israeli in the occupied

areas, how the 'redemption of the land' could serve or be justified by the redemption of the people. The victory of 1967 should have been used to solve past problems, such as the danger of Arab guerrillas, the question of the demilitarized zones with Egypt and Syria, the implementation of the Jews' right to visit their own holy places in Arab Jerusalem (as envisaged in the Jordan-Israel Armistice Agreement). Instead, it was used to create new ones: occupation of Syrian and Egyptian national territories, occupation of the whole of Jerusalem with the holy places of both Christianity and Islam, destabilization of not yet recognized borders, a deepening of the Middle East conflict.

Thus, to the old, insoluble problems new ones were added, but in a situation which no longer permitted postponing the fundamental debate on the nature and task of the Zionist State. The absence at the helm of government of leaders with an historical vision and a personal authority—like Ben-Gurion—made the situation all the more difficult. Just as most of the initiative for the Zionist movement had in the past come from the outside—that is, reaction to anti-Semitism, to social and economic pressures, to Arab hostility—so it was hoped that this time the initiative for a settlement would come from the Arabs, and that the new strength of Israel would attract the necessary support from the Diaspora and the friendly Western countries to solve its other problems, or at least create new conditions in which to face them.

The coalition government of Premier Levi Eshkol, and even more those of Mrs Golda Meir,[37] adopted a policy of military, social, economic, and above all psychological and ideological immobilism, the sole result of which was to sweep under a carpet of conformism and righteous platitudes the old and new problems of identity, legitimacy, institutions, and ideology facing the Israeli State, as a State of the Jews. This was coupled with a phenomenal increase in corruption, social inequality, and waste of human and economic resources through a policy of massive military investment and occupation.[38]

The Arabs and the outside world (including many assimilated Diaspora Jews) were quick to detect, exploit, and emphasize this situation and its inner contradictions. They also seized upon the rationalist and self-colonizing trends in Zionism (which neither the secular leadership of the State nor the Westernized Jew in Israel or the Diaspora was prepared to denounce) and used them to drive a political and psychological wedge between nationhood and religion in Judaism. They elaborated a theory of Jewish-Arab coexistence, based on the principle of religious coexistence in a 'democratic secular Palestinian state'. This was presented as an exact version of an Arab Zionism against which the arguments of Jewish Zionism had little rational impact but which shook the confidence of the Israelis in their own national legitimacy. Like the centipede in the Indian tale, who found himself unable to walk the moment the parrot asked him to explain how he co-ordinated the movements of all his feet, so a kind of emotional-psychological paralysis overtook the Zionist movement and the State of Israel the moment they found themselves forced to analyse and define their own nature in response to external pressure. They could not reach any inspiring consensus, and they lacked the time for reflection and the socio-political logical tools to analyse their problems. Those they had—as in every colonized society—were alien, imported, and unfitted to explain to a people which had largely cut itself off from its own national culture, what that culture was and what their new State was meant to achieve.

And so, after 1967, Israel found itself back in square one as far as the solution of the Jewish question and the definition of its identity were concerned. This in itself was a source of deep concern, insecurity, and anxiety. For the first time, young people questioned the legitimacy of military service and the wisdom of allowing a society born of the craving to put an end to foreign oppression of the Jews to turn into a Jewish society which —certainly unintentionally—was now forced to oppress a million conquered Arabs. For the first time, the Machiavellian dilemma—can a Christian prince be both a Christian and a prince?—hit the Israelis with all the force of its philosophical and moral contradiction. The Government replied, as any other government in the world would have done, that 'reasons of state' required that the end—in this case the search for a true peace, the need for security, the need to oppose Arab radicalism and to exploit the new international situation—must justify the means. It also derived encouragement from the fact that the victory of 1967 triggered a great revival of Jewish consciousness among Jews in Russia and the West, and brought about a new flood of immigration which seemed to prove once more the vitality and the power of attraction of the Zionist movement. What the establishment failed to perceive, unlike many war veterans who returned to their homes with small enthusiasm for the moral effects of the 1967 war, was that the élitist nature of Judaism and the strongest element in Zionism—romantic social pioneering—were not conducive to an easy coexistence between needs and values. An increased abundance led to decreased self-confidence because it raised very serious problems of priorities between aims and means. And the 'quantitative' solutions or justifications given by the government. for its policy ran counter to all that the Jewish people had tried to prove in history, namely that it is only the means which justify the end. When the October 1973 war destroyed the image of material power upon which the feeling of security of most Israelis was based, a deep sense of anguish was bound to pervade the nation. The crisis was all the more profound because of the rapidity with which the whole nation passed from a situation of pseudo-normality to one of a total struggle for survival. The shock of this brutal transition for an entire collectivity created a psychical drama which A. B. Yehoshua has compared to a case of depression in the mentally ill.[39]

Objectively speaking, Israel's situation after the war of 1973 was incomparably better than in 1948; subjectively it had worsened, because the Israeli had been brought face to face with himself, with his split identity and his cultural alienation, and for the first time had no possibility of avoiding a look into the mirror of realities.

What this mirror of realities should have told Israel was that in spite of the very particular historical fate of the Jews, Jewish alienation was not unique, and was to some extent shared by most non-Western societies subjected to European colonization. But it was psychologically very difficult for the Zionists, their Western friends, and their Arab and non-Arab enemies to look at Israel as a colonized society. Self-pride on the one hand, and ideological selectivity against the white man on the other, made this comparison of Israel with the societies of the Third World apparently irrelevant. And yet it is one which could help us to understand many perplexing aspects of Israeli society, and to place in a better historical perspective a Jewish political and cultural experience which would otherwise appear so unique as to defy understanding.

CHAPTER 3

The Two Publics: Israel and Africa

At first glance Zionism and the national movements of the Third World seem to have little in common, particularly as regards Africa. The diplomatic and economic links established by the State of Israel with the new states of the Black Continent were impressive partly because they looked as if they were created *ex nihilo*. The speed with which the Israelis entered the 'African game' in the sixties and the equal speed with which they found themselves ejected from it in the seventies tended to underline the superficiality of these links. There were, of course, interested rationalizations of this newly found 'brotherhood': the story of King Solomon and the Queen of Sheba was stressed to give an historical dimension to a very new co-operation; the role of the 'Zionist' and 'Messianic' African churches and sects, and the possible latent influence of Jewish lore on certain African tribes, such as the Poeul or the Ashanti of Ghana, were dusted off and used in many ambassadorial speeches.[1]

More serious and consistent were the efforts to evaluate the impact of Zionism on African political consciousness in the nineteenth century, when the Jewish and Black movements of emancipation and national liberation showed common signs of a utopian character and aspiration. In both cases, for instance, the search for the 'national' identity was linked less with a specific territory than with the consciousness of sharing a common tragic fate. In both cases the individual and collective self-image was to a great extent influenced by the respective diasporas and by a similarly dependent condition in different historical situations. In both cases there was a rapid loss of the indigenous cultural energy and a willing acquisition of values drawn from the alien, metropolitan-prejudiced environment.

Africanism, like Zionism, is essentially a movement of ideas and emotions and was directly influenced by the efforts of the Jews to combine Redemption with Return. Edward Wilmot Blyden (1832–1912), the West Indian-born, Liberian diplomat and scholar, forefather of Pan-Africanism, went on pilgrimage to Jerusalem as early as 1866 and became an ardent admirer of political Zionism thirty years later because of his metapolitical views of both Jewish and African destinies. His essay on *The Jewish Question* (Liverpool, 1898) followed Herzl's *Der Judenstaat* ('The Jewish State') two years later and recognized the need for an organized return of Herzl's Jewish contemporaries. 'There is hardly a man in the civilized world,' wrote Blyden, 'Christian, Mohammedan or Jew, who does not recognize the right of the Jew to the Holy Land; and there are few who, if the conditions were favourable, would not be glad to see them return in a body and take their place in the land of their fathers as a great—leading—secular power.'[2]

At the same time, Blyden advised the Jews against aiming at political aggrandizement: he believed that the primary contribution of the Jews to world civilization—as of the Blacks, inside and outside Africa—was a spiritual element which he already saw as dangerously lacking in a modern Western world completely 'immersed in materialism'. In 1919 Dr W. E. B. DuBois, promoter of the first Pan-African Conference, wrote: 'The African movement means to us what the Zionist movement must mean to the Jews, the centralization of rare effort and recognition of a racial fount.'[3] This is not surprising since both Zionism and Pan-Africanism were the outcome of the process of emancipation started by the Enlightenment and by the moral, religious, and romantic reactions produced by the French Revolution in the cultural climate of Europe and England. Moreover, both movements developed outside their 'homelands' and strove more for human dignity than for political independence—at least in the beginning. The ideology of return in Zionism and Pan-Africanism drew much of its vigour from the persecution suffered by Jews and Blacks and, in both cases, was a reaction to a discrimination which was resented more for the lack of human dignity it produced than for the lack of political independence. In both cases a Messianic ideal, in which the religious ingredients acted both as a coalescent factor of the new identity and a solvent of the colonial dependence, served as legitimation of the revolt. Some of the great nineteenth-century Black uprisings in America were justified by their leaders on the basis of Old Testament texts which called for leading the Jews out of bondage: just as biblical heroes became inspiring symbols for modern Jewish national revival.

Zionists were less interested in Africa than were Pan-Africanists in Zionism. Theodor Herzl did devote part of one of his utopian novels on the revival of the Jewish society in Palestine to the African colonial question, and promised that, once having achieved independence, the Jews would aid the Blacks.[4] Conversely, an American Black nationalist, Marcus Aurelius Garvey, leader of the unsuccessful 'Back to Africa' movement between the two world wars, took pride in calling himself a 'Black Zionist', although he knew very little about the Jews and Palestine. But when these trends and declarations are put in their proper historical perspective it becomes evident that the links between Israel and Africa are very thin, that no comparison can be made between Zionism and African national movements in terms of their political, ideological development, and even less in terms of their organization and historical experience. What can be usefully compared is the psychology of the political élites of Israel and of the new countries of the Third World, especially in Africa.

The most profound and lasting similarities between Jewish and African nationalism are in fact the result of the exposure of Jews and Blacks to the impact of Westernization in a situation of great political and cultural dependence. For an 'enlightened' African, as for an enlightened Jew, becoming Westernized meant simultaneous identification with a source of prestige and oppression. One must, of course, be very careful to avoid thesis-mongering, mixing ideology, political fashion, and academic evidence. The differences in the historical, religious, social, economic, and cultural experiences of Jews and Africans must continuously be borne in mind. The impact of Europe on the Jews, even on those of Eastern Europe who kept a separate social identity much longer than the Jews of the West, was totally different from the impact of European culture on African colonial society. Geographical, cultural, political, and social environments are not comparable, and any attempt to apply emotion-loaded terms, such as 'imperialism', 'colonialism', 'slavery', to the two cases will prove useless, if not self-defeating.

Things, however, change when a closer look is taken at the psychological impact which Westernization and modernization have had on Jewish and African intellectuals, faced with the problem of national revival. In matters concerning national identity, legitimacy, and the relationship between modern and traditional social structures, the dilemmas and the behaviour of African and Jewish nationalist élites show some striking similarities. This is not surprising considering the effort which both Jewish and African intellectuals, as representatives of traditional societies, had to make in order to adapt to the exigencies of external centres of cultural and political attraction, while struggling to differentiate themselves from these same powerful influences in order to justify their claim to total independence. For both Africans and Jews the identification with Western culture was simultaneously a source of prestige and frustration; for both, cultural Western alienation often meant a total break with their own national traditions; for both, this break meant the adoption of foreign-created images of themselves and the development of a feeling of social and cultural marginality to parent and adopted society; for both, this feeling of marginality manifested itself in expressions of self-hate and irrational attraction to, and rejection of, the West.

The relationship between colonized and colonizer has been the topic of many studies.[5] It may be pointed out parenthetically that in works on colonialism such as those of Frantz Fanon and Albert Memmi, the Jews and the Blacks are constantly intermingled. The comparison attempted by these authors deals principally with the psychology of the colonized man—Jew, African, or other. What interests us here, however, is whether similarities between African and Jewish political institutions can be found, and in sufficient quantity to permit a meaningful comparative examination of Zionist/Israeli political experience and that of non-European political societies.

Among the scholarly studies of African political societies, the work of an African political sociologist, Peter P. Ekeh, has special relevance. Ekeh developed an interesting theory to explain some of the effects of colonization on the élites of the new African states. Although the studies are mainly concerned with Nigeria, his conclusions seem relevant to many other new states, including Israel. Ekeh claims that 'the experiences of colonialism in Africa have led to the emergence of a unique historical configuration in modern post-colonial Africa: the existence of two publics instead of one public, as in the West'.[6] In the West, the private realm and the public realm have common *moral* foundations: in Africa and in many new countries of the Third World, they do not. There is one private realm, founded on indigenous tradition and culture, and two public realms, each with a different type of moral linkage to the private realm. One public realm, says Ekeh, 'can be identified with primordial groupings, sentiments and activities which nevertheless impinge on the public interest. [It] . . . operates on the same moral imperatives as the private realm', and is activated and legitimated by the traditional culture. Next to it, however, there is another public realm which—at least in Africa—is historically associated with the colonial administration and which has become identified with popular politics in post-colonial Africa. Although it provides essential civil structures, such as the military, the civil service, the police, its chief characteristic is that it has no *moral* linkage with the private realm. Peter Ekeh calls this the 'civic' public and underlines the fact that in Africa this second, civic, public lacks the generalized moral imperatives operative in the private realm and in the primordial public. 'The native sector', he concludes, 'has become a primordial reservoir of moral obligations, a public entity which one works to preserve and benefit. The Westernized sector has become an amoral civic public, from which one seeks to gain, if possible, in order to benefit the primordial public.' Hence the corruption which has permeated the political life of new states in Africa, the difficulty for the new governments to mobilize the masses for the benefit of the state, the contradiction between parallel manifestations of total involvement and sacrifice of the individual and the group for the benefit of the 'primordial' public sector—the extended family, the clan, the tribe, etc. —and of apathy shown towards the 'civic' administrative public sector by the same individuals or groups.

Ekeh also notes that the conflict between what he calls two 'bourgeois groups', the foreign and the indigenous (probably the term 'élites' would be more appropriate), is characterized by an acute sense of insecurity due to a crisis of legitimacy. In fact the emerging indigenous ruling class is 'composed of Africans who acquired Western education at the hands of the colonizers and their missionary collaborators, and who accordingly were the most exposed to European colonial ideologies of all groups of Africans'. For this reason, 'although native to Africa, the African [élite] depends on colonialism for its legitimacy. It accepts the principles implicit in colonialism but it rejects the foreign personnel which ruled Africa. It claims to be competent enough to rule, but it has no traditional legitimacy. In order to *replace* the colonizer, it has to invent a number of legalistic theories to justify that rule.'

Many elements of this analysis can be applied to Israel. Here, too, the 'civic public' was not founded either on Jewish political values or Jewish 'primordial groupings', despite very strong 'primordial' Jewish national sentiment. The civic public of the Jews of Palestine both before and after the establishment of the State was, indeed, strongly influenced by the cultures, customs, institutions, ideologies which the early Jewish Zionist settlers brought from their lands of origin. There was, of course, a strong element of original Jewish culture, but concepts such as socialism, democracy, secular nationalism, as well as institutions like the co-operative farm, labour unions, political parties, theatre, painting, school systems, etc., had little or no connection with the traditional Jewish culture which had been practised in the Diaspora for over eighteen centuries.

It is, of course, legitimate to ask to what extent the Diaspora preserved indigenous political values within the special institutions which developed in the unique historical and social conditions of a nation-in-exile, and if, in fact, such political values ever existed. This problem is discussed elsewhere (ch. 4): it will be sufficient here to say that it is inconceivable that a whole dispersed nation could retain its homogeneity, its communal autonomy and an extraordinary religious-cultural unity in spite of its geographical and bureaucratic decentralization, without the existence of a very particular, distinctive, and accepted common consciousness of its identity. Furthermore, it is equally inconceivable that such a consciousness should not apply to political problems and decisions taken by Jews, as such. The history of the West and of Islam is full of instances in which Jews were involved in political action for their own sake or for the sake of others, or for both. The idea, on which more will be said later, that because Jews did not possess a nation state there could be no Jewish politics or Jewish political thought is a colonialist concept as unfounded as the idea that most African peoples had no history—or at least no history worth recording— before the arrival of the Arabs or the Europeans on the Black Continent. What is true is that in the wake of the Emancipation of the Jews in Europe and the weakening of the Jewish traditional society, from the eighteenth century onwards, Jewish national consciousness and Jewish institutions entered into a deep crisis, similar to that of most colonized African polities in the eighteenth and nineteenth centuries. And like the newly independent African states, Israel, the reborn Jewish polity, took over political concepts and institutions from the West, developing variations of social and political habits often in contrast to those of traditional Judaism.

This was already true of the Jewish, Zionist immigrants who came to Turkish Palestine before the First World War, the members of the famous Second *Aliyah* (second wave of immigration, 1904-14), to which many of the State's future leaders—Presidents Ben-Zvi and Shazar, Premiers Ben-Gurion and Levi Eshkol, etc.—belonged. The Second *Aliyah* had little in common with the Jews of the old Palestine community, created by the continuous religious urge which in every century had pushed Jews to emigrate to the Holy Land. The discrepancy between the two types of settler was so marked that, almost until the Allied victory over Turkey, the *Halutz* (secular Jewish pioneer) was often regarded as an anathema by the old Jewish *Yishuv*—religious and secular. The process did not stop with the creation of Israel, because the immigrants who came in their thousands to populate the new State, including most of those who came from Islamic countries, had been subject to varying degrees of Westernization, an influence which they and their fathers had been more than ready to accept. The Zionist élite of European origin drew its inspiration directly from the *Haskala* revolution, the Jewish version of the Enlightenment, which gave birth to a new, secular Jewish élite in open opposition to that of the religious rabbinical traditional Jewish culture and society. In certain cases the new emancipatory ideas were carried to the Jews of Eastern Europe on the muzzles of conquering guns, as was the case with the Africans. Napoleon, of course, gave his conquests a revolutionary and ideological dimension and appearance which was lacking in the colonial conquests in Africa, the theory of the White Man's Burden notwithstanding. But the similitude in the effects produced by the more or less violent encounter between Jewish and African traditional societies and Westernization in the eighteenth and nineteenth centuries can be seen in the way in which the Jewish and African élites absorbed the ideas and prejudices of the imported culture. In both cases the traditional, religion-imbued establishment rejected them, while both Jewish and African intellectuals absorbed Western values and beliefs with enthusiasm. In the case of the Jew, as in many colonial societies, the Westernized intellectual regarded himself as standing in a 'neutral' position between indigenous and foreign values. He believed that the elements which he admired most in the West, as holding the secret of power of the Europeans—science, political institutions, military organization, etc. —were 'neutral' instruments which could be adopted without losing one's own identity. From this rational, 'neutral' point of view, both the African *évolué* and the Jewish *maskil* (intellectual) criticized their own traditional society, called for sweeping reforms and, in the case of the Jews, for the 'normalization' of the Jewish people. The adoption of the Gentile society's social structure, consisting of wide strata of workers, artisans, and soldiers with few intellectuals, in contrast to the 'lazy' and unproductive structure of Jewish society—the pedlars, the pious rabbinical scholars, the petty financiers, or just the masses of 'miserable' middlemen—was one of the main claims of Zionism, and was indeed considered by Socialist Zionism to be an indispensable condition for the revival of Jewish independence.

The African élites did not produce personalities like Moses Mendelssohn, who went so far as to regard the 'power compulsion' of Jewish communities as an imitation of the Christian Church. [7] Nor did the Africans ever develop, either at home or in European capitals, fashionable salons like that of Mendelssohn's converted daughter Henriette Hertz, who attracted and galvanized the leading intellectual personalities of Berlin, and from whose salon Judaism could be denounced as a 'dull practice of mechanical observation'.

Yet if we look at the arguments which the liberal Gentiles and the *Maskilim* used to criticize traditional Jewish society, we find that they were somewhat similar to those employed by the European colonizers to discredit the local indigenous societies, and which African *évolués*—as well as American Blacks—often internalized and accepted as part of their own collective self-image.

It was, of course, more difficult for people of Christian culture to denigrate the Jewish past, since they possessed a common root. But there was no objection to assailing Jewish tradition as a backward and wrong interpretation of Jewish history, and the Jews themselves as enemies of humanity. Jewish anti-Semites did so with particular viciousness, from Karl Marx on the Left to the pro-Nazi, Austrian-Jewish political writer Arthur Trebitsch on the Right. They were 'self-haters', an ultimate expression of that process characteristic of the alienated people of every colonized society. [8]

The difference between the Jewish alienated assimilationist and the African alienated *évolué* is, of course, considerable. Yet both suffered from the psychological dichotomy of the Westernized native; both sought their individual promotion in the acceptance of their cultural submission to foreign culture and values and in the legitimation of such dependence. For the assimilating Jew, as for the assimilating African, the parting from the 'superstitions' of his own tradition and the acquisition of a foreign education were the conditions for joining the ruling colonial élite. In the colonies, Western education also meant an escape from manual work, which was considered degrading. In the case of the Jews it was more a switch from one non-manual work situation to another, but in both cases the perceptions of colonizer and colonized were similar: they identified Westernization and modernization with progress, superiority, promise of social advancement. The fact that the Jews could avail themselves of Western educational facilities to a far larger extent than the Africans was a question of quantity, not of quality. In both cases it produced two results: it helped to promote and preserve 'the aura of charisma which formed the legitimacy for European rule'; and it contributed to enlarging the cleavage between Western institutions and traditional ones, giving to the latter that connotation of *'naïveté'*[9] which was the basis of 'the condescending distinction between the Westernized and "naive" sectors' in traditional societies.

This process of assimilation to foreign values and cultures was responsible for creating situations in which, despite all the obvious differences in objective conditions, the members of the new élites of assimilated Africans and assimilated Jews were caught in the same dilemma of simultaneous adaptation to two opposed systems.

The Africans, says Ekeh, 'claim to be competent enough to rule but have no traditional legitimacy'. They are therefore compelled to 'invent theories' to justify that rule. This is also true to a considerable extent of secular Israeli Zionist élites. In the case of the Africans, these theories are well known to students of colonization.[10] First there is an acceptance of that Western interpretation of African history which currently assumes that African history did not exist before the Europeans arrived in Africa. Next there is the belief that the essence of colonization represented, in the framework of society, 'what conception and education [represents] in the family'. The belief was made acceptable to the native by a subtle presentation of scientific, philosophical, and ideological concepts about the values of colonization, all aiming to establish European metropolitan cultural superiority over the colonized society. In the field of science such superiority remains unshaken to this day. At all events, these efforts at cultural colonization met with no serious opposition.

The Jews went through a similar process more quickly and more thoroughly than any other colonized people because of their high level of education, their longer involvement and physical presence within the culture of the Western host societies to which they soon became active contributors, and, of course, their common cultural roots with the Christian world. For a long time social restrictions did not allow them to participate in those activities considered important for generating power in Western society: the army, agriculture, heavy industry, banking, mining, etc. In the beginning, at least, most Jews lacked the capital to invest significantly in those fields, and those who did so, like the Rothschilds, the Ginzbergs, the Hirsches, etc., automatically assumed the role of leaders within the Jewish community, even if they had broken away from traditional Judaism.[11]

Science, communications, and teaching, which were later to become major sources of power, were considered in the nineteenth century to be still relatively marginal occupations as far as real power was concerned. They were therefore left more open to the Jews than other fields of activity. The deep Jewish penetration of the host society's culture only increased the detachment from traditional Jewish cultural sources and values.

The process was not, and—as has already been said—could not be, stopped by the creation of the State of Israel and its emergence as a new focal point of interest and identity for the Jewish people at large. In fact, the advent of Zionism increased the process of Jewish alienation from tradition in two ways. The Zionists, and later the Israelis, like their colonized counterparts in Africa and Asia, saw in the imitation of the West—especially in its military, economic, and ideological performances—the quickest way to catch the train of progress and modernity. Furthermore, by the creation of a state based on the first secular Jewish community in the history of the Jewish people, Zionism aspired to 'normalize' the Israeli Jew according to non-Jewish rather than Jewish norms, since foreign norms were considered indispensable to the achievement of political independence. The most important result was that Zionism contributed to switching an existing and powerful assimilationist trend from the individual to the collective level. The ultimate—and generally unexpected—consequence turned out to be the creation of an Israeli society different from (and often antagonistic to) all previous forms of Jewish society. But at the same time the emergence of a state devoted to the task of bringing the Jews physically back to their ancestral homeland was bound to affect the revival of Jewish indigenous culture.

As a result, and despite the many differences, one finds—surprisingly enough—the Jewish and the African Westernized nationalist fighting on three similar fronts simultaneously: against foreign political oppression (anti-Semitism and colonialism respectively), against institutionalized traditionalism, and against the vested interests of those among their own people who identified totally with the West, while at the same time searching back into an often legendary past to discover symbolic connections with the people's traditions. Two passages, taken at random from speeches by a Zionist and an African nationalist intellectual, delivered years apart and well before the recovery of political independence, denouncing the evils of cultural and psychological assimilation, will suffice to underline the similarity of the self-colonization process in two apparently completely separate historical and cultural experiences.

The French-Jewish doctor and political writer Max Nordau said:

Jewish misery has two forms, the material and the moral. In Eastern Europe, North Africa, and Western Asia—in those very regions where the overwhelming majority, probably nine-tenths of all Jews live—there the misery of the Jew is to be understood literally. It is a daily disaster of the body, anxiety for every day that follows, a tortured fight for bare existence. In Western Europe . . . the question of bread and shelter and the question of security of life and limb concern them less. There the misery is moral. It takes the form of perpetual injury to self-respect and honour, and of brutal suppression of the striving for spiritual satisfaction which no non-Jew is obliged to deny himself.

The Western Jew, continued Nordau, had bread, and yet he did not live by bread alone; the old forms of misery had been replaced by new, for the inner character and purpose of the Emancipation had been misunderstood by Jews. It had not been instituted to remedy an ancient injustice but as a function of the logic of the men of the French Revolution and because the philosophy of the Revolution decreed—although popular sentiment rebelled against it—that principles must be placed above sentiment. The Jews had hastened, in a kind of intoxication, to burn their bridges, to cut themselves off from the self-contained life of the ghetto. With the new outburst of anti-Semitism, the assimilated Jew discovered that he had

. . . lost the home of the ghetto, but the land of his birth is denied to him as home. He avoids his fellow-Jews because antisemitism has made them hateful. His countrymen repel him when he wishes to associate with them. He has no ground under his feet and has no community to which he belongs as a full member. The emancipated Jew is insecure with his fellow beings, timid with strangers, even suspicious of the secret feelings of his friends. His best powers are exhausted in the suppression, or the difficult concealment of his own real character. He becomes an inner cripple. [12]

Frantz Fanon probably never read a line of Nordau's writings, but as a psychologist he knew that 'an anti-Jewish prejudice is no different from an anti-Negro prejudice'. He was not thinking of the Jewish condition when he expressed ideas similar to those of Nordau, that

. . . exploitation, tortures, raids, racism, collective liquidation, rational aggression, take turns at different levels in order literally to make of the native an object in the hands of the occupying nation. This object-man, without means of existing, without a *raison d'être*, is broken in the very depth of his substance. The desire to live, to continue, becomes more and more indecisive, more and more phantom-like. It is at this stage that the well-known guilt complex appears. . . . The inferiorized group has admitted, since the force of reasoning was implacable, that its misfortunes resulted directly from its social and cultural characteristics. Guilt and inferiority are usually the consequences of this dialectic. The oppressed then tries to escape these, on the one hand by proclaiming his total unconditional adaptation to the new cultural model or on the other hand by pronouncing an irreversible condemnation of his own cultural style. . . . Having judged, condemned, abandoned his cultural forms, his language, his food habits, his sexual behaviour, his way of setting down, of resting, of laughing, his general behaviour, the oppressed flings himself upon the imposed culture with the desperation of a drowning man. [13]

The solvent effect of the encounter between non-developed and developed societies becomes evident, where the meeting of the West with both Jewish and African cultures is concerned, when one looks at the inability of the recipients of modernization to borrow piecemeal, that is, to take from the outside only what is considered most fitting to the needs of their own structures.[14] The feeling of frustration shared by the masses and the élites seems proportional in this case to the age and functionalism of the indigenous structures, or to what the recipients—rightly or wrongly—think them to be. The masses see the old structures—in particular the family ones —destroyed without being replaced quickly enough by acceptable new ones; the élites struggle, often in vain, to regain control of both old and new structures, while feeling in continuous danger of being swept away by the process of modernization which they have embraced. This is particularly visible in the case of the Arabs, for whom the encounter with Israel has been a powerful and uncontrollable solvent factor, within the larger and equally uncontrollable solvent process of Westernization.

The conflict between the Arabs and the Jews could probably not have been avoided in view of the time and place in which it developed, and the historical circumstances, the economic and strategic local and international interests involved. It seems legitimate, however, to ask whether the intensity of that conflict would have been the same if Israeli and Arab leaders had been reciprocally more conscious of the similarity of the problems faced by Jewish and Islamic traditional cultures in modern times.[15] The fact that, from the outset, Zionism presented itself to the Arabs in secular, Westernized, socialist and nationalist garb and as a break-away from the traditional Jewish past, undoubtedly reinforced in the Arab mind the image of its total, and negative, identification with the European colonial world.[16] On the other hand, the abysmal Arab ignorance of Judaism, their unquestioning acceptance of stereotyped Western interpretations of Jewish culture, Jewish character, and Jewish national aims, as part of the general process of Westernization of Arab society, made it difficult for Islamic and 'secular' Arab nationalists alike to look at Zionism except through the spectacles of Western political experience, from which, for totally different reasons, both Jewish and Arab nationalists sought to escape.

In the Arab-Israeli struggle what Geertz calls the 'interest element' has received exaggerated attention at the expense of the 'strain element'.[17] It is, of course, always easier to explain a conflict in terms of measurable factors, such as territory, economy, or military hardware, than in terms of cultural, psychological, or internal collective tensions. The latter type of analysis has to deal with more confused and confusing questions of symbolic formulation, which have so far attracted limited attention from political and social scientists.[18]*

*The relevance of imaginary thought and metaphor to traditional Jewish culture will be discussed in chapter 4; suffice it to say that recent studies

It is within this context of symbolic formulation that interpretations of the dynamics of African society become relevant for the understanding of the dynamics of Israeli society. The reader will recall Ekeh's analysis of post-colonial Africa where, contrary to what happened in the West, collective national values and behaviour change when passing from one level to another in the native society. Because an imported culture impregnates the native society, especially in the public domain, the African's personality is split in two. The resulting bureaucratic mismanagement, corruption, internal tension, and many of the political and administrative mishaps, usually attributed to chance, pragmatism, native character, etc., are simply the result of a dualism created by historical circumstances; they cannot be solved until the élites ruling the countries recognize the true, deep causes of their troubles. Let us take a brief look at some recent and publicized problems of the Israeli society in the light of Ekeh's thesis, which claims that 'the native sector has become the primordial reservoir of moral obligation, a public entity which one works to preserve and benefit. The Westernized sector has become an amoral civic public, from which one seeks to gain, if possible, in order to benefit the primordial public.'

Considering the pluralism of Israeli society, its high standard of education, industrialization, military organization, social mobility, and civic motivation, it seems inappropriate to talk of 'primordial' and 'civic' sectors in the sense used by Ekeh. Yet it is not difficult to perceive in Israel also, a profound dichotomy between the respective values of traditional Jewish culture and the imported Western or Islamic cultures of the Israelis; between the legitimacy of an élite basing its claim to rule on the authority of alien institutions and ideologies, and an élite—or several élites—which contest this authority on the basis of old Jewish tradition, or of a new, nativist one, which is itself already a mixture of several cultural trends.

This dichotomy has become more evident since the 1967 war and has been at the centre of a national debate between the so-called 'hawks and doves' of Israel's political establishment ever since. The 1967 war, instead of stabilizing the *de facto* situation created by Israel's War of Independence in 1948 and transforming the armistice lines, with some changes, into permanent, recognized frontiers, destabilized the Israeli situation internally and externally. It heightened the debate on the legitimacy of the State of Israel by sharpening—*inter alia* because of the historical opposition between Jewish traditional and Israeli secular nationalism—the ideological

of the difficulties encountered in the direct Israeli-Egyptian negotiations show that the introduction by the Arabs of biblical passages into official statements is perceived very favourably by the Israelis, while the inclusion of Koranic passages by the Israelis is perceived as insulting by the Arabs. This seems to be a clear case of misunderstanding due not to opposing interests but to conflicting processes of symbolic formulation.

radicalism of the Palestinian Arabs. It raised the question of how the state could remain democratic without conferring equal rights on those who had come under its control, and how it could remain a Jewish state if those rights were indeed granted and accepted. It forced the country's leadership to face the dilemma of developing an economy entirely dependent on aid from, and trade with, the Western capitalist world but subject to all types of controls, because of security necessities, marxist ideology, and the vested interests of its socialist power élites.

With military victory, occupied territories, and increased immigration brought about by the great hopes raised throughout the Jewish world by the war, came massive foreign investment, growing general expenses, easy money, an increase in corruption, and a surrealistic feeling of power which tore large holes in the older pioneering, egalitarian, and austere socialist fabric of Israel. The values on which the old system was founded were not specifically Jewish: like Zionism, other Israeli ideologies, such as social-ism, agrarian romanticism, liberalism, were imported from the West. But the atmosphere of the state prior to 1967 was more Jewish than after the Six-Day War for a number of reasons. The memories of the Holocaust were nearer; the education of even the most secular leaders of the country—like Ben-Gurion or Levi Eshkol—had still been traditional; the preoccupation with physical survival had kept the Israeli 'family' united; and the rela-tively small income gap between the various interest groups kept the grow-ing social inequality between Western- and Oriental-born Israelis manageable —at least at the level of individual income.

The sudden, smashing victory of 1967 changed all this: everything seemed big and possible; gone was the feeling of claustrophobia; the fear of being destroyed, the sense of paucity. With the new sense of power and security came not new values but new needs, all inspired by the desire to imitate the Western consumer society. While soldiers were still dying in the long war of attrition along the frontiers, newspapers were full of descrip-tions of the new high-society life, parties, *dolce vita*, and economic compe-tition with the full participation of the military, political, and bureaucratic élites. To be a General now also meant being a candidate for a managerial post in a newly created economic enterprise; to be a senior official also meant being an effective or presumed source of capital and influence; to be 'in' no longer meant being a kibbutznik or a war veteran, but an object of attention by the press.[19] The economy developed at a rapid pace, and so did the national debt. The construction of massive fortifications along the new borders was not only a source of security, it was also a source of quick gain and corruption for many of the contractors involved. Some critics of the system believe that these colossal and unimaginatively planned fortifications were the turning point of a relatively honest, productive economy into one dominated by parasitism and 'black' money.[20] This view may be exaggerated, and has been challenged by official and non-official economists.[21] What is certain is that 'Sapirism'—the economic system named after the late and all-powerful Minister of Finance, Pinhas Sapir—favoured the rapid development and industrialization of the country through manipulation of foreign investment capital, discriminatory alloca-tion of economic privileges, and disregard for the social consequences that the creation of sudden new riches might have on the population, particu-larly on the poorer strata, almost exclusively made up of non-European Jews.

The financial scandals and the steep rise in the level of crime were the natural consequences of the social disintegration resulting from rapid modernization and industrialization which did, nevertheless, help to strengthen Israel's overall economic and military ability to withstand hos-tile pressure from outside. In a sense, these scandals were an indication of the vitality of a pioneering society, which had broken new ground in all directions and was now searching for new norms with which to comply. But—as in the case of the two publics in Africa described by Ekeh—the astonishing growth of corruption, accompanied by an equally astonishing display of military and civil virtues in times of emergency, showed the existence of a dichotomy in collective behaviour which had developed as a direct consequence of the Israeli public's divided dependence: on indige-nous and on imported values.

On the one hand, one could see how the traditional Jewish values had remained strong in all fields of the Israeli society as a consequence of the dramatic events faced by the State over such a short period of time. The fifteen days of total national mobilization and anxiety before the 1967 conflict, for instance, had plunged the whole Israeli population once again into the haunting atmosphere of impending destruction so familiar to the Jews of the Diaspora. The then Chief-of-Staff, General Itzhak Rabin, summed up the mood of the nation thus:

> The strain of battle, the anxiety which preceded it, cracked the shell of hardness and shyness [of the Israeli soldier] and released wellsprings of emotion and stirring spirit. The paratroopers who captured the Wailing Wall leaned on the stones and wept—in its symbolism an act so rare as to be almost unparalleled in human history. . . . This scene on the Temple Mount, beyond the power of words to describe, revealed as though by a flash of lightning truths that were deeply hidden.[22]

No less significant was a pamphlet—one of the many which have since appeared in all the intellectual circles of the country—published a year later by the Hashomer Hatzair kibbutz movement, representing the most leftist and secularist trend in Israeli socialism, which said: 'You can call it reactionary, you can say it is no good, that it is medieval, but . . . it is a fact. . . . We are now in a period of return to tradition, towards the Jewish people and our connection with it.'[23]

Six years later in 1973, during and after the Yom Kippur War, those Jewish values became even more prominent. They expressed themselves in a number of ways: in the voluntarism of large strata of the civilian population; in the passionate, almost masochistic need for collective self-criticism; in the increased interest in Jewish studies and continuous public and private debate about the identity and legitimacy of the Israeli state in terms of Judaism and Jewish interest; and in the growing political influence of extra-parliamentary groups (such as *Gush Emunim*—'The Bloc of the Faithful', a non-party organization devoted to the Judaization and settlement of Judaea and Samaria) and of the religious establishment in general.

Side by side with this renewed interest in traditional values was an opposite tendency: a trend towards emigration rooted in disillusion at not being able to achieve an affluent Western society in Israel; the loss of credibility and authority of the Israeli labour establishment which had proved incapable of coping with the social and moral needs of the country; the indifference of the Government towards the growing psychological and economic gap within the population; and the increased reliance of the administration and the army on Western technological and bureaucratic experience to cope with human and cultural problems.

The immediate political result was the defeat in the 1977 elections of the Labour Coalition after thirty years in power, and the unexpected rise of the Right and of Mr Menahem Begin. This will be discussed elsewhere. Here it is sufficient to point out that the Begin phenomenon is, to a large extent, the result of the need to find an authoritative father figure to bridge the gap between the old, national, collective memories and Jewish values of the Jewish people, and the new, national, collective memories and imported values of the Israeli nation. This gap is certainly different from the one analysed in the two-publics model of Ekeh. But it is close enough to justify the claim that the dynamics of the Israeli society cannot be understood *only* in terms of Western political experience.

The works of another student of the cultural colonization and decolonization process, Albert Memmi, the Tunisian-born, French-educated, Jewish sociologist, are of relevance in this connection because they specifically compare the cases of the coloured African, the American Black, and the assimilated Jew, even though Memmi does not relate them to Israel and its cultural problems. In an important study on Jewishness and Negritude,[24] Professor Memmi distinguishes between three concepts: Jewry, Judaism, and Jewishness, and compares them with three similar concepts relevant to the African case: Negrity, Negroism, and Negritude.

Jewry, he says, means a group of Jewish persons, just as Negrity means a group of black people. In its widest sense this concept may include all the Jews of the world (or all the Blacks, as the case may be), and in its narrowest sense it may refer to the Jews (or the Negroes) of one specific place, of New York (or Cotonou). Judaism, on the contrary, is 'the whole of the teaching, beliefs and institutions of the Jews': namely Jewish culture in its widest sense including, of course, religion. To this definition of Judaism one can apply the definition of Negroism. Finally, says Memmi, there is Jewishness, namely 'the fact and manner of being a Jew; all the objective sociological, psychological and biological characteristics which make a Jew; the way in which a Jew lives, and at the same time his belonging to Jewry and his integration with the non-Jewish world'. Jewishness corresponds to Negritude in so far as by this word it is possible to define 'the manner of feeling oneself to be a black man, by belonging to a particular group of men and by adherence to its values'.[25]

These definitions help us to see how we can and how we cannot make comparisons between the Israeli and African societies when dealing with the problem of their respective colonized cultures. If we try to compare the situation—social, historical, or economic—of a certain group of Jews (Jewry) with that of a certain group of Blacks (Negrity), obviously we cannot reach any valid conclusion. It is useless, therefore, to attempt to draw parallels between the status of the Jewish community in Palestine under the British and, say, the Kenyans under the British, and claim—as has sometimes been done by Israeli propaganda—that there are similarities between the two cases because both were subject to the same imperial rule. It is equally purposeless to try to find common points between Judaism and Negroism: the two civilizations have developed independently and on totally different principles.

Yet, if we focus our attention on the way of being a Jew, and more specifically an Israeli Jew, and on the way of being a Black, and more specifically an African, Western-educated Black, then it is possible to trace important and reciprocally illuminating parallels. Both societies have been, and still are, exposed to the same influences and face a similar fundamental cultural dilemma: how to graft a foreign, imported culture on to an ancient, indigenous, and non-Western root, and how to act and react in a situation in which the search for collective identity often clashes with the desire for change and modernism, calling for deep involvement in, and a growing acceptance of, alien cultural values.

The similitude exists because both Jews (and this includes the Israeli Jew) and Africans have lived in what Memmi describes as

. . . special and aggressive circumstances which made it difficult for them to regard themselves objectively; [circumstances in which] illusions were born of the accusations of others and through self-rejection, just as myths were created to counter the accusations. Obviously this abnormal condition of oppression cannot be compared to that of the people who are masters of their own destiny, for whom the relationship between religion and culture, for example, has taken a totally different form.[26]

Although Memmi does not say so, it seems clear that the fact that the Israeli Jew has become master of his own destiny makes the comparison between his Jewishness (i.e. his way of being a Jew) and the African's Negritude (i.e. his way of being Black) not only possible and legitimate, but extremely important for an understanding of the behaviour of both.

The Zionist revolt against the Jewish condition of oppression in nineteenth-century Europe (as well as Jewish participation in revolutionary movements of all types) is not totally dissimilar, though the circumstances differ, from the revolt of the Blacks in the United States (through violent movements such as those of Malcolm X) or in Africa (through the Mao Mao), in the sense that these types of revolt are 'first of all the acknowledgement of an impossible situation'. In these conditions, 'myths are born of the necessity to overcome a situation of aggression which at first seems unchallengeable'.[27] In fact, in every case the oppressed people needed the most powerfully destructive myth as a battering-ram to attack so apparently impregnable a position. 'The Hebrews needed the Column of Fire and the offer of the Promised Land to persuade them to leave Egypt, and these myths have been revived in their entirety by present-day Zionism. Without them, where can the oppressed, who has lived so long in subjection, ever find the strength to break with his slavery?'[28] If the modern Hebrews are today in trouble, it is because the myths of pre-Israeli Zionism, interpreted in the simplistic vein of nineteenth-century Western romantic nationalism, are no longer sufficient. What is needed, in Israel as in other colonial societies, is a conscious collective effort to tear down the image which the non-Jewish world had attributed to the Israelis and which they had, willingly or unwillingly, consciously or unconsciously, made their own, and to replace it with more credible images.

The present cultural, ideological, political malaise of Israel is essentially due to the fact that there is not yet a consensus on how these images should appear. As in many African countries, so too in Israel it is clear that the process of decolonization cannot be an artificial revival of a dead past, or an unconditional break-away from it through imitating other cultures, even if their technical products are of generalized use. What is needed is the elaboration of institutions and collective habits in which tradition and modernity can coexist. No one can say at this moment whether Israel will be capable of making such an effort. What can be said is that the centrality of the problem not only exposes the Israeli society to deep internal doubts but makes it a testing ground for an experience of decolonization which, despite its particularism, is of essential relevance to the major causes of conflict in contemporary society.

CHAPTER 4

Traditional Jewish Political Thought

To defend the relevance of Jewish tradition to modern life means, among other things, facing two difficulties: that of proving that Judaism is not only a religious faith but a comprehensive way of life, with values and a logic of its own which make sense even in our times, and that of overcoming the prejudices of science.

In the Western world, where most of the Jews have lived since their emancipation, Judaism, for the last two centuries, has increasingly been considered as a religion: an open contradiction of the age-old opinion that the Jews were a nation.[1] Religion has been identified with the realm of faith and excluded from the realm of the day-to-day political realities; secularism has become one of the attributes of democracy and of material progress. All these facts had contributed to relegating the traditional way of life of the Jews to the domain of faith and metaphysics, to the 'unreal', or at least to the 'impracticable'. An attempt to make Judaism fit into modern life, therefore, seems to most people a purposeless and hopeless task.

Scientism, on the other hand, contends that all the problems of humanity, be they social or moral, can be solved through proper scientific methods (and that the only valid methods for proving realities are scientific). The Jewish problem should not be an exception, as 'scientific' dialectical materialism, as well as pragmatic Zionism, have tried to prove. But the Jewish question has so far defied all solutions, and Judaism has escaped all 'scientific' rational explanations because both its realities and its inner logic belong to an historical, cultural, and social framework which, however much it has been influenced by Western or Eastern cultures, cannot be identified with either of them.

Before the French Revolution, Jews would hardly have taken notice of other people's civilizations. And this goes for Western science as well. They felt culturally and socially superior, and in fact regarded the host society as barbarian. But from the moment that Judaism began to be explained by Jews and Gentiles and accepted by emancipated Jews as a 'science',[2] it was bound to be judged according to a new scale of values. There were many reasons for the loss of Jewish cultural self-sufficiency. Some of them, belonging to the general historical process undergone by the Western world and by the Jews who lived in it, have already been mentioned. The importance of the colonizing factor has also been underlined. Indeed, the attempt to explain Judaism as a 'science' and the Jewish question in terms of sociological analysis discredited assimilated Jews, since rationalism denounced anything which did not conform to the norms of experimental science. People like Diderot and Voltaire, and later Marx and Toynbee, as well as many anti-Semitic or pro-Semitic rationalistic thinkers, could easily shatter the logic of the Jewish religious belief or, for that matter, of any religious belief, by pointing out the inconsistencies of the authoritative sources upon which all revealed religions rely, as well as the contradictions between myth and reality.

To the assimilated and emancipated Jews, the corrosive criticism of rationalism brought about a deep feeling of abnormality which added to their already inferior position in Western society—a society into which they wanted passionately to enter, while trying to escape from their own.

It was, as already noted, a typical situation of cultural colonization, but with one major addition: the nation which had developed the idea of monotheism and which, more than any other, carried on the fight against all types of natural idols, found itself facing the ethical, philosophical, and social challenge of a Christianity which still claimed to be the 'verus Israel' or the true heir, even while embracing new forms of paganism.[3]

Clearly it would have been easier to claim that the Jews had no history had they been in the situation of an unknown, non-European tribe. It would then have been natural to say about them what even reasonable European historians said about African societies of which they knew little or nothing,[4] namely that they had no culture or past. This was, of course, impossible for European Christian historians because of the intimate connection between Christian culture and Judaism, even if they believed that Jewish culture was corrupted, corrupting, and based on superstition. After the middle of the nineteenth century, prejudices against Jewish culture were reinforced by the fact that to both non-Jews and the new generation of assimilated and ignorant Jews themselves, the Jewish heart seemed scarcely to be beating. It could be claimed more easily than before that—with few exceptions—Jews were that 'miserable lot' concerning whom Heinrich Heine claimed, 'you must be careful not to look at them if you want to take an interest in them'.[5] Indeed, as early as 1840 a socialist Jew, Bruno Bauer, could safely compare his co-religionists to the Africans, calling them 'white niggers' who lacked the crude and uncouth nature and capacity for physical labour of their black brethren.[6] But ignorance and malice could not change the fact that the central problem for the co-existence of Judaism with other cultures was the recognition of the ahistorical character of the Jewish people, or at least the fact that its history was different from that of the rest of humanity. Such recognition could be acceptable on a theological level, not on a social, political one.

The secular Zionists, despite their love for Zion and their strong sense of Jewish dignity, did not want to be judged on any metapolitical parameter. Their pride was to be 'realists' even if their aim sounded dreamlike. Nahum Goldman, the future president of the World Zionist Organization and the World Jewish Congress, argued in 1916 that the Zionists, unlike 'just Jews', were much closer to the German national spirit than to that of the assimilationists who had received their inspiration from the liberal thinkers of Britain and France,[7] implying by this that national progress could only be achieved by becoming less Jewish and more German, less a nation based on ideas and more a people whose identity was strengthened by common territorial political aims.

What Zionists were not prepared to face was the revival of the need for a Jewish culture, as a consequence of the success of a national enterprise which had begun as a conscious revolution against many of the values of traditional Judaism. This traditional Jewish culture clearly expressed itself in the rabbinical literature, and inspired the daily life of the Jews as long as they lived in compact and organized communities. More important, this literature, as well as common Jewish historical memories and experiences, the system of education and the selection and promotion of Jewish élites (which will be discussed later), all helped to strengthen the isomorphism of those Jewish communities' functionalism. Jewish traditionalism perfectly fits the requirements of modern theories of social character such as those of Erich Fromm, who claims that 'in order that any society may function well, its members must acquire the kind of character which makes them *want* to act in the way they *have* to act as members of the society or of a special class in it. They have to *desire* what objectively is *necessary* for them to do. *Outer force* is to be replaced by *inner compulsion*.'[8]

Zionism, of course, claims that the outer force of anti-Semitism was a stronger motor for the revival of the Jewish people than its inner compulsions. Historically, Zionists appear to be in the right, but their pragmatism could not avoid contributing to the destruction (already at an advanced stage) of the very social structures which had helped the Jews to survive as a people for so many centuries. The moment the outer force lost most of its traditional image and increasingly turned from anti-Semitism into anti-Zionism or anti-Israelism, as happened after the creation of the State of Israel and the destruction of the Nazi regime, it became increasingly difficult for the secularized and culturally Westernized Jewish-Israeli society to find an inner logic to sustain its claim to a separate and unique identity, and even harder to support the claim that the Jews were automatically a people different from the host nations among which they lived.

Such a claim, couched in a language which was not that of the rabbinical literature, could be made by Zionist Jews and non-Jews, who argued the persistence of inner reasons for modern Jewish uniqueness on the basis of metaphysical, logical, and conventional scientific knowledge, which could validate the special claim of the Jews or explain their uniqueness as in the past. One of the most passionate contemporary arguments in favour of the metapolitical justification of Jewish uniqueness is to be found in the writings of the Catholic philosopher, Jacques Maritain. Well before the Second World War he claimed that Israel 'is to be found at the very heart of the world's structure, stimulating it, exasperating it, moving it. Like an alien body, like an activating leaven injected into the mass, it gives the world no peace, it bars slumber, it teaches the world to be discontented and restless as long as the world has not God; it stimulates the movement of history.'[9]

Maritain's conception of Israel, elaborated in his *Mystery of Israel*,[10] derives less from his conception of Judaism than from his epistemological theories. The central argument of his book, *Degree of Knowledge*,[11] is that it is necessary to distinguish among the various levels of thinking in order to grasp the unity of the object thought. In the case of Judaism, the distinction and the understanding of the multiple and often contradictory levels at which the Jews act, are the primary conditions for understanding the Jewish phenomenon.

Professor Marcel Dubois, Head of the Dominican Convent of St. Isaiah in Jerusalem and the only Christian monk ever to have been a regular member of the Hebrew University faculty, follows Maritain's epistemological rule when he argues that it is possible to classify various forms of expression of the Jewish existence with the help of some fundamental conceptual pairs: religion and nation, Israel and Diaspora, faith and observance, particularism and universalism. Of these 'couples', says Dubois, the most important and also the most misunderstood is the binomial religion/nation. 'The special trait of Judaism is in fact that religion and nation meet each other not as a synthesis or a combination of two elements but as two poles of the same reality.' For Dubois, the Jewish soul, even today and in a secular society like Israel, continues to show such a vocation for the Divine as to confirm that impression that it remains 'built' for the search for the absolute.

It is a marvellous and terrible gift since the soul which is marked by it is also condemned to idolatry the moment it no longer turns itself towards the Divine. . . . It is the story of the Golden Calf. Jewish subjectivity is constructed in such a way that it transforms all earthly objects into idols, because he [the Jew] carries within himself a search for the absolute which can only apply itself to a living God.[12]

This explains why there is a Jewish way of being an atheist, just as there is a Jewish way of being a Marxist or an anti-Zionist. Jewish anguish and despair or self-negation are to Dubois 'signs of a Jewish subjectivity gone mad'.[13]

An entirely different explanation of Jewish uniqueness can be argued, as philosopher Joseph Agassi does, on the basis of conventionalism of knowledge.[14] Agassi's thesis is the following: the philosophy underlying Western legal reform and Western legislation is largely naturalistic. The naturalist school views the laws of society as the laws of nature, and thus as the true laws. But in practice what happens is that society, even when it proclaims its attachment to naturalism, follows a more or less gradual conventionalism. To avoid admitting the discrepancy, philosophers like Pierre Duhem went out of their way to explain that one should make a distinction between facts of science, which are liable to change with the change of the scientific conventions of language, i.e. scientific theory, and facts of common sense, which are final because they are couched in ordinary language. The Talmud rejects such an artificial distinction. The purpose of its obsessive, minute, and complicated system of discussion is to justify, through highly sophisticated casuistry, the right to add new rulings and precedents to old ones and live with the dilemma of constant interaction between new knowledge and old without allowing the new to cancel the old. Such a philosophy, says Agassi, never fitted the Greek acceptance of a dichotomy between nature and convention. This fundamentally different approach to nature and convention has helped significantly to develop a unique form of Jewish pragmatism, Jewish conventionalism, which continues to influence, consciously or unconsciously, the individual and collective way of thinking of the modern Jew. In a way it could be said that it is a matter of metaphors.

Metaphor, maintains Robert A. Nisbet, is much more than a simple grammatical construction or figure of speech.[15] It is 'a way of knowing'; one of the oldest, most deeply embedded, even indispensable, ways of knowing in the history of human consciousness. He quotes Sir Herbert Read, who claims that 'metaphor is the synthesis of several complex units of the one commanding image; the expression of a complex idea not by analysis, nor by direct statement, but by sudden perception of an objective relation'.[16]

This definition of thinking through metaphor comes very close to the claim of traditional rabbinical scholars, who believe that much of the special Jewish way of thinking is due to the impact of talmudic learning on the mentality of the Jewish people. It is, or should be, common knowledge that the Jewish people is not the people of the Bible but the people of the Talmud. The Talmud is, in fact, the central, cumulative, and creative factor in Jewish culture. Without it no Jewish community has ever been able to exist for a long period of time, while the contrary has been proved correct even in times of the worst persecution. The revival in popularity and in diffusion of talmudic learning in modern Israel is certainly one of the most significant facts pointing to the strength of traditional Jewish learning as well as of the Jewishness of the Israeli society.[17]

It would be beyond the purpose of this book to attempt even a superficial presentation of the role of the Talmud in the history and formation
of the Jewish culture. Yet it is impossible to answer the question whether
there is a specifically Jewish way of thinking without giving some indication of how the Jewish mind has been and probably continues to be
moulded by the talmudic system of learning and values.

The formal definition of the Talmud is 'the summary of oral law that
evolved after centuries of scholarly efforts by sages who lived in Palestine
and in Babylon until the beginning of the Middle Ages'.[18] In reality, the
Talmud is the repository of thousands of years of Jewish wisdom, a conglomerate of laws, legends, and philosophy, a blend of unique logic and
shrewd perception of history and science. It is a collection of paradoxes
which treats abstract and totally unrealistic problems in the same manner
in which it refers to the most prosaic facts of everyday life. The Talmud is
thus the quintessence of living Jewish culture, its formative framework and
the most authentic expression of particularism of a civilization which is at
the same time parochial and universal.

One of the many components of this conglomerate of paradoxes can be
perceived in the fact that, contrary to current modern Western thought,
the traditional Jewish way of thinking throughout the ages has shunned
the use of abstract terminology and concepts. It has replaced them with
pictorial, intellectual models and imagery. Ideas such as authority, discipline, spirituality, statehood, opposition, not to speak of more recent concepts such as psychology, epistemology, etc., are subject-matters arising in
long and pertinent discussion in the Talmud. But they are expressed
through pictorial models. Some of them become so precise and fixed as to
turn into a collection of technical terms of their own. For instance, the
'horn' or the 'foot' of the bull is a figurative concept used not only in
problems connected with bulls and other animals but also, like a modern
mathematical model, in circumstances and to clarify problems which have
no relation whatsoever to the original case of the talmudic bull.

In a sense, these imaginary concepts, once formulated and finalized,
operate as ideographs. Like the written Chinese ideographs, their inhibit-
ing influence as far as the absorption of novelty is concerned has been
grossly exaggerated by Western scholars. But since every form of logic is
related to a given form of culture and language, these imaginary concepts
and other forms of talmudic scholarship and methodology tend, with time,
to create a logic of expression of their own. The trouble with it is not the
ability or inability of such a system to cope with modern problems: it
derives from the fact (as has been the case for a long time with Chinese
culture and other non-European civilizations) that Israelis take for granted,
sometimes even more than Western logicians, that Western logic is the
universal logic of human reason.[19] This, incidentally, is another typical

expression of that cultural dependence which is here named Jewish self-colonization.

To return to Jewish traditional thinking, it has also to be noted that these imaginary concepts and models which the Talmud has developed are original and precisely formulated systems of investigation. For instance, the system which operates on the principle of deducing the possible from the impossible, allows dialectic analysis of problems which appear to be intellectual casuistry. As an example, the debate on the question of whether religious conversion to Judaism is valid without circumcision and its application to the conversion of women is a typical debate on something which is biologically impossible but logically valid and therefore can serve as a refined tool of intellectual research, independent of the real subject-matter which originated the debate.

An aspect of the talmudic method of discussion which has currently influenced the way of thinking of traditional Jews is the fact that the subject under discussion, even when it deals with exclusively religious matters, is never conceived as a question of religion, still less as an elaboration of religious principles. It is always approached in the spirit of clarification of facts, however much the facts are related to the Divine. As a result, there is a lack of differentiation between major and minor issues, between the useful and the irrelevant, the sole objective being to arrive as near to the truth as possible. Such an approach imitates, and indeed surpasses in its scope, the widest framework of modern pure science and accounts for one of the most startling aspects of talmudic dialectical reasoning (*pilpul* in Hebrew): the inability to accept simple and apparently satisfactory proofs, and the continued search for incontrovertible evidence.

The fact that talmudic learning and methodology have been the central pillar of Jewish culture for centuries, and that Jews did not feel any need to step outside the talmudic sphere of influence to satisfy their intellectual needs, has created a paradoxical situation in modern times. On the one hand, talmudic culture remains unintelligible to all those who are not familiar with its particular techniques. On the other hand, in so far as it remains the backbone of Jewish knowledge and continues to influence, directly or indirectly, large strata of the Israeli élites and population, it also continues to condition their thinking, the behaviour of the society and the process of elaboration of its identity. In other non-Western societies this process, or even a type of cultural phenomenon far less important than the Talmud, might have been heralded as a proof of collective efforts towards decolonization and a search for a native cultural identity, but in Israel it has not yet found conscious and explicit expression. This causes the often surprising Israeli reaction to appear anomalous, irritating, or irrational to a Western observer, and thus a source of suspicion, misunderstanding and inexplicable tension. What is commonly missing in this psychological and cultural confusion is a clear realization of the fact that talmudic scholarship is a sacred form of intellectualism, not a religious one. As such, and in spite of its sacredness (which is certainly very unpopular in a secular modern society), talmudic culture still conditions the way of thinking of the Israeli Jew and is responsible for marking Israeli society with that particular blend of profound faith and questioning scepticism which has characterized Jewish traditional society throughout the ages.

It is in these terms that one can relate to a specific traditional Jewish way of thinking in Israel. The incessant self-criticism, the constant awareness that behind every fact there might be an unexpressed deeper reality, is to a visible extent a reflection of the very old Jewish approach to life. In the past this approach acted as a powerful instrument to promote level-headedness, legitimated a system of conventions which gave preference—at least outwardly—to non-material status competition, combined reality with mysticism and the political with the metapolitical, while at the same time it did not lose sight of man's limitations and capabilities. In sum, talmudic teaching was a singular system of education and values aimed at maintaining sanity in the midst of growing madness, and this is what still makes it meaningful to many Jews in modern times, quite apart from its moral religious values.

Another conscious or unconscious impact of Jewish traditional thinking on Israeli society and political culture has been what Professor Dubois calls 'the special fate of the Jewish soul for the Divine' and what Maritain describes as 'the mystery of Israel'. Tacitus, many centuries earlier, put it in a sharper, anti-Jewish form: "The Jews consider profane everything which is sacred to the Romans, while what the Romans regard as impure is popular among the Jews.'[20] Tacitus would certainly not have believed that the Jews, both culturally and politically, would outlast the might of the Roman Empire.

But what about the content of this traditional culture, especially in those domains not related to religion or morality? Can it still be claimed that it has something of its own to contribute to modern society? A field relevant to all other domains of human action, and one which at first sight seems to have received the least contribution from Jewish traditional culture, is politics. An important cluster of ideas which could be described as Jewish political thought may be uncovered, despite the fact that Jewish independence in Palestine ended in the first century CE. The Jews of Babylon remained a strong, autonomous community with considerable political status and power until the tenth century. There were many Jewish 'statelets' in Arabia, and Jewish influence was felt on the political élites of many countries, from North Africa to Russia throughout the Middle Ages.[21] And finally, as has been pointed out, the Jewish communities of Europe, up to the end of the eighteenth century, maintained internal

structures and external relations important enough to justify a rich accu-
mulation of political experience.[22] And yet there is no Jewish political
literature to fill the shelves of university libraries under the heading of
'Jewish Politics' or 'Jewish Political Ideas', as there is for, say, French,
Islamic, Chinese, or American politics or political ideas. A people which
for almost nineteen centuries retained its national culture, a cohesive
internal authority, and a financial organization without any sovereignty or
army, through sheer collective discipline, endurance, and superb diplomatic
skill, paradoxically appeared to have produced no political literature at
all.[23] The phenomenon should occasion no surprise, since it is typical of
all colonized societies. African history, for instance, for a long time 'did
not exist' for Europeans and only began to unfold itself with the first
signs of independence, as part of the process of decolonization.

One of the arguments claiming to refute the existence of significant
Jewish political thought is that the Jews, having been deprived for so long
of their political independence, were unwilling or unable to develop a consistent body of political ideas of their own. In other words, no state—no
political ideas; no practice—no theory. The argument is unconvincing: as
has already been said, even if Jews, over a long period, were not involved
in politics as members of a sovereign Jewish state, they were nonetheless
involved in the politics of their own system and of the Gentile system in
which they lived as members of a marginal but organized community.
Until the Age of Enlightenment these communities successfully struggled
to defend their religious, cultural, administrative, and judicial autonomy,
often enjoying important privileges, as was customary for every estate at
the time. The *Encyclopedia Judaica* lists over 120 entries on the history
and various other aspects of Jewish autonomy through the centuries. All
this is not to equate administrative autonomy with political self-government.
However, at different times and in different places Jewish communities did
develop independence, sometimes even to a considerable degree.[24]

The long, agonizing, Jewish struggle for the survival of a religious and
cultural identity (in which elements of political identity are also ingrained)
might by itself have contributed to distinct political thinking even without
a fully sovereign organization. But Jews thought and acted in political
terms at every period of their long history. The political experience of
ancient Israel as recounted in the Bible 'is of central importance to biblical
teaching because of the highly social character of biblical concern with
achieving the good life which leads to an emphasis on the good commonwealth. . . . Most important in the political experience of ancient Israel
remains the foundation of the Jewish political world view, particularly as
it pertains to the organization and government of the Jewish people. In
traditional terms, Judaism is essentially a theopolitical phenomenon, a
means of seeking salvation by constructing God's polity.'[25] The record of

that experience 'represents the oldest stratum of western political thought and since the record is derived very directly from the experience, the latter is in itself an important factor in the development of western political institutions. If this is more difficult to perceive today than it was in Spinoza's time, it is because the study of the political experience of ancient Israel has been generally neglected since the Puritans and the philosophers of the seventeenth century paid serious attention to it in shaping the political views of the modern men who at the very onset of the modern era were to reject Scripture.'[26] This rejection—in both Western and secular Zionist political thought and practice—is an additional proof of the desynchronized parallelism of institutional development in Western and Israeli democracy.

True, the idea of the state was never formulated in clear terms; there are no talmudic books or passages on the Jewish State similar to the innumerable passages existing on the people, the king, or the army. Some recorded historical deeds seem to have a very precise anarchic meaning. There is probably no other recorded evidence of a leader like Joshua, who stood at the head of a powerful, victorious, united army and people, and then destroyed this unity with his own hands.[27] He not only promoted decentralization and tribalism; he did not even appoint a successor. Other political ideas—that of royalty, for instance—which were developed by the Jews, have remained scattered over the whole vast Jewish literature. Further, there was a great deal of rabbinical literature about politics which, however, remained scattered because of the lack of a commandment to rebuild the State. Instead, talmudic discussion concentrated on specific issues: the crowning of a king, the problem of national frontiers, the legitimacy of political power, etc. The consistency of these discussions is easily made evident when the relevant passages are taken out of their original unclassified places in the text and put together. Rabbis in talmudic times often had divergent opinions about the policy to be followed *vis-à-vis* the ruling powers. Many were not recorded, or were recorded by allusion alone, or were recorded and later omitted. One must remember the permanent state of suspicion in which the Jews, as a people, lived in the Roman Empire, both in its pagan and later in its Christian phases. One must also bear in mind the rabbis' advice to the Jews whenever they were faced with difficulties. They must adopt the attitude of the reed, which sways with the wind but remains firmly rooted in its place.[28] This attitude is understandable when the ordeals the Jews had to endure in order to maintain their religio-cultural identity are recalled. The fact that they could and did find the courage and the ingenuity to record their political opinions, occasionally cryptically, in times of persecution, dispersion, and destitution greater in every sense than that of any colonial dependence, is perhaps indicative of the vitality of their way of thinking.

No less important is the historical explanation for the apparent lack of focus of the traditional literature on theoretical political issues. Quite apart from the special methodological approach described above which, in politics as in other domains, avoided abstract intellectual constructions, the price which the ancient Jews repeatedly paid for their attempts to restore political independence by military means induced the rabbis to favour the dismembering of Jewry as a body politic. They sought to guarantee its survival through institutions which would appear to be politically disjointed, and thus less liable to be the object of political repression by the oppressive authority. The result was an enormously flexible, decentralized polity—the very first in history. The central idea behind the creation of the first Talmudic Academy at Yavneh by Rabbi Johanan ben Zakkai was the shifting of the emphasis of Jewish efforts to survive from politico-territorial to politico-academic, non-territorial channels.[29] In fact, the new academic centre also provided a legitimate authority for the co-ordination of a highly centralized polity.

The idea of decentralization (-cum-centralized legitimation) invented by the talmudists may be opposed on the grounds that whereas decentralization is a general concept, the talmudists invented a very specific, parochial system:[30] there is not, and there cannot be, a Jewish political thought, distinct from other trends of Jewish thinking, because, it is said, when Jews think *Jewishly* they think in religious terms. Their terms of reference, whether in economics or agriculture, in love or in death (so runs the argument), are religious. It has already been shown that talmudic thinking is an intellectual system based on social rather than on religious elements. But assuming this is incorrect, to claim that Jews can think only in terms of religion is like saying that they are no longer thinking Jewishly except in the religious domain. Or, to put it another way, it is like saying that the political thinking of the Jews is either parochial religious thinking which may be political, or political thinking but not specifically Jewish.

To this charge of parochialism one can answer that religion in itself does not exclude politics. For such paradigms of secular political thought as Hobbes and Locke wrote their political treatises not in opposition to but as an integral part of the religious system of ideas of their own age. The charges of atheism levelled against Hobbes by some of his contemporaries were indeed charges against a conception of God different from that traditionally held by Christianity. It is understandable that the bishops, and in particular the Anglican divines of the time, did not like the idea that their dignities derived from *Regis Gratia* rather than from *Dei Gratia*. But one cannot dissociate Hobbes's political writings from religion: the Sovereign, he holds, is the supreme pastor and the source of all authority connoted by that name, and he—and only he—has his authority 'under God'. His rationalism in politics is not anti-religious: nearly half of the *Leviathan* is devoted to an exposition of the theological and ecclesiastical principles that support its moral and political theory. In this sense, Locke's theory of natural rights and of the separation of powers turns out to be far more removed from religion than any of Hobbes's political ideas. But even for Locke, the right of resistance was 'an appeal to Heaven'. Locke's plea for religious toleration is certainly not a plea for secularization of the society. The Calvinist or Puritan political ethic which inspired it was the very opposite of secularism. Similarly, in the same sense much could be said about political ideas in Islamic society, past and present. No doubt the Muslim political thinkers differed from the Christian, yet we accept them as political thinkers and as Muslims (or Christians, as the case may be). The idea that this is parochialism is one which must be rejected: it is an outdated, anti-religious prejudice of the eighteenth and nineteenth centuries.

By the same logic, political ideas in biblical and post-biblical literature should be examined for their political value and meaning, independently of, but without ignoring, their religious setting. They remain political whatever the environmental or psychological frame in which they developed. Even though one cannot speak of the politics of the synagogue—at least after the fourth century CE (there has been no central hierarchy in Judaism since the end of the authority of the *Sanhedrin* in Palestine and Egypt in the fourth century and that of the *Ge'onim* in Babylon in the twelfth century)—as one can speak of the politics of the Church, one can still speak of Christian and Jewish political ideas, even if they are an integral part of their respective religious systems.

This obviously requires the development of proper methods of research to avoid, *inter alia*, the pitfalls of the 'Black Studies' type. It is well to note that the emergence of Jewish political thought and institutions took place some seven centuries before the Greek political institutions; that is, in an epoch for which we have relatively little direct reference material of comparative type. Biblical thinking is certainly less articulate than Greek thought. Furthermore, the Bible does not give any comprehensive description of a political theory, for reasons already discussed. But just as expanded knowledge of ancient Middle Eastern societies and institutions has promoted a better understanding of the civilizations of the Bible, so it should be possible to improve our knowledge of Jewish political thought and practice in Roman and medieval times, not only through co-operative historical studies but through 'careful examination and analysis of the text with special attention to receiving patterns and the reconciliation of apparent contradictions. . . . Theory must be induced from the discussion of the political history and hopes of the Israelites and from the biblical critiques of institutions not fully described.'[31]

There are those who argue that while Jewish political thought may exist, it has been polarized between two traditional Jewish models, neither of which is of any practical use. One model is the Kingdom of David in the past; the other is the Kingdom of the Son of David (the Messiah) in the future. The former symbolizes the perfect integration of Jewish politics and Jewish religion: but it is so ancient, so little articulated, so idealized by subsequent generations, that it has become the symbol of the Golden Age of political Judaism and has thus blocked all Jewish attempts at rational political analysis. As far as the modern secular student (Jewish or non-Jewish) of politics is concerned, the ancient Kingdom of David can be ignored as nothing more than an interesting historical entity. The second model, the future Kingdom of David, the Messiah, cannot, however, be so easily ignored. In the first place, the Messianic Kingdom was not always connected with the redemption of Israel 'at the end of days'. Both in the Second Temple period and in the Middle Ages, the eschatological view of the Messiah was accompanied by a down-to-earth, political conception of the Redeemer. The High Priest and the Messianic King, two messianic figures derived from the Old Testament Book of Zacharias, find their way into the rabbinic literature. In the eschatology of the Dead Sea sect, this High Priest becomes more important than the Davidic King, and to these two is added the Prophet of the Last Days. They express the three main functions—Kingdom, Priesthood, and Prophecy—which should coexist in the ideal Jewish state. The Roman occupation enhanced the hope for the Davidic Messiah—the leader/redeemer—over the others. His qualities seemed to be personified in Bar Kokhba, the greatest of the Jewish political rebels against the Romans after the destruction of the Temple, and in whom Rabbi Akiva thought he recognized the Messiah.[32] A similarly earthly political conception of the Jewish Redeemer was defined in detail by Maimonides in the last two chapters of *Hilkhot Melakhim* (*The Rules of the Kings*) at a time when most of the Middle Ages literature on the subject had taken a definite apocalyptic turn. This latter attitude has, in more recent times, been upheld by Reform Judaism, while the Orthodox remain faithful to the traditional doctrine of the Messiah, scion of the House of David, who will rebuild Jerusalem. In this sense, although the Orthodox strongly opposed Zionism for its claim to substitute a purely human redemption for the Redeemer sent by God, it has become more acceptable to them because of its national achievements. The State of Israel today is officially regarded by the Rabbinate as the 'beginning of the growth of redemption', and consequently blessed as such in the Sabbath and Festival Prayers in almost all synagogues in Israel and the Diaspora.

On the other hand, the fact that one of the apocalyptic, utopian definitions of the Messianic state is inscribed in enormous letters on the wall of the United Nations building[33] should remind us not only of the political impact of the biblical utopia on the conscience of mankind, but also of the political relevance of what is often considered merely esoteric Jewish allegorical literature. The Kingdom of the Son of David, the Messiah, has been an esoteric Jewish utopian concept of political import for the Jews throughout the centuries. The expulsion from Spain—that religious, economic, and political catastrophe which befell the Jews at the end of the fifteenth century—stimulated a new type of mystic cabbalistic thought and literature, centred at Safed, Palestine. Its mysticism, as Gershom Scholem points out, aimed at the achievement of spiritual domination in Judaism in order to transform its esoteric doctrine into a widely accepted way of thinking. 'To mobilize and free all forces capable of provoking "The End" became once more the principal aim of mystics. The messianic doctrine, which up to now had interested only apologists, became for a moment an aggressive propaganda.'[34]

If so, this must have been true for more than just the elaboration of some political ideas in the mystical literature of the time. Although it was allegorical, such literature was then also a kind of 'blueprint' for action—to be executed if and when conditions became ripe. What Scholem calls the 'volcanic eruption', with the appearance of false messiahs like Sabbatai Sevi (1625-76), could not have produced the hysterical mass reactions of the Jews had the cabbalistic literature which preceded its advent not prepared the ground for the will to translate mythical allegory into practical action.[35]

Thus, even the idea of the Kingdom of the Son of David, the Messiah, should not be considered as a concept unrelated to political practice, regardless of its mystical character. It should, rather, be looked upon as an 'incubator' which added a wider dimension and scope to the political activities of many Jewish leaders who, mystics or not, remained at all times involved in the politics of their own communities as well as in those of the many countries of their residence.[36] It is this belief, as much as the demands of the political situational logic of the times, that determined the psychological prism of Jewish political culture through which the Jews viewed their political reality.

There is no doubt about the esoteric quality of both the Jewish utopia and Jewish symbolism. Yet they both interacted with Jewish political action and thus with the political actions and thoughts of their neighbours —and of the Western world at large. More important, in spite of its esoteric nature, Jewish political thought was coherent.

The continuity of Jewish political thinking is due first and foremost to the integrated and compact nature of Jewish biblical and post-biblical literature. As long as the Jews lived in communities run by religious rabbinical tradition, their terms of reference were the written and oral law, which gave basic and real cohesion to the Jewish culture of the diverse and dispersed communities, and continuity through many centuries. As in other areas of Jewish thinking, political thought is no exception. It may have been exposed to widely divergent situations, different in terms of place and time; it may have been exposed to widely conflicting influences, again different in terms of place and time; and it may have been expressed in widely differing terms; but as long as it remained linked, however tenuously, to the interpretation of the Law, it developed in an interconnected and continuous manner. Thus, although occasionally diffuse, Jewish political thought exhibits a certain consistency. Every word of the most important Jewish thinkers was quickly diffused among the widespread Jewish communities; correspondence between scholars was intense at all periods and was rapidly published and incorporated into the tradition. The language—Hebrew—and the traditional values were kept in common, in principle. This is well known. What has passed all but unnoticed by most students of political science is the intensity, the originality, and the pertinence of Jewish political thought. These qualities become evident when, as noted, relevant political passages in the biblical and post-biblical literature are collected and classified according to classical political questions such as those relating to sovereignty, legitimacy, political institutions, opposition, types of government, legitimation and limitation of power, and so on.[37]

Although investigations have thus far covered only part of the biblical and talmudic literature, sufficient evidence has been collected to arouse more interest in the continuity and development of Jewish political thought through further centuries and locations.[38] Two themes among the many seem to stand out within the awesomely massive record of evidence already visible in the Bible and the Talmud alone—the rule of law and the legal rights of the opposition. These two themes alone may suffice to indicate the measure of interconnectedness and continuity of Jewish political thought.

The idea of a covenant regulating the relations between the ruler (God or man) and the ruled, is one of the leitmotivs of Jewish biblical and post-biblical literature. There are the early pacts between God and the Patriarchs, which on the surface do not seem to possess political meaning. Yet even here some authoritative Jewish rabbinical interpreters have found a distinct, extra-religious meaning.[39] The political content of the 'covenant' is no longer doubted after the Exodus from Egypt, whether relating to the right of the people to inherit the Land of Canaan or to the legitimacy of the House of David as rulers.[40] Conversely, it is because the 'covenant' was broken, we are told, that political disaster befell the People of Israel.[41] King Josiah of Israel, on the other hand, renews the covenant between God and the people as a politico-religious measure to restore popular unity.[42] The same procedure is followed by Nehemiah the Scribe, to mobilize the people for the reconstruction of Jerusalem after their return from the Babylonian Exile.[43] His constitution is standard for subsequent declarations of this type.

Professor Elazar distinguishes four constitutional periods through which the Israelites passed, from the time of the Exodus to the completion of the biblical canon, each period lasting some 300 years, or 10 generations.[44] The first period starts from the founding of the Israelite tribal confederacy (1300 BCE) and continues until the establishment of the monarchy (1000 BCE). This period is, of course, marked by the Mosaic constitution-giving, by the creation of what was probably the first true federal system in history, and later by the appearance of regional leadership—the Judges, acting as 'proto-national' leaders.

The second period—the monarchy—was brought about by external military and political pressure. This period, with King Saul and the prophet Samuel (first defined as *Nagid* = Governor), introduces the idea of limited government under God's continuing sovereignty and the no less original and consequential idea of authority divided between Governor and Prophet. The failure of Saul and the rise of David to the rank of full-fledged monarch, limited by a traditional constitution, the tension between King and Prophet, between government and opposition, dominates the political life and thought of ancient Israel. It finally ends, through the reaction against the great violations of the traditional constitutions in both the Northern Kingdom of Israel and the Southern Kingdom of Judaea, with the major constitutional reform under King Josiah[45] whereby the limitations on the monarchy which the prophets had tried to sustain were brought together to form a written constitution, the Book of Deuteronomy. This started the third constitutional stage, which ended the monarchic chapter in biblical history (and, except for the Hasmonean interlude, in Jewish history as a whole).

This period witnessed the disappearance of the monarchy as a viable institution and its restoration was transformed into part of Israel's Messianic dream. The need to develop new modes of group survival in exile enhanced the importance of the written constitution as a source of authority in Israel, with prophets turning their attention to expounding its principles and elucidating its promises for future political success rather than being solely responsible for the maintenance of the constitution.

The fourth constitutional period is the one known as the Second Commonwealth, which brought about the restoration of republican government though within a single polity rather than on a federal basis. It was inaugurated by the proclamation of the Torah, by Ezra the Scribe, as a constitutional document. This constitution was, in fact, the first of its kind and has served as a model—with its preamble, main body of articles, and list of signatures—for many subsequent constitutions, that of the USA included. It exacted a system of rule by council which shared power with the high priest and the 'scribes' in what must be considered an early example of the separation of powers. Such a separation was indeed inborn in the spirit and the letter of the Mosaic constitution,[46] but of course a political structure of this kind must be understood in the terms by which Jewish orthodoxy looks at the sovereign power of the Lord. His power is, of course, supreme, but He, Himself, once the covenant is signed, is voluntarily subject to its rule. The power of 'God in Parliament', to speak metaphorically, is the only aspect of the divine power which is limited. 'By the customs of men', says the Talmud, 'a King of flesh and blood takes a decision which, if he wants, he fulfils; if he does not want—others fulfil; but the Holy One, Blessed be His Name, does not behave like this, but when He takes a decision He fulfils it first. Why is this so? [Because it is written] Keep my guard, I am the Lord, I am the One who has respected the commandments of the Law from the beginning.'[47] Or again, it is stated that God has to comply with the decision of a rabbinical judgement: the Torah, once given, applies to everyone.[48]

For Spinoza (1623-77) the only way to overcome the problem (insoluble, for instance, to Rousseau) of true democracy is the transfer of the legitimacy of power to a body outside the body politic—to God. 'None of the Jews had renounced his rights', he wrote, 'but all had democratically cried: "Here we are (without any intermediary) to do what the voice of God will tell us": they could keep unaltered their reciprocal equality, all having equally the right to consult God, to receive and interpret the laws, and to provide with equal and absolute authority the needs of Government.'[49]

Spinoza is by no means unusual: indeed he speaks here as a typical Jew in two senses. First, the power of the ruler is restricted both by the covenant he signs with the people and by the transfer of absolute sovereignty—as distinct from absolute rule—to God. This is 'democratic' only because God, too, is restricted by the covenant. It regulates not only the spiritual, moral conduct of the Jew but establishes the terms of a real, all-embracing contract, including a political relationship at the highest level between man and God, ruled and sovereign. This is possible 'because God is the central source of right and justice, two of the highest concerns in politics, while the covenant is the means by which human beings are granted freedom, a third concern'.[50] But there is another aspect of Jewishness which Spinoza's philosophy underlines. Although detached from the mainstream of Judaism and considered enough of a 'non-Jew' to be excommunicated, the way in which Spinoza reaches his heterodox conclusions remains typically Jewish. The Latin of his *Tractatus Theologicus Politicus*, the mathematical order of his propositions and argumentation, and the unorthodox interpretation of the Scriptures, do not succeed in concealing the impact of the rabbinical education and talmudic logic to which his mind had been exposed. Just as there is a Jewish way of being an atheist, so there is a Spinozan (and very Jewish) way of being a pantheist.

As a polity, the Jews always functioned as members of a system aimed at embodying the covenant idea. Ancient Israel reaffirmed this in various

ways from the time of Abraham to the time of Ezra, originating three of
the most fundamental modern political principles: federalism, republicanism, and constitutional monarchy.

The God of the Bible certainly has the power of direct intervention in
human affairs, as the miracles of the Exodus clearly show. But as the
Hebrew tribes develop into a nation and the age of miracles gives way, so
to say, to the age of human responsibility, God remains the source of
legitimacy, the depository of sovereignty. He also remains distinguished
from the ruler, who is the depository of political power. As a logical and
historical result, the king and the prophet become the central, institutionalized figures in the political game. They are part of a system in which
the balance between values and interests, between aspirational strategy
and operational tactics (to use the jargon of modern political science) is
maintained by the right and duty of dissent.

If we turn to another central political trend in Judaism, namely to the
right of opposition, we see that this right is consecrated by a precise and
very ancient biblical commandment: 'Thou shalt rebuke in any wise thy
neighbour',[51] repeated in various but passionate forms throughout the centuries and the Jewish literature. The prophet Ezekiel cries out to the community leaders, 'When I say to the sinner that he will die (for his sin) and
you have not warned him to change his ways, he, the sinner, will die, but
his blood will be on your head.'[52] In the Talmud we read of Rabbi Jocha-
nan's proclamation: 'Why has Jeroboam obtained the Kingdom? Because
he criticized [King Solomon].'[53] And in *Midrash Tanchuma* it is stated:

Whosoever could reprimand the members of his house and has not done
so, will be held responsible for it; who [could reprimand] the people of
their town [and did not do so], will be held responsible for them; who
[could reprimand] the world [and did not do so] will be held responsible
for the whole world. Rabbi Hanina said: Which is the reference? The Lord
will come to [the place of] judgement with the Elders and with the Ministers of His people (Isaiah 3:14). If the Ministers are culprits, why are the
Elders [culprits] as well? Because the Elders did not protest against the
Ministers.[54]

Opposition against the ruler is thus naturally kept quite distinct from
opposition to the Sovereign. Nathan's criticism of King David and Eliahu's
of King Ahab are 'true messages from God'.[55] In fact, they are expressions of legitimate opposition. The value of the opposition is brought to
its ultimate and paradoxical conclusion in the Sanhedrin ruling, which up-
holds the principle that no man can be sentenced to death by a unanimous
ruling of the judges. Only when there is a majority condemnation opposed
by a minority may the culprit be executed.[56]

From the three principles of constitutional monarchy, republicanism,
and federalism there emerges, according to the *Encyclopedia Judaica*,[57] a
picture of the ideal political commonwealth, another central idea developed

by Jewish political culture. Two principal descriptions have been canonized, one in the Book of Joshua and the second in the prophecies of Ezekiel. The former is an idealized version of the conquest and settlement of Canaan and a description of what the ideal Israelite polity should be. Ezekiel's utopia looks not to the past but to the as yet unrealized future. In both utopian accounts the theocratic principle is fundamental: politics serve theo-politics, which are the means to achieve and maintain the Holy Covenant. God is sovereign: He exercises this sovereignty through his servants, who act as national leaders, and through the traditional institutions of the people, which are federal and republican in character. This biblical ideal commonwealth became a major force in the political thought of the Western world and has permeated Jewish political thought and Jewish traditional culture ever since.

To retrace the circuitous development of these trends of political thought from post-medieval times to the modern period, and to sort out the inter-connections and reciprocal influences between Jewish and non-Jewish society, is an historical enterprise which has never been attempted in spite of the growing number of studies on the life of the Jewish communities in the Diaspora. One can even ask whether such an enterprise can be attempted in view of the disproportion between the visible and active political role of the Jews in the Diaspora and the impact of biblical thoughts and values on the nations among which they lived, mainly in the West. From the large, structured reservoir of traditional culture created during the time Jews lived as an extensive political entity in Israel and later in Babylon up to the tenth century, only a trickle of recognizable original political thought passed on to the autonomous but marginal and usually oppressed world of the powerless Jewish communities of the Diaspora. In the coming Emancipation and, with it, the growing trend of assimilation, political Judaism can perhaps be recognized in the style of Jewish politicians operating within and for non-Jewish societies—from Lassalle to Trotsky, and from Disraeli to Blum—but certainly not in a consistent genuine Jewish manner. With Zionism, the Jews once more became actors in history, and with the creation of the State of Israel, the Israeli felt the revolutionary transformation of the Jew who ceased to be an object of history and became master of his own fate.

It is at this point that the roots of Jewish civilization began once more to put forth the sprouts of a traditional culture which had been inhibited for a long time in its political expression. It poured out as in the case of almost every decolonized non-Western society. To ask, then, today in Israel whether Jewish political thought is the result of the application to politics of certain values peculiar to Judaism or, on the contrary, the result of the unique historical circumstances in which Jews have lived, is like asking which came first, the chicken or the egg. It is the application and modification of given principles to diverse circumstances. Every culture is made up of values and responses, and the same holds for Judaism. What is certain is the fact that one major reason for the confusion existing about Jewish political thought is the difficulty in differentiating between types of political ideas: those drawn by Jews from non-political sources (from religion and morals, for example) and the political ideas developed in response to historic circumstances imposed on Jews from the outside. Both sources, of course, have had some direct bearing on the articulation and evolution of indigenous and absorbed Jewish political thought. However, to believe that Jewish politics can be studied or understood only in terms of Jewish non-political values, or alternatively, to believe that Jewish politics can be studied or understood only in terms of external circumstances, are both equally unwarranted.

Such polarization of sources creates confusion and over-rationalization in the study of all history of political thought, old and new. Innumerable obstacles to the understanding of contemporary politics ensue, particularly when it is applied to a cluster of space and time configurations such as the Jewish Diaspora, not to mention the added complexity of a new Jewish State. The polarization of sources into all-innate or all-absorbed sources forces both secular and orthodox Jews, for instance, to go through all sorts of intellectual contortions to prove (in the case of the secular Jew) that modern Jewish national consciousness is 'non-religious', or (in the case of the orthodox Jew) that modern Jewish national consciousness is not theocratic. Jewish Marxists who believed, with Lenin, that the Jewish question is mainly a product of historical social circumstances are, incidentally, in the same boat: circumstances have changed profoundly in the past fifty years, in Russia as well as in Western Europe, but never has Jewish identity been more evident than in our time.

Are we then to search for something else, something additional to the reasons for the particularism already mentioned—metapolitical, conventional, and logical, as well as exclusively Jewish; something which can throw some light on the question that the Church of Rome to this very day officially calls 'the mystery of Israel'—the mystery of how the Jews maintained, through the ages, a distinct national culture of their own? Despite geographical dispersion, despite diversity of ethnic origin, despite different but all-too-often prolonged immersions in foreign cultures, in foreign economies, in foreign political systems, how did they preserve intact a specific, compact, national, religious and political culture for over three thousand years?

The contemporary French religious historian, Henri Daniel-Rops, believes that the distinctiveness of the Jewish culture can be understood if one remembers that no history gives in a greater degree than does that of Israel the impression of having obeyed an internal development, of having borrowed from circumstances only the means of being more completely it-self. If this is so, how is this 'internal development' to be defined—as a divine plot, or as a fortuitous interlacing of values and environmental acci-dents which, in the words of Arthur Koestler, makes modern Israel 'a freak of history'?[58] Or can it be defined as an original, purely intuitive creation of 'national' genius, as the late Professor Y. Kaufman claims in his monu-mental *History of the Jewish Faith*?[59] One must return to the original text to look for an alternative approach.

The text of the Written Law, and the interpretation of the Oral Law (the Talmud) with its commentaries, is permeated by what seems to be a general taboo on the hybrid in Jewish tradition. There are precise prohibi-tions on 'mixing' things which nature, so to speak, has set apart, and a whole tractate of the Talmud—*Masehet Kila'im*—deals with this subject. For instance, Jews may not plough a field with two different types of ani-mal yoked to the plough; they may not wear clothes made of fibres from both plants and animals, or sow two types of seed in the same plot; they may not graft together different plants nor interbreed animals of different species.[60] If mixing is to be contrasted with purity, then the list of con-trasting pairs can easily be multiplied.

Anthropological research seems to support the thesis that from the out-set Jewish modes of thought were shaped by a metaphysical interpretation of the phenomena, dominated by the sense of opposition, of polariza-tion:[61] for instance, the distinction between native/foreign; between im-mortal God/mortal man; father/son; holy/unholy; pure/impure, etc., all of which found symbolic expression in Jewish religious commandments. If this interpretation is correct, it would tend to fit in with the older Jewish conceptual matrix which has favoured the development of those dialectic, linear, non-systemic patterns of thought which seem so typical of Jewish culture and which talmudic methods of analysis and teaching have helped to articulate and systematize.

The structuralist method of anthropology may help us to understand, if not to explain, why the rationalists of the eighteenth century regarded the Jews as being incapable of contributing to political theory. Western politi-cal culture is traditionally founded on systems and myths, and until recently shared with Judaism one defect—being as ahistorical as possible. This being so, one of the explanations for the apparent indifference of Judaism to Western political thinking may well be not the alleged Jewish inability to think politics, but a Jewish inability to think politics *in a cer-tain way*, namely in a Western systemic and methodological way. Only an historical perspective on both Judaism and rationalism will reveal the error of the rationalists.

Political theory, in so far as it is systemic, has remained alien to the Jewish way of thinking. Jewish political pragmatism has no sympathy for

systems or myths which base their interpretation of the complex human
situation on dogmatic principles, such as that the real world starts after
death (Christianity), or that all men are born equal (The American Declaration of Independence), or that history is fulfilled by and through the state
(Hegel), or that society develops through the class struggle (Marx), and so
on. The detailed theories which one can build up on these principles may
be elegant and appear more and more authoritative. Their role, indeed, was
often to justify the principle—in so far as they succeeded in appearing
more and more universal—and in explaining with greater or lesser success
certain political and social phenomena. But Judaism ignores the kind of
myth which has to be rejected or endorsed with certainty. This is not to
deny for one moment the existence of Jewish (indeed, peculiarly Jewish)
kinds of myth: for example, the Messianic inspiration, or the myth which
sees the Jews as a people chosen to serve by virtue of the principle of
'noblesse oblige', being both outside and deeply involved in world politics. The difference between these myths and the Western, non-Jewish
myths of political system building, of political 'wholes', entities, totalities,
must be recognized. All political concepts like *collective soul, national
mind, popular will, 'thinking' class, 'achieving' race*, and so on look like
idols to Judaism, and the traditional Jewish mode of thought has no kind
word for idols.

In the case of political Zionism and Israel, one is tempted to wonder
whether the trend towards collective assimilation and the ease with which
Jews have developed and accepted processes of self-colonization, do not
have a much older cause, namely the permanent struggle between the Jewish monotheistic vocation and polytheism. The dilemma of identity, the
difficulties encountered by the State of Israel in defining its Judaism, seem
to be less the result of the departure from, or non-acknowledgement of,
Jewish traditional ideas (which, as has been argued, exist, even if only in
an unco-ordinated and unstudied form) than the consequence of the adoption by secular Zionism of a political rationale based on a very un-Jewish
way of thinking: by, and through, systems. Systems, whatever their nature,
operate according to the functional logic of their connecting parts. In the
specific field of politics, systems such as nationalism, socialism, racialism,
liberalism, fascism, and democracy are all founded on universalist ideas
which for the traditional, asystemic Jewish way of thinking have the
appearance of idols, each one supported by its own godless religion—the
religion of the state, of class, race, etc.—each one defended by its more or
less authoritarian secular bureaucratic priesthood.

Jewish traditional culture seems to reject these modern idols, rationally
accepted by contemporary Jewry, including orthodoxy, much as the body
rejects a transplant. It is not so much the speed of change in modern
society or the pressure of external enemies which makes life difficult for

the Zionist state, but the vitality of an unarticulated political traditional culture which refuses to adapt to the *modus operandi* of alien states, not only because they are alien but because they are fundamentally pagan.

The paganism of the State of Israel has found a most passionate and articulate critic in Professor Y. Leibowitz. For him the state can only be an instrument, not an end in itself. The State of Israel can be Jewish and fulfilling a legitimate Jewish historical aim only if it is an instrument towards the realization of Judaism. But if Judaism and the Jewish people are to be identified with a 'state like any other state', a state which makes its own laws and does not submit to the Jewish law, then such a state will in fact create a new people, the Israeli people, which is not the continuation of the Jewish people.

There are certainly Jews in the State of Israel for whom the people is God, the state a religion, nationalism the law and a supreme value. They are Fascists, some of them conscious ones, many unconscious, and they are attached with passion to the idea that the Jewish people be defined according to their State. . . . There are many Jews among us who raise the [concept of] the land to a level of holiness. This is idolatry pure and simple. . . . The land is neutral like anything else in the world. Only One is Holy . . . and apart from Him nothing is holy, neither in history nor in nature nor in man; but it is possible to sanctify all things through the service of the Lord.[62]

Other analysts of Jewish traditional politics in Israel are less brutal but reach the same conclusion.[63] Jewish history, for instance, may be seen as a series of encounters within which the fundamental principles of Jewish religio-political life have been expressed in different ways. Within such a framework the relationship of Israel, as a community, to the land of Israel, can be examined to understand the way in which the forces of geography work to mould the people. Israeli labour legislation, for instance, can be understood in the spirit of the biblical affirmation of the relationship between labour—which binds man to the forces of creation, and freedom in the land—which is absolutely essential as a precondition for political freedom. Zionism can thus be seen as a natural outgrowth of Jewish political ideas and an important factor in the renewal of the colonization process in the land of Israel. But the very attempt to look for similarities poses the theopolitical question of the direction in which the secular Zionist state will develop: that of the traditional covenant or that of the materialistic modern world.

CHAPTER 5

The Crisis of the Israeli Élites

'Peoples have the governments they deserve', goes the popular saying. How well does this fit the case of Israel? On the one hand, and according to Western political standards, few nations deserve better leaders in the light of Israel's military and civil qualities; of her outstanding success in building up—almost alone among the new nations of the post-colonial era—a viable state out of literally scattered national ashes, and considering her determination to uphold the principles of true freedom and democracy in spite of the crushing moral, political, and economic burdens of her thirty years'—and still unfinished—war with the Arabs.

On the other hand, anyone coming into even superficial contact with responsible Israelis, or reading the vast literature produced by concerned Jews and non-Jews on the present situation and on the future of the State, is struck by the depth of its multiple crisis; by the inability of its leadership to make decisions; by the difficulty some of its institutions have in functioning properly; and by the lack of consensus in the Jewish nation, inside and outside the boundaries of the Israeli state, concerning the type of legitimacy justifying its existence.

Crises of leadership, institutions, and legitimacy are, of course, intimately linked with one another. Any attempt to dissociate them when discussing the Israeli case would be artificial. Furthermore, crises of this sort, and especially a crisis of legitimacy, become acute as soon as people start being apologetic in their efforts at self-explanation. The compelling need felt by the Israelis and Jews involved in the great Zionist adventure constantly to analyse their intentions and actions is one of the clearest symptoms of an inner insecurity, felt equally at the levels of Jewish leadership, institutions, and ideology. At the roots of this malaise one always finds the unresolved struggle between Jewish and alien culture, a struggle which, as has been pointed out, is neither new in the history of Judaism nor solely linked with the modern confrontation between Jewish and Western ways of life. On the other hand, the 'shining idols' of modern, progressive, Western society (secular humanism, rationalism, liberalism, and Marxism) were crushed, together with their Jewish and other devoted worshippers, in the camps of Auschwitz and Siberia. The result of such a momentous and startling event as the creation of Jewish polity was the attempt to rationalize the Israeli crisis into something more than simple criticism or apology. The world outside Israel judges it according to a special set of theatrical standards and not by rational political standards applied to other countries.

The crisis of Israeli leadership is manifested in the fact that Israelis have always shown themselves better equipped to face the enemy from without than to cope with problems from within. As a result, their élites, who not only share the confusion of the common people but increase it through their greater rationalizing ability, are constantly faced with choices which they are incapable of making owing to their lack of a basic consensus on the role of a modern Jewish state. The reference here is not so much to basic political aims, such as survival, rejection of a Palestinian state, security, or welfare, but to much deeper questions, such as the laicity or the orthodoxy of the state itself, socialist and capitalist conceptions of economic and social development, and interpretation of what is meant by Western and Oriental Jewish communal and cultural rules.

Here it is necessary to repeat a point which will also be stressed in the following chapters dealing with the crises of institutionalization and legitimacy: such crises cannot be dissociated from the general malaise created in the contemporary Western and non-Western world by the process of modernization and change. Israel's élites, like the élites of all developing countries, struggle with the problem of rationality and conformism, that is, with the need to use increased rationality to explain their decisions rather than rely on the principle of historical legacy. There is nothing Jewish in the way problems of bureaucracy are dealt with in Israel. Like many other new states, Israel was born with an old-fashioned bureaucracy, the productivity of which cannot increase faster than the scope of the activities bureaucratized. Since most of these activities are linked to a goal already realized—the creation of an independent Jewish polity—the Israeli bureaucracy reduces its productivity as the scope of the activities in which it is engaged shrinks. Similarly, Israel shares with all developing countries a problem of societal control and co-ordination. Quite independent of the political system adopted, these problems always affect the collective behaviour of societies in which the traditional structures—family, clan, tribe—are major elements of the collective solidarity.

Another common aspect of Israeli and non-Israeli élites is Faddism, a phenomenon defined as 'a relatively rapid and intense alteration and application of means for relatively fixed ends'.[1] Faddism contributes to the creation of unstable status values and images. It introduces into the society symbols of class distinction or power, like motor cars, foreign fashions or domestic gadgets, which at first are the privileges of the rich and with time become the possessions of the poor. Here prestige is associated with goods purchased, not persons buying them. The result is that people are caught in what anthropologist Lloyd Fallers calls 'the trickle effect',[2] that is, illusion of social upward mobility similar to the illusion of movement perceived by a person sitting in a standing train passed by a moving one. It is a source of frustration and a cause of permanent resentment on the part of the ordinary people towards the élites.

Finally, and perhaps most important, Israel, like all other developing countries, cannot escape the fact that the structure of modernization is always subversive of the *status quo* of non-modernized societies. Traditional patterns will always be invaded by external factors when these factors are stronger. Major sources of control held by members of traditional societies or groups become eroded and, with them, élite authority over the masses, especially when these masses belong to a different cultural, psychological, and economic background from that of the élites, as is the case in Israel.

Consensus and authority have been shaken many times in the long history of the Jewish people by their coming into contact with different civilizations. The years in Egypt, the period before the Exodus, and the forty years that the Jews wandered in the desert are punctuated by as many rebellions or attempts at rebellion against the Mosaic rule as by acts of acceptance of the tremendous innovations brought about by the break with Egypt and the new rule of behaviour imposed by the Sinai revelation. Consensus and authority broke down when the nomadic Jewish tribes came into contact with the sedentary and materially superior civilization of the peoples of the land of Canaan, and again after the Babylonian exile.

Yet the more Jewish history unfolded, the clearer became the fact that the very existence of the Jewish people evolved around the unique relationship between a certain concept of God and a certain concept of the Jewish destiny. Josephus Flavius was the first to use the word 'theocracy' to describe the system thus created—a concept which has given rise to multiple interpretations. Some of these will be discussed in a later chapter dealing with the Israeli crisis of legitimacy. Whatever the meaning of this unique relationship, one most important practical result was the creation, side by side with the theocratic ideology, of a comprehensive system of education and power distribution aimed at producing the leadership responsible for the translation of the lofty social and political concepts of Judaism into practical day-to-day norms of behaviour. The total conformity, or at least the conscious and sustained effort to achieve such conformity, has made the Jewish people what it has been throughout millennia, moulded its special identity, and interiorized the idea of national exclusiveness to such a degree that for centuries, until the Jewish Emancipation, the Jews understood and accepted their solitude among the nations as a natural status of superiority.

Of course, this sense of superiority had nothing to do with 'nature' (there are no such things as Jewish chromosomes of élitism); it arose as a consequence of natural solitude and unique aloofness. Whatever the causes, the evolution of separateness sprang from a highly elaborated traditional education which enabled Jewish leaders in any community to elicit consensus and imitation, as well as to adjust to changing political and social situations and institutions while still maintaining intact the special self-image which the Jews had of themselves as a chosen people. The incarnation of values and aspirations derived from the peculiar belief which formed the sole essence of Jewish collective identity was broken during the period of political Jewish Emancipation by the enthusiastic acceptance of an alien process of cultural colonization. The crisis of the Israeli élite today derives, therefore, from the fact that it is called upon to lead a people that displayed extraordinary vitality in the establishment of a Jewish polity on principles of non-Jewish ideology such as socialism and nationalism, while disregarding the cultural and ideological tools which in the past had provided the élites with the capacity to fulfil the special Jewish aspirations of the Jewish nation. In any inquiry into the crisis of contemporary Israeli élites, the first question to be asked should therefore be how the traditional, Jewish élite-promoting system functioned, at least from the second century onward but probably before, and how it compares with the one at present in existence in Israel.

The first characteristic of the traditional Jewish system of élite formation was its mass recruiting; the second was the informal, merit-based promotion of these élites. The third characteristic was the elaboration of a system of education and a network of institutions which integrated the principle of mass power participation with that of high selectivity in the exercise of authority. The result was the establishment of a regime of popular aristocracy, operating according to a logic of its own which fitted the existentialist needs of the Jewish society. This society could not, nor ideologically wanted, to rely on external, non-Jewish cultural or institutional contributions. At the same time it needed a very high percentage of top people in order to defend its solitude and replace the permanent lack of quantitative resources with an equally permanent supply of qualitative ones.

The concept of democracy in ancient Israel preceded the one developed in ancient Greece by many centuries. It is expressed formally in the Sinai covenant (Exod. 19:8), where the Divine choice is offered, not imposed, and collectively accepted by the Jewish people. The Bible, however, does not provide for recurrent consultation of the popular will, as in modern democracy. The people's consent may be required for the establishment of a new political regime, as in the case of the replacement of the federative tribal system with a centralized monarchic one. This was done at the time of Saul in spite of the expressed reservations of the Lord and the prophet Samuel (1 Sam. 8:12). The people's consent is 'conceived as a historical decision, binding on future generations . . . it is also a commitment, a moral obligation. . . . The nation is conceived here as a collective entity with a long, perhaps eternal, life of its own, and not as an assembly of short-lived individuals.'[3]

Democratic principles coexisted in the biblical political system with the principle of the absolute rule of the Lord since that rule cannot be imposed but must result from a free commitment by the people. Indeed, the basic roots of revolt against authority probably lie in this freedom of choice, which may well have given rise to that very special brand of Jewish self-confidence and penchant for anarchy which has been a marked trend of the Jewish character through the ages.[4] Just as the will of the many is subject to the will of the Divine, so is the will of the few, or the 'best', subject to the same absolute will. This is one of the leitmotivs of the Bible which became the inspiring principle of Jewish governance until the nineteenth century. 'Moses received the Law [from the Lord] on Mount Sinai'—so begins the first chapter of the talmudic tractate *Abot*, which is read every Saturday from Passover to the Jewish New Year. The Law passed on to Joshua who related it to the Elders who transmitted it to the Prophets who handed it over to the members of the Great Congregation—and the chain of legitimation of command does not stop there. In the time of the Second Temple, the Sanhedrin, the highest judicial body numbering 71 members, exercised its authority as the interpreter and the applier of the Divine Law. Subsequent generations of rabbinical scholars and community leaders, whether in Judaea or Babylon, in Spain or Germany, in Yemen or Afghanistan, considered themselves as strictly bound by the established legal tradition as had the preceding generations.

Thus Jewish leadership in its most varied institutional form was the expression of the 'best' who judged, ruled, guided, educated in the name of the divine authority. This was certainly not a combination of power, of 'mixed rule' similar to the one suggested by Aristotle or followed by modern representative democracy. The Jewish political system, notes Roshvald, works on a triangular relationship: the people, the élite, and God who remains the essential link between the people and the élite. What makes this relationship dynamic and allows the spirit of criticism to develop, as well as makes possible social mobility on a much larger scale than that required by élitist ideology and the survival needs of a people permanently lacking material power, is the idea that the entire House of Jacob—that is, all the members of the nation—can attain the spiritual–moral perfection of the genuine aristocrat, with all the duties and privileges which go with it. 'You shall be unto me a kingdom of priests and a holy nation' (Exod. 19:6) is the operative biblical passage for this open-aristocratic blueprint. A very early practical expression is the story of Eldad and Medad (Num. 11:29). They were the two Jews who were not called upon to join the institutionalized élite upon which the divine spirit descended after the Sinai revelation in order to relieve Moses of his almost singly performed leadership role. But they were seen prophesying as passionately and, probably, as authoritatively as the consecrated elders. The immediate political reaction of the newly formed aristocracy, expressed by Joshua, then acting as chief-of-staff, is to put them into prison. No, says Moses, let them go free and hope that one day the whole House of Israel may turn out to be a house of prophets. Within the framework of the divine discipline all are equal and the distinction of the higher ruler, of the *primus inter pares*, is measured in terms of humility, not in terms of splendour. The leader should not 'lift his heart above his brethren' (Deut. 17:20), an idea which has been taken over intact by the Church when it calls its supreme leader, the Pope, *Servus Servorum Dei*, the servant of the servants of God. This is by no means fortuitous: the Church is the Christian tradition of *Verus Israel*, the true Israel, operating, like traditional Judaism, on the principle of an inverted pyramid model aimed to enlarge the top as much as possible for the benefit of the base. As a result, the Jewish traditional social system, no doubt spurred on and conditioned by a prolonged situation of defenceless isolation, was characterized by its ability to turn out numerous élites, quantitatively superior, relatively, to those of the host countries. In their turn, these élites were able to lead the Jewish masses through the hazards of new environments and political situations without breaking their unity or the ideological continuity with that concept of inborn solitude which for generations was considered by the Jews, and by their enemies, as the mark of their chosenness.

There is no foundation for the belief (sometimes shared by ignorant Jews with vulgar anti-Semites) that Jews are in some way different from other people and thus capable of greater virtues and more sinister crimes than other human beings. What in fact gave them, relatively, a quantitatively richer leadership and self-confidence was the fact that for centuries the social structure of the Jewish communities permitted greater upward mobility and a more thorough mobilization and education of the most capable elements of the people. This upward mobility derived from Jewish political ideology, inspired, as noted, by the mixed democratic-aristocratic-theocratic biblical system. Jews did produce a larger élite than most other peoples because their society geared itself ideologically and practically to the task of realizing in its day-to-day behaviour the principle of *noblesse oblige*, this being the most fitting ideological tool of survival for a small people particularly vulnerable in its lack of material resources and its consciousness of having been chosen to perform a revolutionary task: to witness, through its behaviour and ahistorical fate, the presence of the absolute in history. Whether the necessity of opposing quality to quantity as a means of collective physical survival preceded or followed the biblical idea of the 'chosen people' is, of course, an open question and a matter of opinion.

What seems clear is the fact that the combination of a special élitist consciousness with a system of very particular mobilization of élites helped
the Jews not only to survive against impossible odds but also to retain a
common identity despite geographical, cultural, and ethnic dispersion.

Let us now take a closer look at how this system of popular aristocracy
worked. The idea of education is central in the Mosaic teaching. The in-
junction, 'Thou shalt teach them [the commandments] diligently unto thy
children' (Deut. 6:7) is repeated twice daily in prayer. Josephus Flavius
writes: 'Our principal care of all is this, to educate our children well' and
the first establishment of general education is attributed by the Talmud to
Joshua Ben Gamla, a High Priest in the first century CE, although as far
back as the first century BCE Simon Ben Shetah introduced the first
known system of community-supported public education, an unheard-of
feat not only in ancient times but for most states even in modern times
(*Baba Batra* 21 A). During the talmudic period, a Jew who could not read
or write was so rare that he was assumed to have been taken prisoner by
barbarians as a small boy and released only as an adult.[5] Education was
not only universal and obligatory but also integrated. Its goals were to
transmit knowledge and skills from one generation to the next, to broaden
the range of man's knowledge and skill, and to concretize cultural values
into the forms of accepted group and individual behaviour. In ancient
Israel these goals—religious education, the learning of occupational skills,
and military training—were pursued indiscriminately at various levels.
Later, when military training became obsolete following the loss of political independence, unprecedented attention was given to religious study
and to the methodology of learning and teaching, so that the talmudic
age saw the development of researches, models of analysis, epistemological
discussion, and a curiosity to understand nature and man's place within it,
that produced one of the most refined types of scholarship ever known.
Every Jewish boy went to school at the age of 5 or 6 and usually continued
to study up to the age of 13, if he was unfit to become a scholar, and all
his life if he was among the select few to be trained to become a *Talmid
Ḥakham* (wise scholar). Selection was much stricter than even in the presti-
gious scientific institutions of the twentieth century. One thousand people,
says the Talmud, enter upon the study of the Bible (the lowest level, the
first five years of a standard Jewish curriculum); 100 embark upon the
study of Mishna (the second level of education); 10 reach the study of
Gemarrah (the third echelon). Only *one* becomes a teacher. In this way the
best minds were devoted to the teaching of others. In addition, the idea of
compulsory, universal, highly selective education went hand-in-hand with
an even stricter social promotion through scholarly meritocracy. As in
noble Gentile families—but on an open social basis—élite membership was
reinforced by a system of family alliances through marriage. The daughter

of the *Gvir*—the leader of the community—of the rich merchant, the man with power, whether rabbi or layman, was 'reserved' for and automatically bestowed on the *Talmid Ḥakham*, the brightest young talmudic scholar of the community, irrespective of his family or economic status. What determined the alliance between money and brains, between power and merit, was the standard of traditional values inherent in the individual, not his clan, although marriages between 'dynasties' of rabbis, the intermarriage of 'brain with brain', is still very much in existence in 'rabbinical courts'.[6] In this way the Jewish élite could be recruited from every level of society, and perpetuate itself according to established meritocratic principles which allowed for the recruitment of the largest number of potential leaders in any generation.

The situation was not profoundly different in the Jewish communities of the East. The *Gvir* or the man possessing power and riches was more frequently a scholar among oriental Jews than among European Jews. The main reason for this is historical. In the East, Jewish political autonomy lasted until the twelfth century and was expressed, *inter alia*, by the position of the Exilarch, who, under the Parthians, Sassanides, and Arabs (140–1240), usually held the third rank of protocol after the Emperor. The Jewish traveller Benjamin of Tudela, visiting Baghdad in the year 1168, reports that the Exilarch, Daniel ben Hisdai, was received every Thursday by the Caliph and travelled to these audiences in a carriage preceded by horsemen calling for the clearing of the way before the 'Son of David'.

In more recent times there are many recorded cases of famous oriental Sephardi scholars combining great influence and great wealth, accumulated because they were both the spiritual and the political leaders of the community. Some of the great Sephardic families of Palestine Jewry were originally linked to the leading social position of an outstanding Rabbi. The European Ashkenazi scholar was generally far less involved with material concerns and was thus freer to maintain an uncompromising moral and intellectual detachment.

Another important difference between Ashkenazi and Sephardi leadership is due to the special relation between the oriental Jewish scholar and the school teacher. In Islamic countries a wide net of modern educational institutions was established through the good offices of the Alliance Israélite Universelle.[7] The Alliance teacher was by no means anti-religious; but he represented the colonial power, culture, and dynamism—three elements which were willingly accepted by the Sephardi rabbis. This acceptance contributed to a break in the internal balance of the authority of the oriental Jewish communities and in time to reducing the leadership role of the indigenous Jewish scholar.

The fact that merit and power were usually united through marriage reinforced the social system to such an extent that the training responsibilities of the leaders in the traditional Jewish communities extended well beyond marriage. It was, in fact, one of the duties of the rich father-in-law to accommodate and financially maintain the young *Talmid Hakham* for a number of years in order to facilitate his further studies. This was an institutionalized family scholarship system (known in Yiddish as *Kest*)[8] through which the richest helped the brightest not only to improve themselves but to learn the ways of the powerful—even if only to reject them at a later stage.

The result, as we have already said, was an integrated educational and socio-economic system which permitted the mobilization of the greatest potential leadership available. It gave the Jewish people not only the moral and psychological training to maintain unity in spite of dispersion and to face the hardships of exile by opposing quality to quantity, but indeed the means suited to approach the ultimate national goal, set out by the biblical revelation: the creation of a whole nation of 'priests and princes' through an open aristocracy relying for its survival on the strictest observance of the rule that *'noblesse oblige'*.

Two facts emerge from this dicussion of the traditional educational system. The first is that even after two centuries of self-colonization, assimilation to Western culture, and wilful breaking with traditional Judasim, it is still difficult for even the most secularized and Westernized Israeli to free himself completely from the deep-seated influence of an old, powerful, all-embracing, traditional sociocultural system. To an extent which it is difficult to gauge, Israeli society remains a popular aristocracy, often against its knowledge and will. We shall elaborate this point later when dealing with some of its particular institutions, such as the kibbutz and the army.

What is clear, however, is that, independently of the degree of conscious or unconscious preservation of traditional Jewish popular aristocratic elements in the Israeli secular, capitalist/socialist, and often closed democracy, the image of the new Jewish polity among the nations is one of confused—and, for its enemies, frightening—possibilities. None the less, it becomes almost impossible to raise the banner of Jewish civilization, especially on the political scene, and then expect the new Jewish state to content itself with fulfilling the historical role of a country of similar geographical and demographical size and natural resources, such as Haiti or Albania. These expectations, friendly or hostile (not to speak of the permanent war situation), combine to strengthen the consciousness of uniqueness and inborn solitude of the Israeli. This is true even if he no longer relies on any ideological or cultural justification of his own to explain the strange, old/new fate of the Jewish people. One of the reasons for the present antagonism to Israel is the inability of its leaders, because of their lack of Jewish traditional culture, to offer an explanation acceptable to the modern, Westernized, rational mind, of why Israel is so dissimilar to other modern nations, and also different from any known type of 'closed' aristocratic society as well as from modern, materialistic, 'closed' or 'open' regimes. One has only to recall the élite of the American system described by C. W. Mills[9] or Djilas's account of élites in the communist system[10] to realize not only the differences but the challenge which the Jewish combination of merit, power, and anti-materialism represent for all existing political regimes.

The second fact which bears underlining is the extent of the change which has taken place in the social and educational structure of the Jewish nation through the process of emancipation and self-colonization discussed in previous chapters. The old élite-recruiting system has broken down together with the traditional, rabbinical educational system. This is partly through its own inability to adapt to the requirements of modern life, but even more through a deliberate policy of political populism. The constant call for quality in the Israeli army is paralleled by anti-intellectual trends within Israeli political culture, as expressed in the electoral belief of leaders like the late premier Levi Eshkol that the entire academic population of the country did not 'weigh' as much as a *ma'abara* (new immigrants' transit camp)—a clear demonstration of the paradoxical coexistence of entirely different types of existentialist logic.

The desire to be like any other nation, explicitly and implicitly expounded by Zionist ideology and by nineteenth-century liberal, democratic, socialist ideas, increased the speed at which the native Jewish élitist system of social promotion and education was destroyed. In modern Israel, personal intelligence and integrity are still appreciated but not rewarded economically. Once the 'fountains of honour' started to draw their waters from alien sources two important changes took place. First, the state and its institutions became the major source of social promotion and reward, on a basis of standards which gave greater premiums to non-élitist than to élitist qualities. The rule of democracy, by definition the rule of the greater number and operative by consensus, inevitably favoured mediocrity and penalized skills and excellence. The coexistence of parallel and competing élites diminished the number of available members for each. But most important, a system based on values was replaced by one based on needs. The result was the collapse of the élitist traditional system of recruitment and promotion of leadership which had kept the Jewish nation alive despite extraordinary stress. Status is no longer determined on the basis of excellence in scholarship, and marriages, as in other democratic societies, are contracted, for the most part, among men and women belonging to the same social and economic classes. As a result circles of existing or emerging vested interests and institutionalized plutocratic groups are crystallized, and these necessarily represent much smaller markets for a meritocracy than the traditional Jewish ones. The old, popular, rabbinical aristocracy has broken down and been replaced by a loose federation of more or less closed élites with few common values, with the result that the smaller the Israeli élite becomes, the less articulate are they or capable of facing external pressures—which remain hostile and call for the maximization of quality. More important, these new élites tend to subtract themselves from the control of more exigent social and moral values, and in their new conformism favour a downward alignment, at the level of the lowest possible denominator, which sometimes contributes to their transformation into negative social élites.

All this was inevitable from the moment the Israeli society abandoned the traditional social model of the 'inverted pyramid' of an open aristocracy, with its harsh but effective system of education, in favour of the 'normal' pyramid of Western democracy. The Israelis were right to accept the Zionist theory that the abnormal Diaspora conditions of the Jews could be cured by their return as free men to their own land; but they were wrong in believing that a Jewish state could do away with the old Jewish values which had maintained the Jewish identity for millennia. These values were, in fact, the very source of that inner strength, self-assurance, and self-respect which had permitted and could still permit the Jewish nation to face the trying fate which history has imposed upon it. No Western ideology, no nationalism, and no socialism could in the end fulfil that same role.

The social and ideological aspirations of Zionism to 'normalize' the Jews by transforming them into a people organized according to the social pyramidal model of other nations—namely a large stratum of peasants and workers, a smaller stratum of service people, and an apex of intellectuals-cut deeply into the typology of the Jewish nation. The pyramidal model was, of course, the one existing in the agricultural societies of those Central and Eastern European states in which most of the Jewish masses lived during the nineteenth century, and it was only natural that the first Zionists—Eastern European-born—should try to imitate it. For a people which for centuries had been forcibly restricted in its economic and social activities, forbidden to own land, forced to survive through commerce and moneylending, the return to primary agricultural production seemed to be —and indeed was—a real necessity. The inverted pyramidal structure of Jewish society in the nineteenth century did not appear to its members to be a model similar to that of a rapidly industrializing country like the United States, where the absence of 'peasants' was proof of the modernity of that society. On the contrary, in the historical and social framework of an oppressed minority sharing the hopes and illusions of Enlightenment and Emancipation, an inverted pyramidal social structure seemed to be not only absurd and abnormal, but the unbearable result of the restrictive coercive conditions imposed by the Gentile world upon the Jews, to which Emancipation had put an end. What was not perceived was the fact that in Europe, where the transformation of the inverted pyramid model of the

Jewish society might have reduced the anti-Semitic reaction against the sudden flooding of a native middle class by 'foreign upstarts of Jewish extraction', it could not take place for lack of ideological, economic, and social incentives. On the other hand, in Palestine, where to some extent the inverted pyramid model was changed, the competition between the new Jewish worker and the indigenous Arab worker was one of the elements of friction between the two communities, while the anti-intellectual trend of the new Jewish pioneering society hampered at that time, and still hampers today, the absorption of immigrants from the developed countries. In the final analysis, the working population of Israel was not composed—as the Zionist idealist A. D. Gordon preached—of intellectuals converted to the new purifying religion of normal work, but of destitute Jews from Islamic countries, abandoned by their communal leaders, who were hampered in their social and economic progress in Israel by the lack of that middle-class professional education which the Zionist, pioneering neo-proletariat so profoundly criticized. The trouble with this anti-intellectual trend was not its existence—especially at a time when it carried with it a strong charge of deeply felt, and actually lived, egalitarian ideology—but rather that the pioneering spirit quickly turned into pioneering symbols with considerable content. To be officially registered as a 'tractor driver' or a 'charwoman' was, until recently, regarded as a status symbol by some top Israeli leaders who had not touched a tractor or a broom for years. At the same time the creation of the State brought in its wake crucial changes in the definition of élite roles: it transformed the pre-state élites into ruling groups which, when faced with the need to govern, ascribed old ideological concepts to new and often totally opposed realities. It became 'pioneering' to work in a government office, while a higher price was attached to organizational and manipulative ability than to ideological merit. More attention was paid to competence than to character. A renewed appreciation of intellectual work developed with a parallel growth of academic institutionalization and formalization, in open contrast to the illusion of informality in which both the Zionist pioneering and the Jewish rabbinical traditions continued to believe. (It is certainly not by chance that the 'workers' of the 1930s and 1950s became the 'employed' (*me'usakim*) in the national contracts of the 1960s and 1970s, and that Archie Bunker, the American TV type, has turned into a national hero for the common Israeli. Bunker is a caricature of lost ideals and of persistent prejudice.)

These few general remarks will suffice to underline the variety of problems facing the Israeli élites and some of the reasons for the present leadership crisis which are peculiar to the Israeli society. It should also help in understanding why it is so difficult to locate the exact whereabouts of the country's new élites. In fact, the crisis which they are undergoing is not only a consequence of their lack of stability, proper education, or legitimation, but also that of the unclear patterns of 'circulation'—to use Pareto's word—of the élites themselves. Eisenstadt attributes this confusion, *inter alia*, to the fact that the classless views of the Israeli society bear no connection to reality, and to the fact that in the pre-state ideologies of modern Israel there was no reference to the distribution of power as a basis for social status.[11] Another reason could be the difference in the 'symbol languages' which the various élite groups use to express themselves, resulting from the different historical and cultural contexts in which these different symbol languages developed. Karl Deutsch argued that even when all other conditions are satisfactory, a unification process may fail because the communication capabilities of an élite are underdeveloped.[12] In this sense, communication difficulties among the new Jewish élites of Israel may indeed be a major problem.

Whatever the cause, these élites, while differing profoundly from the traditional Jewish ones, do not fit either into the patterns of Western society or those of the Third World, especially if one tries to apply to them the theoretical classifications elaborated by political sociologists.

Two alert Israeli journalists, Yuval Elizur and Eliahu Salpeter, in a popular study published just before the Yom Kippur War, noted that in 1972, 51.4 per cent of Israelis were employed in one or another kind of public service or managerial private job that made them feel 'very important'. The upper echelon of the present Israeli élites, they also note, crystallized in the 1930–40 period and is, on the whole, characterized by four facts: first, the Israeli élites are not, or do not see themselves as, a distinct social class, the son of the rich industrialist standing side by side with the orphan who survived the Nazi Holocaust or the founder of a new kibbutz; second, there is a high rate of absorption from the general public into the élites; third, as in other immigrant countries, Israel presents a non-homogeneous multiple type of élites; and finally, there is a high degree of mobility within the élites themselves, which explains their rapid changes of quantity and quality.[13] The behavioural scientists Weingrad and Gurevitch do not disagree with these findings. They add that élites are comparatively young and well educated and tend to be European in origin. Even though the percentage of Middle Easterners and North Africans is higher in the political élite than in other sectors, their representation in this category is still minor. Exclusive memberships are normal.[14]

It is always difficult to evaluate any élite numerically. In terms of occupation, it has been shown that some 13 per cent of the Israeli population can be regarded as belonging to the upper class, with a further 9 per cent added on the basis of educational criteria.[15] This confirms what has already been said, namely that despite its proclaimed egalitarianism, Israel has a large group of citizens (some 80 per cent) who are not included, or who do not perceive themselves as being included, in the upper class. It also shows that the 'upper class' has become relatively extended, since it includes 20 per cent of the total population. This is not a bad percentage if one considers the rapidity of the changes which have taken place in a quarter of a century within the demographic, military, ideological, economic, and educational structures of Israel. It is, however, a profound change from the situation which existed in the Jewish settlement in Palestine, the *Yishuv*, prior to the establishment of the State, when a large proportion of the population consisted of highly motivated people, with a high percentage of university and high-school graduates among them. Their participation in the Zionist movement and in the pioneering groups epitomized the traditional role of the intellectual as a rebel against the established order. This has radically changed: with the increased, non-selective immigration, urbanization, bureaucratization of the state, and with the establishment of group differentiation of communicative, scientific, and other 'cultural' roles, the place of the intellectual is today reduced and in any case no longer clear. In Israel a considerable variety of intellectual types has emerged, bureaucratic, professional, academic, freelance. These often overlap and are conformist, or critical of the government, religion, and society. They are also often apathetic towards wider public affairs, and on the whole accept the state as the fullest manifestation of the value of Zionism and as a focal point on to which they can transfer their feelings of identification. The tendency to 'idealize the state', which people like Professor Leibowitz denounce as outright idolatry and potential or actual fascism, coupled with the passage of time and the increasing routinism of state activities, has given rise (as Professor Eisenstadt had already noted in 1966[16]) 'to a feeling of emptiness and moral crisis demanding ideological explanations which remained unsatisfied'. This dissatisfaction in turn gave rise to an ideological 'conservatism' which is at the same time critical of the Government but faithful to pioneering values and is often a source of apathy and cynicism. As it became more difficult to transform ideological trends into cultural life, civic spirit weakened and civic responsibility, voluntary association, and dignified relations between public bodies and the general public deteriorated. These observations received tragic confirmation in subsequent years. The Yom Kippur War underlined the false self-confidence of the political and military establishment, while the economic difficulties which followed the war uncovered the extent of social corruption which had developed within the Israeli society. The élites seemed to be particularly responsible for this state of affairs and for their own evident lack of a sense of direction. In fact they were no worse, probably much better, than in many other countries. They were simply not Jewish enough—in spite of their Jewishness—to cope with the permanent, central problem of the Jewish nation: its solitude, and the need to transform this unique and uncomfortable situation into a source of strength and status. They had forgotten the talmudic obligation to question constantly.

Could things have been done differently? The Jewish people, the most colonized, traditionalist, and persecuted national minority in the Western world (and in the Islamic East), not only had an undisputed right to renovate itself and to achieve a larger measure of equality with the rest of the nations of the world, but had no alternative way of survival except through modernization. Modernization meant, first of all, Westernization, which in turn meant the acceptance of moral, social, and economic values opposed to the solitary aspirations of traditional Judaism. More important, however, was the adoption of an educational system which was totally unfitted to prepare the new élites to defend and perpetuate the élitist self-consciousness of the Jewish nation. Both assimilationists and Zionists concurred in their belief that the Jews, in order to survive physically, had to 'normalize' themselves, giving up their claim to uniqueness. The case of national élites seeking power and freedom in a process of self-extinction through assimilation to the West was not confined to the Jews. In the nineteenth century, when European expansion and technological superiority appeared unbounded, with the 'white man's burden' as the ultimate moral duty of colonialism, many non-European leaders—Japanese, Egyptians in the Khedivian period, Indians, Young Turks—dreamed of becoming like the Europeans and believed that the shortest way to national political renaissance was to break away from their own traditional past. None had to face such a grave dilemma of national revival through cultural assimilation as the Jews of nineteenth-century Europe, who lived in conditions of geographical dispersion, lack of a central political authority, social and economic destitution, and in a deep crisis of identity. To the Zionists, secular as well as orthodox (though the latter were a minority), the creation of an independent State seemed, in these circumstances, to be a primary and indispensable—even if insufficient—condition for putting the Jewish people into a situation where they could once again become masters of their own destiny. The late Chief Rabbi of Palestine, Rabbi A. Kook, stated the problem succinctly when he reminded critics of his pro-Zionist attitude that the builders of the Tabernacle in the Sinai Desert after the Exodus from Egypt, and later on the builders of the Temples in Jerusalem at the time of Solomon and Nehemiah, were not pure men, yet the work of their hands was holy, pure enough to become the dwelling of the Lord.[17] To say that impure people can produce an instrument fit for holiness is, however, very different from saying that any instrument is holy. The builders of the Temple worked within a precise framework of moral, religious, and national concepts. They acted within a parameter of values which unconditionally believed in the necessity of sanctifying the means rather than the ends; but they were not allowed to enter the holy places of the Temple once it was consecrated. This was the very opposite of the Hegelian, Marxist, and Nietzschean conceptions which so deeply influenced the founding fathers of

Zionism: they believed (with a few notable exceptions, like Martin Buber) that the end justifies the means and that a Jewish state was the best framework to allow the survival and self-realization of the modern Jew.

But a state of the Jews which would be an end in itself was a national idol with which even a residual trace of Jewishness could not cope. Similarly socialism, productivism, military efficiency, economic affluence, while acceptable to Judaism as legitimate needs, could never be recognized by it as legitimate values. Owing to this fundamental clash between the Jewish and the Western conceptions of national interest, in the widest sense of the word, the leadership of the state has consistently been unable to achieve any large measure of consensus on any major problem—except problems connected with Israel's physical survival, which are imposed from the outside. The most that a powerful leader like Ben-Gurion could do in this regard was to make the various political groups postpone any decision about the fundamental issues of the state—its purpose, its character, its legitimation, even its written constitution—hoping that time would eventually bring about a solution. There was some justification for this temporizing attitude: the return of the scattered people to their ancestral land, the revival of the Hebrew language, the experience in self-government, the need to withstand external pressures, the very isolation of the Israeli state in international society and the need to define itself—even if only to present a rational image to the outside world—formed a cluster of elements which were revolutionary for the Jewish nation and for the international community, even if not linked to or formalized in a clear, revolutionary ideology or programme. For Ben-Gurion there was no point, therefore, in talking about the identity of a Jewish nation as long as the Jews themselves continued to be, so to speak, half-men: 'In Israel, the Jew is one hundred per cent Jewish and one hundred per cent human, that is, a member of the human race.'[18]

Ben-Gurion's statement, implying that a Diaspora Jew, because of his split personality, is not a full Jew, and not even a full member of the human race, underlines the extent of his belief—typical of many secular Zionist leaders—in the constructive value of Israeli existentialism. Ben-Gurion's Judaism, it has been noted, resembles the Bergsonian *élan vital*, with a dash of Buddhism and more than a dash of Spinozism.[19] The world of Nature and History may certainly testify to a divine movement, but there is no real dialogue between the Divine and the human. It is, to say the least, a very simplistic approach to the problem of reviving Jewish consciousness and original culture. But even if it were true that by some miraculous spontaneous germination, Jewish civilization, one of the most sophisticated in history, could be even partially revived by the magic physical touch of the Jewish hand, it would still leave unanswered the problem of how the Israeli could free himself from the negative image of the Jew which a secular,

European-inspired movement like Zionism had carried with it into Israel. This image was produced by prejudices assimilated from alien sources like those of most other colonized peoples, and by those created by the Jews about themselves and tainted by an exaggerated self-criticism, which joined with the stereotyped belief that the Jew had to detach himself from his Jewishness in order to become a 'modern' Jew.

Self-hatred is a well-known manifestation of anomalous exilic existence. Cultural colonization among subject peoples including the Jews has become prototypical of this psychological self-destroying attitude. The indifference, bordering on contempt, which many Israelis show to traditional Judaism, to the institutions which produced a world civilization of such a standard that, by comparison, the Israeli cultural contribution hardly reaches the level of folklore, is a local version of that same alienated psychology which Zionism believed would disappear in the 'healthy' society of free-born Sabras. Although there has recently been a considerable revival of interest in and revaluation of Jewish traditional culture (a clear sign of a conscious or unconscious process of decolonization), there still remain innumerable signs, both large and small, of the Israeli self-shame complex. The fashion of name-changing is one of the most revealing. The hebraization of foreign names is understandable in a society, like that of the Jews, which was forced for generations to accept ludicrous foreign family names imposed by the petty tyranny of anti-Semitic functionaries in the host countries. No one likes to be called *Afterveilchen* ('Bottom-Violet'), for instance: one can, however, discern a deeper desire for change in Israelis— like writer Dahn Ben-Amotz, for instance, who chose a resounding Canaanite name, *Amotz*, in place of his father's name, *Tehilimsager* ('Psalm-reciter'), or a powerful leader like David Gruen, who felt that by becoming David Ben-Gurion ('Son of the Lion Cub') he was giving an important finishing touch to the new role he wanted to fill. Many African leaders, from Joseph Mobuto of Zaire to Amin Dada of Uganda, have felt the same psychological compulsion as part of their efforts to achieve a greater measure of integrity in their personality and self-image.

The political philosopher Shlomo Avineri, speaking on the phenomenon of Israeli self-hatred, said that one of its manifestations was the desire to 'be like the Gentiles', a desire which stemmed from the Israeli perception of the traditional Jewish society as dejected and despicable. Avineri regards this as a totally wrong perception, unwarranted by historical evidence.

. . . One must possess a very high degree of Jewish self-hatred in order to represent the entire Exilic history of the Jews as a chronicle of persecution and a record of a miserable, spiritless, crippled life. The Jews have been persecuted because they have been better educated, wealthier, and more cultured than the average of the societies in which they have lived. Anti-Semitism should be seen not only as the employment of force by the strong against the weak, but also as the jealousy of the average towards achievement and success. Rather than being proud of a Jewish tradition that is aristocratic in the true sense of the word, though its meaning in Jewish life has always contained an element of living dangerously, we are often ashamed of our own history. This means that Jews too frequently have accepted the criteria of an alien society. It has been noted that the image of the Jew in the eyes of the anti-Semite is remarkably similar to that of the Diaspora Jew in the eyes of the Sabra, educated in the vulgarized form of Zionist ideology.[20]

The Hebrew University scholar goes on to explain that a scarcity of books on modern Jewish history is partly responsible for the Israelis' distorted, vulgar view of the Diaspora. 'If Zionism means negating the Diaspora, then Zionist education has automatically been associated with an approach which not only highlighted the negative and distorted aspects of Jewish existence in the Diaspora but even saw the patterns of existence of the Jews of 19th-century Europe as characterizing all Jewish history since the destruction of the Second Temple. One can ask any child in the street about his image of Jewish life in the Diaspora and find that it is a projection of the East European Jewish *stetl* in its decline. This view has submerged any positive content.' But not only for children: David Ben-Gurion is on record as having stated in an official document his oft-expressed opinion that Israel had '. . . consolidated human dust, scattered and crumbled throughout the exile . . . into the seed of a resurgent nation'.[21]

Author Haim Hazas has a hero in one of his novels declare: 'I am opposed to Jewish history. It is not we who have made our history but the Gentiles —they have made it for us. They made it according to their will and their way of life, and we only received it from them. But this is not our history. . . . Jewish history is boring and uninteresting. It contains no feats, no contests, no heroes, no conquerors . . . only a multitude of sighing people, who weep and ask for mercy.'[22]

The situation could hardly be otherwise in a Jewish State which honours recognized leaders of the Zionist movement like Micha Joseph Berdichewsky, who once wrote: 'We must cease to be Jews with an abstract Jewish faith and turn into just Jews',[23] or another Zionist founding father, Leo Pinsker, who preached that we, the Jews, must turn our soul not to the Holy Land (*Eretz Kodshenu*) but from now on to our own land (*Artzenu*). All we need is a big piece of land, which can be all ours. There was another reason why it could not be otherwise: the only other 'Zionist' group which could have balanced the self-hating tendencies of the dejudaized Jew were the rabbis, the natural defenders of the national tradition. But they, too, were no less culturally and ideologically colonized than the secularized Zionists, whom they fought fiercely right up to the eve of the day on which the State was established.

When the German rabbis, for instance, in the famous declaration of 1897, denounced the aims of political Zionism, they were not raising the banner of a traditional nationalism against the new secularism; with very few exceptions[24] they believed that 'the efforts to create a Jewish state in the Land of Israel conflict with the chosenness of the Jews as expressed in the Holy Scriptures'. This was an attitude that orthodox Jewry, on the whole, maintained (for reasons of Jewish legitimacy which will be discussed in detail later) until the physical destruction of European Jewry by the Nazis, and in some cases even after the proclamation of the State of Israel.[25]

The total result was an inevitable dilemma which the Nobel Prize novelist S. Y. Agnon underlined when he wrote: 'An historic mistake has happened which the creator of the *Halakha* [rabbinical tradition] did not take into consideration. The Jews could not wait for the Messiah and created a state without Him. In this state opinions were divided: a minority said— the *Halakha* cannot bear with the state, therefore the creation of the state was an error and a sin. The majority said—if there is conflict between the state and the *Halakha*, one must do away with the *Halakha*. Or, at best, make a compromise: let the religious Jews live according to the *Halakha* and let us make a [political] coalition with them.'[26]

The trouble was, of course, that the *Halakha* was not just the way of life of the religious Jews; it was the institutionalized expression of Jewish life. Any state of the Jews without the Messiah, to use Agnon's expression, had two choices: to give up being Jewish (in which case, as the Arabs claim, there is no reason to have a Jewish state) or to elaborate a new Jewish élitist *Halakha* for a Jewish State without the Messiah—with or without the collaboration of the orthodox Jews. People as widely different as Aḥad Ha'Am and David Ben-Gurion tried in their respective ways to do just that, showing a deep understanding of the vital role which a system of education aimed at promoting an open popular society would play in the reborn Jewish polity. Aḥad Ha'Am viewed it as part of a utopian community of sages which would be responsible for that 'spiritual centre' in Palestine out of which the reborn Jewish nation would eventually spring. Ben-Gurion was more practical: he put his faith in the army (which he conceived as a school of virtue and as a military instrument for the defence of the country), in the scientific community, and in the puritan life of the desert-conquering pioneer (a life he himself chose when he retired to the Negev kibbutz of Sdeh Boker in 1953—an example which was not followed by many Israeli leaders).

Asher Zvi Ginsberg, better known by his pen-name, Aḥad Ha'Am ('One of the people'), was one of the first Zionist thinkers to perceive the inner contradictions in which the new Jewish national movement would be caught as a result of the clash between a traditional élitist and a secular populist political culture. A man of recognized superior intellectual gifts and a master of talmudic learning, Aḥad Ha'Am, like so many of his 'enlightened' contemporaries, refused to remain within the limits of Jewish tradition. He searched for 'secular' culture, as an expression of the revolutionary passion which burned in the lonely, introverted character of a wholly self-taught moralist. Like many Jews of his time and place of residence (Eastern Europe and Russia), he lived fully in the plenitude of two great cultures: the Jewish and the European. In an article entitled 'This is not the way'[27] Aḥad Ha'Am launched a devastating attack on the pre-Herzlian, Rothschild-supported attempts of Zionist pioneers to establish settlements in Palestine. The settlers and their supporters, members of the *Ḥibbat Zion* movement,[28] erred in the spirit and the tactics of their enterprise. Apart from other considerations (and Ahad Ha'Am was the first to foresee trouble with the Arabs), the concept of a national return to Palestine which was now being focused exclusively on the material wellbeing of individual Jews could not coexist with the idea proper to traditional Judaism that the spiritual wellbeing of the people should be the primary concern of Judaism. He believed that no properly structured society or great collective enterprise can be set up on the basis of private interest alone. His solution for the revival of the Jewish national consciousness was to make the Zionist enterprise an effort aimed not at a 'concentration of the people, but at what must precede it, the concentration of the spirit', with Jewish settlement in Palestine [the Yishuv] transformed into a model workshop in which the regeneration of the Jewish people should be hammered out and from which, by dint of example and teaching, a new and healthy influence would radiate forth.

Aḥad Ha'Am preceded Hermann Hesse in the idea of the Glass Bead Game of utopian Kastalien when he proposed, and in fact established, a semi-secret order of 'Lovers of Zion', dedicated spiritual Zionists, the *B'nei Moshe* (Sons of Moses), for which he wrote the doctrine and the rules.[29] The order quickly foundered, but it showed how a secular Jewish intellectual like Aḥad Ha'Am still remained close to the idea that only through a system capable of producing an élitist Jewish leadership could the regenerated Jewish nation transform itself from 'the people of the Book into a people of the books'—a utopia, but a very Jewish one.

The institutions which Aḥad Ha'Am imagined could aid the revival of Jewish civilization in modern times were as aristocratic as any Jewish traditional institutions could be. But the moment he detached the *Halakha*, the life discipline, of his B'nei Moshe order from the traditional Jewish *Halakha*, he was bound also to detach his 'spiritual' Zionists from Judaism, or whatever was left of it, and to face the same contradictions which he denounced in populist political Zionism.

Ben-Gurion's concept of the new way of life which the Jews should adopt in Israel was different, just as his personality differed totally from that of Aḥad Ha'Am. Ben-Gurion was a convinced socialist, but he believed in the Messianic role of Zionism and claimed that 'where there is no vision, the people perish'. He distinguished between Zionist ideology—the offspring of nineteenth-century Europe—and the permanent Messianic longings of the Jewish people for national redemption in the land of their fathers. He thought that Jews could cure themselves of their split personality merely by living in Israel. Whereas for Ahad Ha'Am the collective 'salvation of bodies' through the establishment of political independence was dangerous and self-defeating, for Ben-Gurion the establishment of a Jewish State was the beginning of a new uplifting for the Jewish people. Freedom, climate, hard physical labour in the land of their fathers, service in a national army, science—all these would eventually revive Jewish civilization, especially if such a revival could draw energy and inspiration directly from the experiences of ancient Israel and ignore, as much as possible, the Diaspora interlude and its alienation. What he failed to perceive was that the end of the separation between Jewish and Gentile societies with Emancipation was an epoch-making event for the Jews—at least as great as the establishment of a sovereign polity—but that the two worked in opposite directions and were not jointly sufficient to recreate a Jewish identity. 'The remote past', said Ben-Gurion, 'is closer than the past two thousand years. . . . There is a leap in history: we are living in our homeland, and every excavation in Beit Shearim or in Hatzor reinforces our affinity to the homeland and to our past in the homeland.'[30] For him, as for so many Israelis, Judaism could be a spontaneous outgrowth of historical contingencies rather than the ultimate refined product of an elaborate civilization.

Like so many Jews of his generation, Ben-Gurion seemed unaware of the extent of the cultural colonization of the modern Jew. He believed in the values of modern civilization, which he considered equal, if not superior, to those of rabbinical culture because of their scientific achievement, and in spite of his patriotism he believed that the value content of Israeli society could best be judged by Western and not by Jewish standards.

But he, too, could only conceive of Israel as an élitist society. 'Only by being a model nation of which every Jew, wherever he is, can be proud, shall we preserve the love of the Jewish people and its loyalty to Israel. Our status in the world, too, will not be determined by our material wealth or by our military valour, but by the radiance of our achievement, our culture, our society—and only by virtue of these will we acquire the friendship of the nations.'[31] Spartacus and Moses—that was Ben-Gurion's utopia for Israel. But if Western tradition could supply the ideology for Spartacus, what, except Jewish tradition, could supply the ideology for Moses? Ben-Gurion had no patience with the tradition elaborated in the Jewish Diaspora; he wanted to go directly to the Bible, in a kind of Jewish Protestantism which should perpetuate the achievements of Jewish civilization without preserving or imitating the painstaking process of acculturation through which Jews become Jews. 'It is impossible', retorted Professor

Leibowitz to Ben-Gurion, 'to erect Judaism on the basis of the Bible, nor is it possible to base it on ethics and messianism. There are those who offer us a substitute for Judaism—bibliotry, the Bible itself, not the Bible within the framework of active Judaism and with the meaning given it by "ism", but the Bible itself, as a document of elevated ethical values and as a basis for secular human-anthropocentric and Jewish ethnocentric education. This approach is a distortion from the Jewish point of view and an absurdity from the human point of view. This bibliotry is not Judaism: it is a strange and highly paradoxical mixture of atheism and Christianity, deriving from atheism in that it deprives the Bible of its religious meaning, and from Christianity in that the latter has always clung to the Bible, using it to attack Judaism.'[32]

For Leibowitz there is no Jewish philosophy or ethics, or specifically Jewish political or social idea, just as there are no specifically Jewish artistic or aesthetic values and no Jewish science. 'The only specifically Jewish creation that actively appeared in history is the *Halakha*, that is, the attempt to organize the rules of human life against a background of law, the aim of which is the service of God.' This was the formative and unique system which produced the utopia of a people—a whole people—turning it into a 'holy nation and a kingdom of priests'. This was the only way of equalizing men upwards, of creating a popular aristocracy.

That the Jewish people could not survive by the Book alone; that the Bible needed a system of interpretation and adaptation to make it consistent with the changing conditions of life and society; and that it had elaborated institutions fitting this purpose, are well-known facts. But since this system had collapsed, if the one proposed by Ahad Ha'Am proved unreal, if the idea of existentialist Messianic redemption put forward by Ben-Gurion was too passionate, crude, and open to alien influences to offer a framework for selective acculturation and promotion of the new Israeli élites, how could the leadership of the State be expected to face successfully the challenges facing the Jewish nation? Where could it turn to find at least some intermediate reference points according to which it could steer a course with the maximum consensus of the Israeli and Jewish people? Obviously help could not be expected from the outside nor could the perpetuation of Jewish values rely solely on the ability of the Jew to respond to external challenges.

The root of the problem seems to be the lack of awareness in the Israeli society of the fact that—as in the case of velocity in flight mechanics—there is a critical level of Jewish culture below which Judaism, its values, and the Jewish national identity cannot be maintained. The crisis of Israeli leadership seems fundamentally to be a crisis of Jewish culture and education, not in the sense that it does not recognize its own ignorance, important as such recognition is, but in the sense that the leadership does not seem to perceive that the very consciousness of the state of cultural colonization by the Israeli society would help create the conditions for the elaboration of a new education system, capable of adapting the élitist principles vital to the survival of Judaism to the challenges of our time. The only organized attempt to deal with the problem has been made by the religious parties, *Agudat Israel* and *Mafdal*, which exert constant political pressure to obtain as large a share as possible of the state's educational budget for their religious schools. The rapidly expanding state and private religious educational network, which already covers 27 per cent of the school population, is not only the most advanced in the country but also the most élitist-oriented. It has not yet produced any outstanding national leader but—as will be shown in subsequent chapters dealing with institutions and the changing political balance of forces—it has contributed to making the National Religious Party (*Mafdal*) the rising centrist force in the parliamentary spectrum. The problem of education, however, even for the religious sector and certainly for the larger secular sector, is not only a matter of pursuing Jewish studies but of trying to see things Jewishly, accepting the reality of the fact that Jews, in Israel as elsewhere, must accept being different in order to be Jews. 'This does not mean', says Adin Steinsaltz, talmudic scholar and mathematician, 'that we are better than others, but when we say that we are different, there has to be something concrete about the difference. We have to work out some way of understanding our own history. We know that there is the law of entropy found in every physical part of the world, according to which all things must run down. . . . [But] within the cosmos in which the law of entropy holds its sway, there is also the realm of biology, and even though the biological realm is contained in the general physico-chemical laws, there is a pulling in an opposite direction. Everything grows up, things develop and become bigger and more complicated. . . . By analogy we have to understand our special history within world history in this manner. The laws of growth, development and decay that apply to other cultures do not apply to our people. Their times of greatness—and their ideas of greatness—did not coincide with ours. Understanding this difference, and trying to identify with it, is the only way we can really know ourselves.'[33]

It is the lack of comprehension of the desynchronization of Jewish/Israeli history with the history of the world which more than anything else explains the lack of direction of the State's élites. It is their unawareness of the depth of the Israeli society's dependence on alien cultural sources that prevents the elaboration of a wider national consensus on the role and nature of the new Jewish polity created by the Zionist movement. But it is also the triumph of the Jewish cause of national liberation which has crystallized in the minds of the Israelis the illusion of their 'normalization' through the acceptance of non-Jewish standards of life.

It is an illusion which must be dispelled before any consensus can be found to face the fact that unless Israel is prepared to accept the tragic solitude of the slave it cannot renounce its élitist posture, which also imposes another kind of solitude.

CHAPTER 6

The Crisis of Institutionalization

'In the beginning,' wrote Montesquieu, 'the leaders create the institutions of the Republic; afterwards the institutions create the leaders.'

In Israel, the pioneers of the Zionist society and the founding fathers of the State created new institutions for the Jewish republic, some very original ones, like the kibbutz. Yet, only thirty years after the establishment of the State, the feeling shared by many sectors of the population is that something has gone wrong; the institutions have become clogged and outdated. Political parties call for electoral reform because the present parliamentary system seems incapable of permitting the formation of authoritative governments; the public demands organizational reforms because the machinery of the State seems to be unable to provide a just distribution of services, taxes, and income. Workers as well as industrialists press for labour reforms because they feel equally damaged by an egalitarian socialist system which is neither egalitarian nor any longer socialist but seems to be conducive to parasitism and a perpetual source of conflict, especially in the areas of nationalized production or those owned by the labour unions. This consumer-materialist system produces a wide stratum of educated professionals which cannot be absorbed in the economic system; this in turn produces frustration and emigration, two phenomena which cut deep into the image of a just society and into the claim that Israel exists for the purpose of gathering in the exiles.

The malaise has been general and admitted by all—as was shown by the electoral programmes and propaganda of all parties in the May 1977 general elections—and had a direct effect on the collapse of the coalition of socialist parties (*Ma'arah*). These parties, in various forms and combinations, had dominated the political life of Israel for more than three decades; their defeat was less the result of a swing to the Right than of the public's wish to punish the socialist establishment for its corruption and for its inability to solve long-festering problems, especially after the Yom Kippur War. None of the parties, however, seemed to be able to produce a remedy, or even to identify the deep sources of the institutional and ideological crises of the Israeli society. The consequences of these elections will be briefly discussed in the final chapter, together with their significance in relation to the process of cultural decolonization which has been referred to throughout this work.

The questions asked here are to what extent the crisis of Israeli institutionalization reflects the crisis of the Israeli leadership described in the previous chapter; whether or not biblical and talmudic Judaism possessed institutions of its own which could be relevantly compared with the new institutions created by Zionism; whether or not the clash between the spirit of these new institutions, copied or imported from the West, and the spirit of the traditional Jewish institutions still consciously nurtured in Israel, significantly hamper or impinge upon the functioning of the state institutions. Finally, does the process of institutionalization of a new society cope with the need to balance past and present in such a way that the former does not suffocate the latter, and the latter is not too violent in its rejection of the former. After all, balance between past and present is one of the main problems of all new nations.

One can, of course, claim that what hampers the working of the Israeli institutions is not so much the inadequacy of their structure or the (lack of) ideology on which they are based, but the difficult objective conditions in which they operate. If there were no wars, for instance, there would be more resources available to raise the standard of living and education of the population, to fight juvenile delinquency, to prevent corruption, and so on. But such arguments have counter-arguments of equal weight: when the external pressure on Israel was much heavier, during the War of Independence or at the time of the massive immigration during the 1950s, the national income rose more rapidly than now; the level of criminality and corruption was much lower; social organization, despite the lack of proper institutions, was more pronounced; not to mention the high level of voluntarism, readiness to make sacrifices, individual and collective moral standards. How is it possible, one may ask, for a state whose whole *raison d'être* is being Jewish, to elicit the interest and loyalty of its non-Jewish population? Conversely, how can a state which professes to be egalitarian and democratic remain particularistic, i.e. Jewish? This dilemma will be dealt with more thoroughly later. Here it is necessary to discuss the often-heard claim that if there was more of everything it would be better. The present crisis of Israeli institutions is at least as much a crisis of means as of ends, and the purpose of this chapter is to examine the problems of ends without reference to means or—for the sake of argument—to the objective situation, which of course plays a major role in the functioning of the institutional system of a country at war and facing a serious problem of a national minority at home.

Let us examine first the hypothesis that institutions cannot function well because they have conflicting aims. The argument here is that the crisis of Israeli institutions stems from the maladjustment of traditional to modern values. Israelis cannot reconcile themselves to this inability to adapt. It is not only a question of the pace of change but of the incompatibility between values inspiring organizations aimed at coping with modernization and change and those existing in a Jewish society, which still lives within conservative structures and focuses its collective aims on aspirations different from those of the Western society in general and of the consumer society in particular.

To be more specific, although only 12 per cent of the population of Israel is 'officially' orthodox and votes for religious parties, 90 per cent of the population of Jewish parentage accepts 'Jewish values', however they may interpret them, as matters of fact. Although Judaism has never been sympathetic to asceticism and has consistently proclaimed its belief that man has to find his salvation and his self-fulfilment in this world, it has nevertheless lived, and indeed survived, through a very strict set of moral values. There is therefore no reason to expect that Jews, when they try to live as Jews—in a traditional rabbinical society or in a modern secular one—should find themselves better equipped morally than other traditional, non-Jewish societies to stand up to the challenge of modernity, particularly since they are no longer protected by their customs and traditional institutions. This becomes evident when one looks at the crisis of Israeli institutions from the point of view of their ability to cope with the problem of development and of their own functionality.

Development is a matter of expectations, which may or may not be fulfilled. Functionality is the capacity of the machinery to 'regulate the practices and administer the rules' most befitting the changing 'system of practices and social roles developed about a value or a series of values'.[1]

As for expectations—many of those held by the Israeli society have been fulfilled. Paradoxically, those which looked most utopian have been realized to such an extent that one of the reasons for the institutional malaise is the widespread consciousness of a lack of present purpose in the institution set up to achieve these utopian aims. For example, once the Zionist expectation of creating a Jewish State was realized, the cumbersome machinery of the Zionist Organization seems superfluous because none of the new tasks which this organization sets for itself can justify its existence —as Ben-Gurion repeatedly argued. This is a typical case proving that, as noted, the productivity of the bureaucrat cannot increase faster than the scope of the bureaucratized activity itself. One does not need a special 'Zionist' organization to deal, for instance, with the main problems of immigration, and no bureaucratic organization will ever be able to create motivation for immigration if the moral, political, social, and economic conditions to activate such immigration do not exist. The same could be said of the socialist expectation: the control of major instruments of production and the sources of economic and political power by the labour organizations and parties has been largely achieved in Israel. And yet things are less than ideal with regard to the functioning of the socialist sector: endless strikes; no working-class solidarity; a disrespectful attitude towards workers and their ideals; inflation; lack of trust in the socialist establishment, have sapped the very sources of power of this sector. 'A wind of madness', noted Golda Meir before the 1977 elections, 'is blowing through this country.' But it was not: it was the Israeli version of the materialist, cliché-ridden Archie Bunker syndrome because all the Zionist institutions have maximized power and have now become unable to administer it properly. The one institution which still operates with close to maximum efficiency is the one whose aims have not yet been fulfilled, namely, the army, which after thirty years of wars and victory is still searching for ways and means of guaranteeing the physical survival of the nation. Nevertheless, despite all declarations to the contrary, the growing bureaucratization of the military, its politicization in the wake of its larger share of control of the national expenditure, and above all the reduction of its cultural horizons through specialization and a lack of basic humanistic education among its locally born officers, have shown their negative effects in battle. Whatever the army's gain in terms of fire power and costly equipment, it lost in strategic and tactical ingenuity and in the initiative of its high command. Nothing could be more significant in this connection than the way in which the Israelis lost their strategic superiority over the Egyptians through the building and manning of the Bar-Lev Line, a bad imitation of an outdated defence concept (the French Maginot Line) and an explicit example of professional conformism due to loss of indigenous cultural identity.[2]

The crisis of Israeli institutions is not, therefore, caused primarily by development or by the pace of change, although the strains of quick development are felt in Israel just as in other developing societies. It is caused by their lack of functionality. The inability to regulate the practices and administer the rules most befitting a value or series of values reopens the question of which rules and laws: the secular, egalitarian, imported ones or those that are Jewish, élitist, and particularistic. The very fact that the Israeli state declares itself to be a Jewish State and that the majority of its citizens—apart from the Arabs—want to remain Jews (however they interpret this) indicates at least one of the major causes for the institutions' malfunctioning. It is impossible to *be* something without knowing why, or, in the case of the Jews, also how. The alternative is a situation of indifference, of collective normlessness, of 'anomie', to use Durkheim's expression, which would make it impossible for the society to support the goals it pursues. One could claim the contrary when looking at the high degree of mass participation of the Israeli public in military and political events, especially in times of crisis. But even this participation is lower than in the

earlier stages of the Zionist enterprise. The state has taken over many of
the voluntarist movements, particularly in the field of youth organization;
the craving for material advantages has blunted the enthusiasm and the
puritanism of the early days. This phenomenon is part and parcel of the
general process of development and modernization which Israel shares
with many other countries. What characterizes the situation in Israel is the
coexistence of two ways of life: one is marked by voluntarism, a civic
sense, and readiness to sacrifice individual for national interest; the other is
operated by a growing egotism in private and public relationships, a lack of
civic spirit in everyday life, brutality expressed in rudeness and in the
highest rate of traffic accidents in the world, in fast-growing organized
crime, and in a general attitude of indifference.

The 'aberrant' behaviour which then ensues, and which is very evident
in the case of Israel, is not, of course, necessarily an indication of the
peculiar Israeli national character. Robert K. Morton speaks of 'a symptom
of dissociation between culturally prescribed aspirations and socially structured avenues for realizing these aspirations' common to many countries,
especially in the Third World.[3] Here the focus is on the dissociation between different aspirations, a common phenomenon of developing countries. In the Israeli case it is therefore important to clarify which of these
aspirations are 'prescribed' by indigenous values and needs, which by 'alien'
factors, and what is the role Jewish traditional culture can play in the
system.

The institutions of traditional Judaism have been defined as those
belonging to a society which regards its existence as being based upon a
common body of knowledge and values handed down from the past. Many
of the factors which for a very long time separated this society from the
outside world served at the same time as a common denominator of Jewish
identity: religious nationhood, Messianic hope, consciousness of a common
fate and being the object of common hostility. These factors continue to
be at the root of the common consciousness of most members of a Jewish
society which is no longer traditional, and many Israelis discover, often to
their surprise, that they feel emotionally closer to a black Jew from Ethiopia than to an Oxford don.

At the same time, since the Age of Enlightenment, the consciousness of
immediate religious destiny and the rationalist belief in the unlimited validity of human intellect have combined, despite their being opposites,
against traditional Jewish society, claiming 'self-deserved authority in
opposition to the acknowledged validity of tradition'.[4] As in the case of
the Israeli élites, here too there is a deep clash of emotional and rational
approaches which makes the process of westernization of the Israeli state
look paradoxical, or at least *sui generis*. Furthermore, in the state of Israel
religious charisma has to a large extent been replaced by the charisma of

state and nation. Although such secular charisma does not possess the same legitimacy, the rise of the new Jewish state (which most orthodox rabbis acknowledge as *Reshit Tsemihat Ge'ulatenu*, the beginning of the growth of our salvation) remains overcharged with feelings which are deep-seated in the old Jewish national religious tradition and have therefore had a strong impact on the minds of Jews all over the world. For entire communities, as geographically and culturally remote as those of Yemen and Russia, the rebirth of Jewish independence has been an emotional and intellectual event often perceived as possessing a supernatural dimension. The whole national history of the Jews is marked by this kind of meta-political element. But there is a distinct difference in the nature of past and present experience. In both the biblical and the Zionist exodus, a mass of persecuted individuals breaks through into freedom and becomes a conquering nation. But in the first case, the ideological purpose of freedom is the special relationship with the Divine which is not only made miraculously clear at the foot of Mount Sinai but is embodied in a formal treaty, the Covenant, and in the written law, the Torah, and the oral law, the Torah she'be'al'peh, which for the next thirty centuries will mould the individual and collective behaviour of the Jews. In the second case, the old purpose seems irrelevant, a new one is not spelled out, and the formal treaty of acceptance within the society of nations is not only contested by a large number of states but, if taken seriously, would mould the collective and individual behaviour of the Israelis in the most heterogeneous and unJewish matrixes possible. One biblical legend serves to illustrate this point. According to the Exodus story (14:9–15), when the Jews were caught between the Red Sea and the pursuing Egyptian chariots, they did not know what to do. Struck by fear, they accuse Moses of having led them to death in the wilderness, and then divide up into four groups each one with its own embryonic institutional aspirations and organizations. The first group tends towards destruction: it proposes to the others to throw themselves into the sea (which rabbinical tradition interprets as the sea of assimilation), and stop existing as Jews. The second group suggests surrendering to the Egyptians and serving them physically and morally in exchange for life. The third group opts for war and calls for military organization. The fourth group calls for prayers and religious sublimation of their tribulations. Moses rejects all four 'solutions'. To those who have lost courage to the point of being willing to lose their own identity, Moses says: 'Fear not, stand still and see the salvation of the Lord' (14:13). To those who want to surrender to the Egyptians, Moses says: 'The Egyptians whom ye have seen today, ye shall see them no more for ever' (14:13), i.e. your masters are more vulnerable than you. To those who want to fight, Moses says dryly: 'The Lord shall fight for you' (14:14). And finally, to those who choose to rely on prayer, Moses briskly orders: 'Keep quiet'

(14:14). What then is the solution? The Lord Himself gives it to Moses. He says: 'Why do you shout at me? Speak to the Children of Israel and tell them to *move on*' (14:15). Move on: this is the operational word for the Jewish leadership throughout the ages and concurrently the main functional purpose of Jewish institutions.

A sociologist such as Eisenstadt, in a totally different framework of thought and in very different language from that employed by the Bible, comes very close to the same conclusion when he notes in a lecture on the heterogeneity of modern Jewish beliefs that 'the constellation of Jewish identity and traditions contained a certain type of response to basic dilemmas of Jewish existence and self-conception which developed from the beginning of Jewish history. One such basic dilemma—that between the universal and the particularist element in Jewish culture—was solved, in a sense, by diving or pushing forward to some future time the possibility of realization of the universalistic element, of a really open dialogue and encounter with the other nations.'[5]

The point Eisenstadt makes is, of course, totally different from the one in the talmudic legend about the crossing of the Red Sea, but it is interesting and relevant to our argument in two ways: the 'pushing forward' of apparently insoluble problems is not a metaphoric or a metaphysical approach to reality. It is a basic, almost inborn Jewish reaction to all major challenges, inspired by long historical experience and legitimized by a strong traditional culture. Theodor Herzl, who knew very little about Judaism, defined his movement—Zionism—as the Jewish people on the march. The pioneering ideology of pre-state Israel owed part of its appeal and authority over the non-pioneering section of the Palestine Jewish community less to its socialist content than to the subconscious memories which the idea of pioneering, of 'moving on', elicited in the hearts of modern secular Jews. Nobody, of course, would dismiss the importance of the cohesive role played by external pressures on modern Israel, but while at least part of this pressure is the consequence of the Zionist decision to 'push forward', the crises of Israeli institutions seem to be caused by the feeling elicited by the creation of the State, that there is no longer an enemy to run away from. Practically, the moment the pioneering ideology lost its meaning and the people started to believe that solutions to Israel's major problems could be found in a dialogue with other nations—especially on economic and ideological matters—the institutions of the Israeli polity lost most of their functionality. To paraphrase Montesquieu, the institutions of Zionism *did* create the leaders of the new Israeli republic but these leaders have not yet succeeded in creating an institution for Zion.[6] Seen from this particular Jewish traditional psychological angle, the relationship between the crisis of leadership and the crisis of institutions becomes clear, as well as dramatic, because for a long time the resulting 'aberrant' behaviour remained 'camouflaged' by non-Jewish and pseudo-élitist ideological patterns such as socialist-nationalism and the call for quality in a materialistic society for security reasons. When the camouflage broke up, the shock was greater and the public was unprepared to understand its causes.

The talmudic legend about the four wrong choices on the shores of the Red Sea becomes very topical: a relatively large percentage of the Israelis, some 350,000, decided to return to the lands of the Diaspora; others sought a solution to the problems of the State in greater efforts to imitate the world around them, whether Marxist, democratic, Arab, or counter-culture; a very large percentage relied on the military option; and others on prayer and strict orthodoxy even if this no longer fitted the requirements of a modern nation. In spite of enlarged territorial frontiers, no one could decide in favour of 'marching on' because the leaders not only had no promised land to go to, but no heart or authority to move. In the absence of Moses, both they and the institutions they had created stood still and deteriorated.

We can now turn to the other two questions asked at the beginning of this chapter: whether or not traditional Judaism possessed institutions of its own which (as in the case of traditional and Western thought) could compare in a relevant way with the new institutions created by Zionism. It is clear that the institutions of a non-sovereign religious community, whose functions catered to the needs and obligations of second-class, persecuted subjects, could hardly fit the needs of a modern polity. But what about the old formative ideas inspired by the necessity to strengthen Jewish identity and the old principle on which stood the consensual authority of a scattered nation? Robert Gordis, professor of Bible Studies at the Jewish Theological Seminary, believes that the three major factors which have contributed to fashioning the Jewish soul and its ideals (and which consequently profoundly influenced Jewish traditional institutions) are the memory of the serfdom in Egypt, the nomadic period of desert wandering, and the continuous heroic social and moral activities of the prophets. These three factors, combined with the permanent political, demographic, and economic weakness of the Jewish people, have made them develop a system of life and government which, in his opinion, had the substance if not the outer form of an ideal democracy.[7] This situation is not surprising in the light of our argument that the Jewish mind and culture shun abstract definitions and prefer metaphors and imagery.

Gordis believes that the Jews realized from the very beginning that democracy was something indivisible which could not be broken down into artificial compartments such as 'political', 'social', and 'economic'. Just as it became impossible for the Jews to draw a clear line between the divine and the human, the particular and the universal, so it became increasingly impossible to distinguish between freedom and justice, liberty and leisure. This 'compact value' attitude could, of course, work both ways, helping to blur the distinctions between the permissible and the permitted, the sectarian and the national, the private and the public—all the negative features one perceives in the Israeli society but which certainly also existed in the past. The prophets and rabbis would not otherwise have dealt at such length with problems of private and public morality, their judgement or prevention. Gordis's implicit presumption that the indivisible approach to democracy might be a source of positive collective social and political behaviour is contradicted by past and present realities. This does not alter the fact that the compactness of the value-approach of traditional Judaism was responsible for making its institutions compatible with a number of those basic ideas and aspirations which, as we have said, aimed to achieve national unity, social co-operation, and voluntarily accepted authority.

One of these concepts is that of 'tsedaka u'mishpat', which could be translated as 'the right way of behaviour and justice'. The fact that the two ideas, correct behaviour and justice, had combined into one operative value, underlining the Jewish belief that one cannot work properly without the other, had a number of practical effects. One, for instance, was the visceral distaste of the Jews for absolute political rule. Jewish monarchy not only remained suspect, it was always sharply criticized by the prophets. But even in the case of the most absolute rulers, like King Ahab, it was always subject to the law. The supremacy of justice-cum-right behaviour (which in the case of the Divine Sovereign became absolute justice-cum-absolute mercy) is exemplified by the theory—unique in the history of religions—that the Lord Himself, the very source of all Law and Life, is subject to the Covenant which He has established with the Jewish People. From this extraordinary and revolutionary idea developed, as noted, the distinction between the Sovereign and the Ruler, which became the essential element of the legitimation and proper working of modern democracy. This element was conceived and translated into practical institutions by the Jews well before the age of Pericles.

Two other fundamental principles of the ancient Jewish democratic system were the *right* to be different and the *duty* to criticize the established rulers. But criticism had to be enlightened in order to be constructive: in this way it contributed to the development of that system of universal compulsory education which traditional Judaism built up also as machinery for mobilizing, selecting, and promoting the largest possible élites. One can get an idea of the pioneering and socially revolutionary nature of this educational system of at least 2,000 years ago if one looks at it, as Gordis does, in the light of the beliefs of the Governor of Berkeley, in the State of Virginia, who in the year 1670 thanked the Lord for the absence of any free school and printing presses in the colony.

Jewish democracy developed an equally original approach to labour. Slavery was still an accepted and legalized practice in the United States in the nineteenth century and was officially abolished in Saudi Arabia only in 1969. Some 1,500 years before the Christian era the Jews limited slavery to a period of six years. Both Aristotle and Moses recognized the fact that the spiritual promotion of man demanded leisure and that it could not be obtained except by reducing physical work and increasing the time allocated to intellectual activities. But while Aristotle contended that the spiritual advancement of free men justified the human animal status of the slave, Moses, by the institution of the Sabbath rest to be observed equally by men, women, slaves, and animals, gave every living being the right to equal leisure. This revolutionary idea was extended to a sabbath of the land via the sabbatical year (in which land was left untilled) and to a jubilee year (once every fifty years), when all debts were returned and family property restored to the original owners. This was not one, but a multiple-system society including issues involving ecology, agriculture, economics, etc., which aimed so high that in practice it was never fully observed by the Jews. However, it served to permeate the Jewish consciousness with the belief that 'the land will not be sold for ever because all the land belongs to Me and you will inhabit it and stay on it with Me' (Lev. 25:23). This concept of the temporariness of material possessions was bound to stimulate the 'nomadic' element of Jewish spirituality, to instil in their *Weltanschauung* the stimuli of a permanent 'push on' behaviour, which had its modern secular version in Zionist pioneering.

If democracy in traditional Judaism means indivisibility of the political from the social, the moral, and the economic, then when such a democracy is translated into practical terms it must find permanent and meaningful ways and means to integrate its needs and values—an aim which appears as utopian as the permanent combination of the universalistic and the particularist. Here again, the Greek and the Jewish approaches are totally different. For the Greeks, need can turn into value; for the Jews, needs and values must remain totally separate. One could search the entire Jewish literature in vain for anything approaching the funeral oration of Pericles. The Jews fought and died as heroically as the Greeks yet they never exalted military qualities or patriotism. The State, says Professor Leibowitz, is a need, a vital need indeed, but of the same type as the need to urinate.[8] It does not become a value, because even the most vital needs are never gratuitous, while gratuity is the distinguishing characteristic both of values and of the institutions which are supposed to cultivate and defend them, i.e. the aristocratic institutions which operate on the principle of *noblesse oblige*. Hence the efforts of Jewish traditional culture to create organizations fulfilling the aspiration to make needs and values, élitism and democracy, patriotism and universalism, right behaviour and justice, coexist.

To say that such an approach is utopian and impracticable is legitimate only if we also say that democracy, which tries to combine the will of the many with the rule of the few, and communism, which tries to maximize equality and participation and minimize organization and public authority to the point that the State should eventually no longer exist, are also utopian. Jewish democracy is certainly singular, but not more utopian or less logical than other political systems. It has a logic of its own which during more than 2,000 years of experience has shown itself both practical and fitting the needs and aspirations of a people with a unique history and some very special social and political problems. It is in the course of this long historical experience, and through the trials of situations which have undoubtedly always been of a very special nature, that solutions such as the separation of sovereignty from rule have been invented. Other solutions were more earthly, like the educational system aiming to produce the largest possible élites, and the two-tier majority to provide a working system for decision-making in a 'democratic aristocracy'. This two-tier voting system was based on a combination of the numerical majority (*rov minyan*) and the 'construction' majority (*rov binyan*), which was called in when issues of special importance had to be decided upon. As in the case of the Security Council at the UN, problems of defining the nature of a decision —for instance, the difference between decisions of procedure and of substance—was not easy. Furthermore, no one could establish what made a man so influential that his moral authority was greater than that of the established governmental or institutional authority. And yet all Jewish traditional culture was geared to this system, which made a simple needlemaker like Rabbi Joshua ben Hananiah more influential than the President of the Sanhedrin himself.[9] Because of this approach, the 'teacher', the rabbi, overrode the President, the *cohen*, in the exercise of power: the prophets eclipsed the king.

All this was certainly not achieved without tension and bloodshed, as the history of the First and Second Temples underlines.[10] Neither was the system foolproof; its functioning depended on the delicate balance between votes and interest, means and ends. It did not prevent great distortions of justice, as the prophets' criticisms amply demonstrate, but it was functional to the aspirations of the Jewish people. It developed a system of research and interpretation (talmudic) which, under the most difficult and unexpected circumstances, was able for centuries to educate the élites who created and guided the institutions set up to produce more élites.

The system broke down in the wake of the Emancipation, through the acceptance by the Jews of alien values, through assimilation of its élites to Gentile—mainly Western—ways of life, and of course under the pressure of economic, political, social, and racial discrimination, which grew too strong to be borne by the majority of the people.

This problem has been discussed in the first part of the book: let us now consider whether or not, and to what extent, the clash between the spirit of the new institutions, copied or imported from the West, and the spirit of the remnants of traditional institutions, still consciously nurtured in Israel, hampers the functioning of the Israeli Republic. The very posing of this question raises a number of other queries: how Jewish is the Israeli society? How does this Judaism express itself? How can one measure the Jewish way of doing things, the Jewishness (as opposed to Judaism and Jewry, to use again Memmi's terminology) in a non-Jewish institution? Without clarifying these preliminary points it is very difficult to know whether Jewish tradition has contributed towards or put obstacles in the path of Israeli institutions.

The editor of the *Encyclopedia Judaica*, Louis I. Rabinowitz, argues in his article entitled 'How Jewish is the Jewish State?' as follows.[11] All the energies of the State of Israel 'on the way' since Hitler were directed towards the sheer human necessity of saving Jewish bodies from extermination. This led to a distortion of the essential purpose of Zionism and the ultimate justification of Israel's existence, which is the survival of the *Jewish soul*. The determination of the Jewish people to develop a way of life and a civilization in Israel which reflect 'the highest ethical and social ideals of Judaism' is the fruit of 'an internal subjective duty'.

The argument is interesting for many reasons. First, it recalls the old debates between Herzlian Zionism and the spiritual Zionism of Ahad Ha'am, concerning the choice of priorities—salvaging the body or the soul of the Jews. This, in itself, is a non-Jewish debate, if we accept the concept of the indivisibility of values and needs discussed earlier. Next, the argument recalls Ben-Gurion's existentialist approach to the Jewish renaissance through the development of 'a way of life and a civilization in Israel' which is rejected by those who, like Professor Leibowitz, see in the Israeli way of life an additional stage of de-Judaization, of collective Jewish assimilation. Finally, Dr Rabinowitz presumes that there is a 'subjective urge' in the Jewish people 'to develop a way of life and civilization in Israel' reflecting the 'highest ethical and social ideas of Judaism'—an urge, he says, which has become more acute as the result of spiritual erosion within the ranks of the Jewish people in the Diaspora. One could easily claim the opposite, however, on the evidence of the material assimilating trends of the Israelis. Yet within this argument can also be seen a parameter of relations between traditional Judaism and Zionism which shows at least one way in which the Israeli society is affected by Judaism. Ideologically it is affected by the struggle between spiritual Zionism and political Zionism; existentially, by the actual living in one place (Israel) which is more Jewish than any other in the world and which, because of modern communications, participates in the rapidly changing non-Jewish world; politically, by the drama of translating into a polity created for the purpose of solving the insecurity of the Jewish situation in the Diaspora, which, with few exceptions, ironically enough, is no longer felt by the majority of Jews living outside Israel.

Dr Rabinowitz is quick to point out that there are few indications that Israeli state institutions in fact deserve to be called Jewish.

Let it be said at once that this theory of the role of the Jewish State, as preserving Jewish values among Jews, and contributing to the progress of civilization as a whole, runs counter to a doctrine which, since the era of Emancipation, has been sedulously propagated as a bolster to Jewish self-esteem in the diaspora. Throughout the centuries, Jewish thought, theology and prayers viewed the *galut* as an unmitigated misfortune and tragedy, the punishment meted out to the Jewish people for their lack of loyalty to God—'because of our sins we were exiled from our land and kept far away from our soil'—and held that the time would yet come when the Jewish people would expiate those sins, and God in His mercy would return them to their land. The post-Emancipation philosophers seized hold of what may be called 'an orphan statement' to the effect that 'Israel was exiled among the nations only that converts might be added to them' (Pessah 87b). On this they built the concept that the exile, far from being a tragedy, was a blessing in disguise for mankind. This was the birth of the theory of the 'Jewish mission'. . . . Reviewing this theory in the light of the facts, one must come to the rueful conclusion that if that has been the appointed role of the Jewish people, either we have been very bad teachers, or the world has shown itself to be a very bad pupil![12]

The first Israeli contribution to traditional Judaism, therefore, is the creation of a state which flatly denies the 'Jewish mission' idea. The existence of the State of Israel has certainly proved one thing: only the concentration of Jews, orthodox or secular, in their own land, and the achieving of political independence, can create the conditions in which Jews can lead a fully Jewish life. This framework alone, therefore, can provide the basis for hope that Jewish ideals will become visible realities. Whatever the gap between ideals and reality, the very fact that Jewish ideals can exercise their impact in Israel in a free and sovereign society creates the basic conditions in which the Jewish factor can play a creative role. The editor of the *Encyclopedia Judaica* sees five main fields in which the Jewishness, 'actual or potential', of Israel can be preserved and in which there is, in fact, an ongoing process of institutionalization within the framework of the 'secular' Israeli state: national formalities, legislation, ethics, education, and the overall atmosphere of the country.

Under the heading 'national formalities', there is, first of all, the calendar of the state which fixes the holidays according to the Bible. Then there are the dietary laws which are observed in the armed forces, air lines, railways, and government institutions. These formalities are no guarantee of any internal content, and in many cases, as mentioned, they may contribute to projecting an image of collective hypocrisy in official Israel. This often adds to the difficulties of the external observer trying to understand the true institutions and nature of the State of the Jews. Yet, as in most of the former European colonies where religion served as a powerful cohesive element, more against the colonizer than among the natives themselves, the formalities and the symbols of national tradition have been taken over by the modern state as part of the paraphernalia of government, if not of faith.

In the field of legislation, the impact of traditional Judaism on the Israeli society has certainly been greater, in spite of a growing demand for a separation of religion and state among secular groups.

The poor electoral performance in the 1977 elections (one deputy only) of the Citizens' Rights Party, headed by Shulamit Aloni, cannot be taken as a sign of the Israeli population's respect for orthodox Jewish legislation and tradition since Mrs Aloni's party represents many other controversial points of view, but it is certainly a proof of the relative importance attributed by the mass public to the call for institutionalized secularism. Nevertheless, legislation in a democratic state cannot be effected unless it is based upon the general will of the electorate. In Israel, despite the proclaimed secular character of the state, this will has supported, or at least has not opposed, a vast legislation which tends to incorporate more Jewish traditional norms than in any other field of Israeli life, starting from the controversial Law of the Return, which confers Israeli citizenship automatically on any Jew who sets foot on Israeli soil, down to the no less controversial decision that Jewishness is legally defined not only according to the rabbinical principle that a Jew is anyone born to a Jewish mother, but also by his non-adhesion to another religion. There is, therefore, a whole body of coded laws and accepted juridical principles belonging to traditional Judaism which cannot be performed by civil officials—matters concerning the personal status of the Israeli, particularly marriage and divorce.

Here again there is a profound discrepancy between the spirit of the Jewish law and the extent to which this spirit has penetrated into Israeli legislation. Dr Rabinowitz stressed the abnormality of this legal system of the state, which is governed by 'an almost tacit agreement . . . between the civil and religious authorities of the state whereby as a *quid pro quo* for the former keeping "hands off" in the sphere of personal status, the rabbinic authorities have agreed to keep "hands off' in civil law'.[13] As a result, the Knesset apparently has had a free hand in every legislative matter, including those which run directly counter to the established principles of Jewish religious law concerning such things as property, adultery, abortion, etc. Principles of native Jewish law regarding civil issues are available to the Israelis should the legislature wish to take them into consideration, but they by no means operate actively within the legislation itself.

In the field of ethical ideals, Dr Rabinowitz notes that Ben-Gurion was

constantly aware of the spiritual purpose of the State of Israel as 'a light
unto the nations'; that Israel has consistently voted against South Africa
on the question of apartheid; that its treatment of its minorities goes far
beyond the mere formal granting of electoral representation, in spite of
the emotion and often pronounced identification of Israeli Arabs with the
enemies of the state. Yet in all these matters one can see some of the
erosion of those ethical principles which has taken place since Dr Rabinowitz published his article in 1972. There is no longer any pretension on the
part of the state to act as a 'light unto the nations', and in fact most of the
efforts of Israeli propaganda today are directed towards countering the
image which her enemies have succeeded in spreading all over the world
and which identifies the Zionist state with a militaristic, racist, and colonialist organization. The moral and financial scandals of the last few years,
especially since the Yom Kippur War, the growing social and educational
gap between rich and poor, the increasing emigration and decreasing immigration, have contributed in no small measure to raising doubts about the
Jewish ethics still operating in the Israeli state and society.

Turning to the educational field, i.e. to the basic institutions which are
supposed to produce the élites of the state and mould the national consciousness and self-image, the most significant fact is that the system is still
divided into 'religious' and 'non-religious' schools. It is difficult to judge
the impact of the religious educational network on the Israeli society, although on the whole its educational system is more developed pedagogi-
cally than the secular school system. What one can say for certain is that
although the religious parties capture only 12 per cent of the Knesset
representatives, the religious schools cover 32 per cent of the school-age
population at all levels, including large numbers of deprived children. If
one includes the *Hadarim* and *Yeshivot* (non-government-supported orthodox schools and rabbinical academies), the percentages become higher.
Over 20,000 rabbinical students studied in rabbinical colleges and academies in 1969–70, which compares very impressively with the 50,000
students at other colleges and universities in the country in the same year.
These figures alone indicate that the Jewish-conscious and overtly religious Israelis form at least 35 per cent of the total Jewish population.

Another important aspect of the religious school system—government
or private—is that it is far more élitist-oriented than the secular system,
and on the whole more ideological. Although the religious educational system has not yet produced any distinct and outstanding national leadership
of its own, it has created a large group of locally born young religious individuals who strongly resent the discrimination from which an observant
Jewish minority inevitably suffers since it cannot fully participate in the
activities of the secular majority (for instance, employment in international
communications, heavy industry, police and diplomacy, where observance

of the Sabbath as a day of rest is certainly an obstacle). Among the reasons for the *Gush Emunim* movement's great appeal to religious youth is not only its biblical nationalism but also the fact that it has offered the young, militant, religious establishment an organized means to advance itself into the forefront of Israeli politics and international public opinion, and to make itself felt in an original way.

If, finally, one turns to the general atmosphere of the country, the differences between the spirit of the Israeli community and of the Diaspora are very marked. Jewishness, of course, does not necessarily have to be the basic factor of this difference: the geographical, social, economic, and cultural conditions of members of a sovereign polity, composed of immigrants and set in the heart of the Middle East, are more than enough to distinguish them from the members of any Jewish minority community in the Diaspora, or, for that matter, from any other polity in the world. But the traditional value traits which have characterized the Jew throughout the ages, according to the talmudic maxim defining the Jews as 'the merciful children of merciful ancestors, full of kindness as their ancestors were', does not particularly characterize the Jews of Israel today. On the other hand, one can point to distinctive characteristics which constitute an almost complete metamorphosis from the Diaspora personality. One is the sturdy and almost exaggerated independence of the individual Israeli, which is seen by Dr Rabinowitz as a positive trait, contributing to the absence of at least outward social barriers. But here again, this 'superb fearless' trait of the Israeli character is not necessarily 'the distilled essence of the fruit of Jewish ethical and social doctrine'. It can only express hopes for the future.

We are interested here in the answer to the question of how the spirit of traditionalism hampers or helps the functioning of Israeli institutions. Thirty years of statehood permit one to affirm that they hamper in every way more than they help them to operate. We have already mentioned the *status quo* between the rabbinical and secular sectors in matters of personal status. A superficial perusal of the government crises shows that they have been caused to a great extent by the controversy between tradition and secularism or—as it is wrongly described in Israel—by an Israeli *Kulturkampf*. This German expression, widely used by Israeli politicians and press, is in itself a description of political experience borrowed from the West without any historical or content relationship to the Israeli case, an illustration of the extent of intellectual dependence of the colonized Jewish/Israeli culture upon that of Europe.

The first Cabinet crisis in the history of the state (February 1951) and the first premature election were caused by the refusal of the secular Minister of Education and Culture, David Remez, to allow the religious educational system to include the children of oriental immigrants in the

Ma'abarot (immigrant transit camps). The secular majority had to give in. The crisis which brought down Rabin's Cabinet and caused the premature election of April 1977 was again started by the indignation of the religious parties at the desecration of the Sabbath by the arrival of two F-15 fighter planes on a Friday evening. In the intervening twenty-five years there have been innumerable clashes between the representatives of the religious minority in the government and the representatives of the majority, ranging from controversies over the kosher kitchen of the Israeli merchant marine flagship, to the inauguration of TV broadcasts on the Sabbath. The most prolonged controversy, which also led to a Cabinet crisis in 1958, broke out over the question of how a Jewish 'nationality' should be defined in the population registry. The religious bloc again won the day, as they did over the question of conversion to Judaism performed by Reform rabbis, and, in July 1978, of army service exemptions to religious girls who do not wish to serve.

These few examples should be sufficient to show the strength of organized political orthodoxy in secular Israel. It cannot be solely attributed to a parliamentary and electoral system which makes the religious parties an essential element of all coalitions. The situation certainly has been exploited to increase the strength of the religious establishment, but this Jewish brand of political clericalism is supported by a deep layer of Jewishness in the population. There is a specifically Jewish way of being atheistic in Israel. In this connection, Eisenstadt quotes a pertinent observation made by the doyen of Jewish historians in America, Salo Baron, concerning American Jews, but which also fits the case of Israel.[14] Baron notes that among the customs which even the most unreligious Jews observe are those relating to the primordial facts of life: circumcision, marriage, and burial, followed by others which are particularly symbolic of collective identity, such as the lighting of candles on Hanukah and on Friday evenings. These patterns of reconstruction of religious symbols, says Eisenstadt, are not necessarily related to a return to orthodoxy. This is especially true in Israel, where side by side with a process of de-Judaization of society in terms of rabbinical traditional behaviour, there is a growing Judaization of collective symbols. We shall elaborate on this in the next chapter, which deals with the crisis of legitimacy. The point here is that, explicitly or implicitly, the impact of Jewish tradition is much more pronounced in Israeli life than would appear on the surface and therefore hampers, or at least impinges on, the functioning of the secularized, Western-imported institutions of the state much more than is currently admitted.

A few examples will suffice. First, let us consider the occupation of Judaea and Samaria after the Six-Day War. Since its occupation, this area, the ancient geographical cradle of Judaism, has brought about a revival of Judaistic consciousness in both religious and non-religious sectors.

Sometimes this consciousness is manipulated by political groups, such as the *Gush Emunim* movement, where religion (as has happened in many other countries) is a by-product of nationalism, with concern for military-security issues equal to concern for religious values. It has cut deeply into all political parties, in spite of their originally secular ideologies.

Another example is the show of unity among Israelis at times of particular danger, such as the three weeks preceding the Six-Day War in 1967 or at the outset of the Yom Kippur War. During these periods the whole country felt itself plunged into an historic, Jewish existentialist situation of solitude, imminent annihilation, and 'no choice' decisions.

We shall have more to say on this later on, but let us here summarize the three answers we have attempted to give to the questions posed at the beginning of this chapter. First, the crisis of the Israeli institutions does reflect, probably to a larger extent than elsewhere, the crisis of the national élites. Second, traditional Judaism did possess institutions which can be compared in a relevant way to the new institutions created by Zionism. Third, the clash between the spirit of the traditional institutions still consciously or unconsciously nurtured in Israel and the spirit of the institutions copied or imported from the West, does hamper or at least impinge very significantly upon the functioning of the state's institutions. Finally, the process of institutionalization has not been able to harmonize tradition into an innovative and coherent system of ideas and practices which would make Judaism an effective mortar in Israel and make that country a spiritual centre for world Jewry. The clashes between past and present and between Jewish and secular Zionism have become evident. We have mentioned some of these clashes at Cabinet and other levels of politics, but they are only the tip of the iceberg. The opposition goes much deeper throughout all strata of the Israeli society. Schematically it could be said that as far as the institutional crisis of Israel goes it expresses itself in five major patterns: the pattern of the Jewish 'national family' opposing itself to the pattern of Western individualistic life; the 'abnormal' inverted pyramid model of the Jewish people as compared with the 'normal' pyramidal structure sought after by the Zionist state; the patterns of Jewish open aristocracy as opposed to the patterns of more or less closed democracy of the Israeli society; the clash between quality and quantity, especially—but not solely—in the military field; and finally, the opposition between Jewish Zionist and Western Zionist ideology.

Some of these issues have been raised in earlier parts of the book: they are mentioned again in order to stress the difficulty of dissociating the historical and moral aspects of the institutional clash from its social and political aspects.

In a recent interview in *The Jerusalem Post*,[15] *Commentary*'s editor Norman Podhoretz said that he believed that Jewishness was not a matter of choice but something inescapable. If one were born Jewish, in his view, one could make a strenuous effort to renounce Jewishness, through radical assimilation or conversion, but such efforts would be spiritually very costly and frequently unsuccessful. Anyone born a Jew is born into a fate; he can be happy or unhappy about it, but Podhoretz believes that it is no more a matter of choice than one's sex or one's physical being. Podhoretz is really saying that the problem of Jewish identity can be better understood if one stops trying to make it fit into the current Western ideological clichés defining nations, races, or religions, and looks at it as if it was the identity problem of a big, dispersed family. This feeling of belonging to one family is not restricted to religion, which in a sense legitimizes the position of God as the group's 'paterfamilias'. It crops up continuously in secular Israel, often in the most unexpected ways. A superficial reading of an Israeli newspaper will show, for instance, that the choice of news is inspired as much by the 'taste' of the clan as by the objective value of the news. There is a distinct element of parochialism in this attitude, but it is not the parochialism of the 'village' or the 'colony': it is the parochialism of a family-culture, which reacts with the same intense interest to the outcome of the Jerusalem International Bible Quiz as to the marriage of a Rothschild—inside or outside the 'family'.

A more serious and significant instance is the behaviour of the Israeli bureaucracy, faced by the surprise of the Yom Kippur War. The whole administrative apparatus practically stopped operating as an impersonal, articulate body: in every ministry the decision-making élite shrank into a small group of people, working together not according to functional, ideological, or political tasks, but on a basis of close personal affinity. There were, of course, many objective reasons which contributed to this paralysis of the administration: the mobilization of large numbers of civil servants, the fact that army headquarters and the Ministry of Defence are located in Tel Aviv, which made the transfer of the government from Jerusalem to the coastal town imperative. But all this does not explain the fact that the largest part of the administration ceased to work for more than a month; nor does it explain why many ministries operated better than before this reduction of activity. One reason was certainly the greater devotion of the civil servants to their work; the greater discipline and sense of responsibility of the population; the reduced extra-military activities of the entire country. But also the administration stopped working 'by rule', that is, operating according to imported Western bureaucratic standards, and began to improvise: it reacted with the spirit of a family in distress, when tasks and duties are dictated by considerations other than those of an impersonal organized administration.

Something similar, but on a much larger scale, happened in 1948 when the new State of Israel had to learn how to survive in the administrative chaos intentionally created by the departing British Mandatory Government. At that time the situation was far more critical than in 1973 because of the comparatively stronger Arab military forces, the lack of arms, food reserves, strategic territorial depth for withdrawal, or foreign allies; and also because of the streams of incoming refugee-immigrants from Europe. It is possible that the birth trauma of Israel and the success of chaotic improvisation have continued to influence the mentality of the Israelis and increased their distrust of institutions copied from abroad.

Israel is certainly not the only non-European country which has shown itself capable of working under stress by relying on patterns of traditional family behaviour. Countries such as Congo, Tanzania, Lebanon, Uganda, and Nigeria have behaved similarly. If they survived in often difficult situations when, according to Western political and administrative logic, they should have gone bankrupt, it is thanks to their ability and the willingness of their members to rely on traditional institutions, operating according to their own logic of family, tribal, or clan systems. It would be wrong to draw conclusions from the African case to fit the Israeli experience, but it cannot be denied that in both, traditional patterns of behaviour become more evident in times of crisis than in times of normalcy.

It is interesting to note that the breaking-up of the 'family pattern' in Jewish behaviour and institutions is considered a source of evil by socialist leaders whom, ideologically, one would expect to hold a different view. Arieh Eliav attributed the corruption, disorders, and creation of new 'feudal nobilities' based on sectarian vested interests rife in many strata of Israeli society, to the abandonment of the old Jewish principle that 'every Jew is responsible for the other Jews'.[16] Yet he, too, though correct in believing that ends cannot be achieved without proper means, seems to overlook the importance of the fact that the 'means', i.e. societal institutions acting as an extended family, as a tribe, cannot be created on the basis of socialist ideologies promoting individual rights and a Western conception of the state.

Another illustration of the open clash between traditional and imported institutions in Israel concerns the 'normal' and 'abnormal' models of the Jewish society. The classic, and still current, view of Zionism was that the abnormality of the Jewish people stemmed not only from its lack of territory or from its attachment to the 'superstitions' of a backward, tribal faith, but from the fact that, unlike other peoples, it possessed a much greater number of unproductive persons, of 'idle' intellectuals, pedlars, parasitic middlemen, etc. This view was deeply influenced by the prevailing non-Jewish ideas concerning the nature of the Jews and the Jewish Question in nineteenth-century Europe.

The Zionists and the assimilationists who wanted—each in their own particular way—to 'normalize' the Jewish people, did not, of course, want to deprive the Jews of their strength. On the contrary, they wanted to give them new vigour, but they had lost faith in the ability of traditional Jewry to achieve this. However, they also believed that the Jews would be more secure in the future if they could add to their traditional type of superiority the new strength of the Gentiles, and more particularly of the Europeans who, in the meantime, had come to dominate the world with science, technology, and secular political systems. What the two groups, Zionists and assimilationists, did not consider was that the one strength—secular technological—could not easily be grafted on to the other—traditional religious. The Jews could not be 'Spartacus and Moses' at the same time, but had to choose—at least temporarily—between the two prototypes, and the values of Jewish tradition and the system of rabbinical education were inconsistent with those of the West. They did not realize that one could not reverse the inverted pyramidal model of the Jewish society without reversing its system of authority and undermining the values and legitimation on which it stood. Furthermore, it did not occur to them that the reversed pyramid model of society was best fitted to face the challenge of modernity. They did not stop to remark that in the leading industrialized countries, such as Britain and America, the general trend was, in fact, to imitate the 'abnormal' Jewish pattern and allow a lot of people to go into the service sectors while reducing the number of those engaged in agriculture. Both Zionists and assimilationists took as their norm the Central and Eastern European states in which they had lived, societies bulging with farmers and poor in services, without realizing that this situation (as, for example, in the case of Russia) was one of the major causes of their backwardness.

The Jewish wish to imitate 'the ways of the world' was normal and understandable in a people oppressed and discriminated against; the fascination of material and political power irresistible to a people which had lacked them for so long. The loss of traditional culture through emancipation suddenly made the Jews conscious that they had become slaves—and therefore needed to revolt. Possibly the 'normalization' of the Jewish people would not have affected its inner strength if the transfer of individuals from the 'unproductive' to the 'productive' activities (e.g. agriculture and industry) had been carried out while maintaining the traditional Jewish system of élitist education and élite recruiting. But this proved impossible, though it was, indeed, one of the major hopes and aims of the kibbutz system.

It is not therefore surprising that in recent years, and more especially since the Yom Kippur War, there has been a growing interest among kibbutz members in the study of traditional Judaism, and an intensive search for integration of old and new Jewish social and moral values.

On the occasion of the 50th anniversary of the foundation of the

Kibbutz Federation, many leaders of the kibbutz movement expressed the conviction that their unique society was no longer an experiment. With 254 settlements and 110,000 members, it had the right to claim to be recognized as a laboratory for a social experiment which—in the words of Yaakov Hazan, one of the Kibbutz Artzi (left socialist) leaders—had an important contribution to make to Israel and to the world at large. It was, he said, 'a holistic society, based on an integrating principle of mutual responsibility and commitment, capable of providing a hint of a message of international importance'.[17]

Sdemot, the literary quarterly of the kibbutz movement, has consistently called for a return to the sources of the old Jewish civilization. Yariv Ben Aharon describes the 'back to the sources' movement as an inevitable part of the third, contemporary stage in the history of the Jewish people. The first was the period of the First Temple, when the nation was led by the kings, and priests and prophets appeared on the scene to challenge the former when they became corrupt. Then came the Second Temple period, when, prophecy ended, the rule of the kings and priests reached its peak—particularly when the Hasmoneans combined kingship and High-Priesthood, and the Talmudic Sages appeared on the scene. Already before the Destruction of the Temple in 70 CE the Sages were challenging the leadership of the kings and priests, and after the Destruction they became the nation's unchallenged leaders, remaining so for the next eighteen centuries. The third stage, today, is that of Zionism. The Enlightenment had seriously undermined the leadership of the rabbis, and Zionism 'overthrew the hegemony of the rabbis and', Yariv Ben Aharon says, 'created a new type—the doers in the spheres of settlement, security, education, etc.—that took over their role as the shapers of Jewish life'.

As a result, the *halutz*, the labouring pioneer, became for Jewish life today what the kings, priests, prophets, and rabbis were in their respective times. And 'not the synagogue, but the field, the factory, the army unit, the schoolhouse, is today the center of Jewish life. . . . In rejecting the rabbis, the *halutzim* also rejected the Jewish sources', said Yariv Ben Aharon, recalling that the bold step of the kibbutz movement's founders in cutting themselves off from *Halakha* was inevitable. For *Halakha* is an all-embracing, all-demanding system, and so was the early Zionist pioneering ethos, with its own criteria as to what is 'holy' and what 'profane'. Yet he does not see any future for this innovation brought about by the kibbutz unless it draws its nurture from the primary Jewish sources.[18]

We have here all the elements of the crisis, but also of the possible renewal: the return to the sources, and the attempt to combine the past and the present, the old and the new, in a harmonious way; an egalitarian institution which is also an open aristocracy; a combination of practical activities and theoretical studies; pioneerism, both in the sense of conquering new earthly frontiers and new spiritual ones. 'The spiritual problem of the kibbutz is, like that of the entire modern House of Israel, to learn to aspire again.' Nowhere is this need more evident than in the field of security where her defence requirements and the immense demographic and military potential of her enemies demand that Israel match quality against quantity in order to survive.

The same can be said about immigration. By substituting imported ethics geared to the satisfaction of material needs and based on Western European values and consumption aspirations for the Jewish qualitative system of education and socialization, Israel has considerably reduced her own attraction for potential immigrants. There is little need for a Western or Soviet Jew to come to Israel in order to live according to an American or French way of life: it is simpler to go to New York or Paris. On the other hand, many Israelis, no longer able to distinguish between Zionist values—after the creation of the State—and Western values in countries in which anti-Semitism is no longer fashionable, have become increasingly frustrated at home and dubious about the 'special tasks' of their State. Hence the growing number of emigrants, especially among the young people born in the country.

In summary, the main points so far discussed in connection with the crisis of Israeli institutions are the following. We have claimed that these institutions suffer, like most institutions in contemporary societies, from the strains of modernization and technological change. They also suffer from the equally general crisis of traditional values. Further, Israeli institutions, in addition to these general problems, suffer also from the special strain of a culturally colonized society because of the substitution of imported values and educational structures for indigenous ones, while retaining many of the social and moral ambitions of the old family-pattern élitist Jewish society. All this creates social and institutional disjunction. The phenomenon is widespread in every type of modern society, and as sociologist Daniel Bell remarked in a recent study of Western society, in every social structure ruled by an economic principle defined in terms of efficiency and functional rationality, culture 'is prodigal, promiscuous, dominated by an anti-rational, anti-intellectual temper in which the self is taken as the touchstone of cultural judgements, and the effect on the self is the measure of the aesthetic worth of the experience'.[19] Obviously, if this is true, Israel cannot hope to develop institutions which can cope with the challenges of her contemporary existence, nor can the West provide her with a valid experience for survival. If she shows such an extraordinary ability to survive, it is because the Israeli political system is already a mixture of imported and indigenous values. Often against its own assimilatory vocation, this mixture has provided the state with a stubbornness which enrages and surprises those friends and foes who cannot grasp its inner logic. As in the past, the Jews in Israel create that kind of inexplicable tension which, in the words of writer A. B. Yehoshua, seems to ignite 'the spark of folly' in the Gentile nations.[20] Once again, like the Jews of the past, Israel confronts the world with an irritating social and political challenge. It irritates those members of democratic societies who no longer believe the West can set an example to other nations and the leadership of Communist states, because it does not share the guilt complex of the former, nor does it follow the rationality of the 'historic determinism' of the 'inevitable' decay in which the Communists believe. Although closely linked, especially in its Zionist experience, to the European world of the last two centuries, the Israeli phenomenon is neither part of it nor solely a manufactured native product of the West. If, as Jean-Paul Sartre once noted, not very long ago the earth numbered two thousand million inhabitants—five hundred million men and one thousand, five hundred million natives, the former having the world while the others had the use of it[21]—then one can understand why the Jews and Israel were and still remain a special case: they are denied the use of the 'world' and do not belong to the natives. Because of this marginal situation, Israel infuriates, while also attracting the admiration of, many nations.

This does not mean that Israel has found permanent solutions to her problems, or is immune to social and institutional crises: it means that the disjunction between social institutions and culture which Bell sees as the main problem (at least in capitalist states) has a different significance in Israel from elsewhere.

One is therefore compelled to regard the strange, emotional, and critical attitude of many Israelis to their society after the Yom Kippur War as a symptom of maturity. It is not only because the Arabs succeeded in shattering Israel's feelings of invulnerability in the first three days of the October war that so many Israelis began to question the meaning, rights, and chances of survival of their State. It is because, having lost even for a very brief period of time their sense of security, they discovered that life in insecurity plunged them right back into the old existentialist situation of the Jew, and to be brought back by events to such a situation was certainly a major psychological shock. For those to whom the State of Israel had represented a final break away from the 'Jewish problem', it was a very painful experience, often leading to despair and emigration. For others, on the contrary, it was the starting point in a search for a Jewish revival.

Under the circumstances, no one should be surprised at the depth of the current crisis of Israeli institutionalization. The same problems affecting all contemporary institutions have to be faced—trying to catch up with the rapidity of technological and consequent social change—while at the same time adjusting to deeper conflicts agitating modern Judaism. None of the typologies created for the use and understanding of other societies fits their particular case. The major question facing Israeli institutions is not whether they can be corrected or improved, but whether they can be changed to the point of transforming their function: from institutions aimed at ensuring equality of rights into institutions aimed at putting into practice the principle of inequality of duties in a free and democratic society.

CHAPTER 7

The Crises of Identity and Legitimacy

Who is a Jew? What does it mean to be a Jew? When Dr Chaim Weizmann was asked this question by the members of the Anglo-American Commission of Inquiry on Palestine in 1946, he answered that it was easier to explain what a Jew was not than what a Jew was. He was not trying to be ambiguous: on the contrary, knowing the complexity, the uniqueness of the Jewish identity problem, he was sticking to the old rule of rhetoric that in a serious discussion one should avoid using arguments the opponent cannot understand. Just as it is difficult to discuss mathematics with someone who has never studied it, so it is difficult to explain what Judaism is to someone unfamiliar with it. Dr Weizmann's reply may also have been prompted by fear of the consequences of misunderstanding the identity of the Jews, if such an identity were explained according to the image which non-Jews hold of the Jew. This misunderstanding is still one of the major sources of conflict between Jews and Gentiles. It is also one of the factors contributing to the persistence of the crisis of identity which pervades contemporary Israeli society: the tendency to reduce realities to simplified and inadequate concepts.

Ben-Gurion was even more aware than Weizmann of the seriousness of the problem of defining Jewish identity. In October 1958 he contacted some seventy Jewish scholars in Israel and abroad, to solicit their opinion and advice. This unusual step was prompted by prolonged argument, within the Israeli government and among the public at large, which shook the coalition in Jerusalem and turned an apparently minor administrative proposal of the Minister of the Interior into a major ideological and political quarrel between the secular and the religious parties. In the wake of the decision to issue new identity cards to Israeli citizens, the Registrar thought it logical and necessary to make the entries concerning religion and nationality according to the declaration of the citizen himself. If an Israeli wanted to declare himself a Jew by nationality but an atheist or a Christian or a Muslim by religion—so be it. This proposal seemed quite natural and in line with the Israeli Declaration of Independence, which guaranteed the citizens of the new state against racial, religious, or sex discrimination. The religious parties, however, refused to recognize as valid any definition of nationality for an Israeli Jew other than the one determined by rabbinical law, *Halakha*, according to which only a person born of a Jewish mother, or converted to Judaism according to Orthodox practice, is considered a Jew (even against his will). In practice there were two problems confronting the Government: one was the definition of the Jew with reference to the Law of the Return, which grants immediate citizenship to any Jew returning to his ancestral land; the other was the definition of the Jew with reference to the competence of the religious courts in matters of marriage and divorce. By virtue of the Islamic Ottoman law, which Israel had inherited from the British and which (though for different reasons) neither Orthodox Jews nor Muslim Arabs wished to see changed, these courts had sole jurisdiction in restricted but important fields of private law. 'The opinion has been expressed', wrote the Israeli Prime Minister to the 'saviours' of Israel, 'that since the Registry is a civil one and not used for religious purposes, the registration should not be governed by purely religious criteria. Others say that since "Religion" and "Identity" are inseparable, and since religious allegiance is naturally a religious question, only religious criteria should be followed in registering both religion and nationality.'[1] What should the Government do? It seemed a simple, almost a rhetorical, question, but in fact it forced the Israelis to face the problem of their identity, namely what it meant—at least officially—to be a Jew, in the first community of Jews in history which proclaimed itself secular, and, conversely, what it meant for a Muslim and a Christian Arab to be a citizen of a Jewish state.

Ben-Gurion's decision to ask the advice of the 'wise men' of Judaism was in itself an extraordinary move. Not only were these sages not part of any organized Jewish body, but some of them were scholars of renown only in secular fields of learning. Yet the very fact that they were asked to give their opinion, and that almost without exception they answered, underlined the unique character of the link uniting the Jewish 'family', and the singularity of the concept, or at least the feeling, of Jewish identity. No less interesting is the fact that the great majority of answers, including those of non-orthodox Jewish scholars, called on the secular authority of the state to respect the religious-national principles by which Jewish nationhood had been traditionally defined. These principles were, in fact, later incorporated into the legislation of the state by Ben-Gurion's successors in a much more precise way than by Ben-Gurion's governments.

The collection of the *responsa*, despite the juridical limitations imposed by Ben-Gurion's questions to the 'sages' (the question of registration of children born of mixed marriages, for example), forms an illuminating document on the complex meaning of national Jewish identity in modern times.[2] In its simplest traditional form, being a Jew means, as noted, being either a person born to a Jewish mother or a recognized convert. Once a person is a Jew, either by birth or by conversion, he cannot cease to be one whatever he does, including conversion to another religion. It is curious that secular Israeli legislators have imposed some religious restrictions on the definition of Jewishness which had not occurred to the most orthodox rabbis. For the Israeli state, a Jew is not only a person born to a Jewish mother or converted to Judaism according to the rabbinical law, but one who at the same time does not profess another religion. This restriction originated in some major legal cases brought by individuals against the state which underlined the complexity of the definition of Jewish nationhood in Israel.[3] We shall not discuss them here, since what interests us is the variety of approaches to the idea of Jewishness which transpires from the answers given by the 'sages of Israel' to Ben-Gurion's questions.

For Rabbi Y. Y. Weinberg, for example, a leading talmudic authority in Europe,[4] the Jewish people 'is not a religious sect or a political party in the usually accepted way'. It is *a religious unity*, the greatest and the noblest of all'. For the Israeli secular historian Y. Kaufmann, the traditional *halakhic* definition of the Jew is the only acceptable one because 'Judaism is not merely a system of belief but also a *Covenant* uniting a community and forging it into a congregation of *sons of the* Covenant'. He recognizes the fact that Jewish religion is in essence a universal religion, but—he writes in his reply to Ben-Gurion—certain historical factors have confined the Jewish religion to the Jewish people and made this universal faith the heritage of the Jews alone. Therefore 'the word *Jew* indicates both a religious and a national relationship'.[5]

The philosopher Abraham J. Heshel believes that any theory which proposes that there is a Jewish people without a religion necessarily implies that there is a Jewish religion without a people. If the Jews were like all other peoples, and the Torah like all other religions, then the first change would bring about the denial that the Jewish people exists, while the second would turn the Jewish religion into a church or a sect.[6] Such a dilemma does not exist among Western nations in which the separation of church and state has not created an unbridgeable gap between the two. In Christian society the linkage of the two was an imported concept, in fact a Jewish concept, even if in the Roman city religion and state were closely interwoven. But it was a connection profoundly different from the biblical one, just as the Roman *Pietas* and the Christian *Grace* are concepts totally different from the Jewish *Kedusha* or *Shekhinah*, which are sometimes employed as translations.

The Jewish link between nation and religion is not an historical accident but a defining quality of an ancient but continuing situation. Furthermore, there is no way to understand the 'wholeness' of Jewish nationhood by simply assembling its constituent parts. If only one aspect of Judaism is stressed, says Rabbi Menahem M. Schneersohn, head of the Lubavitch movement, this will increase the dangers already existing in the State of Israel 'that a new generation will grow up, a new type bearing the name of Israel but completely divorced from the past of our people and its eternal and essential values'.[7]

These concepts of Judaism sound strange to modern ears. They stand in contrast to the existentialist belief that, in the last analysis, Judaism in the modern world is what Jews are and, more important, that there are stages of development for Judaism as for everything else. The traditional vision of Jewish destiny does not, however, conceive of progress as a criterion of success. One of the scholars consulted by Ben-Gurion is categorical about this: 'It is success which often constitutes the most powerful factor for decline or even death. Such success Judaism has never known. It has only known sharp and incessant battles which have assured it an extraordinary perpetuity.'[8] One is reminded of the famous objection uttered by the Jewish-German philosopher Herman Cohn (1842–1918) against Zionism: 'The bastards want to be happy.'

Judaism is an 'organic' cell. Because religion and nation cannot be separated, they represent a *unity* which stands in opposition to modern concepts of both religion and nationhood. Because of this opposition, the unity perpetuates a battle—even in secular times, and even in Israel where political Zionism has created the first non-religious community of Jews. And because of this battle, the triumph of Judaism and of the Jewish nation in any specific field becomes improbable. Yet the situation of non-success is the existentialist condition for Jewish survival because, through a dialectic historical process, it helps to develop those qualities of strength, ingenuity, and perseverance which are the best guarantee of Jewish prosperity, provided such prosperity is self-contained within moral and material boundaries.

Seen in this perspective, Jewish tradition is less a religious system than a permanent effort to transform the needs of an unchangeable Jewish national identity into practical solutions. It has already been stressed that the nature of this identity does not depend on time or territory but upon a certain idea of God—as an active presence in history—and of a people linked by a formal treaty, the Covenant, to this manifestation of the Divine. The difficulties encountered by the State of Israel in so far as it remains connected with any part of traditional Judaism or with the destiny of the Jews, are thus evident: the decadence of Jewish culture in modern times and the disruption of Jewish traditional society (a phenomenon common to all developing countries exposed to the impact of Westernization) make it even more difficult for Israel to elaborate a new national cultural framework fitting the special nature and needs of both Jewry and a Jewish state.

For some Israeli authors Judaism, Jewry, and Jewish statehood are simply incompatible. Three belief-systems will illustrate this point—one philosopher, one novelist, and one world-famous architect. Gershon Weiler, the Tel Aviv University philosopher, has made a major contribution to the debate on Jewish identity in his book on Jewish Theocracy.[9] His central thesis, supported by a deep knowledge of Jewish, Greek, and Western philosophical tradition, is that rabbinical Judaism as expressed in the *Halakha* stands in open opposition to the idea of Jewish statehood. It is, therefore, impossible to conceive of a Jewish state or to build a modern state on the basis of *Halakha*. As in the case of Machiavelli's dilemma concerning the impossibility of a political leader being both a Christian and a Prince, the two vocations belong to conflicting and equally consistent moralities. A state—according to Weiler—cannot be Jewish because statehood and *Halakha* belong to different moral, historical, and philosophical spheres.

Another interesting view of the problem of identity is developed by the novelist A. B. Yehoshua, most of whose literary work is focused on living with the question of the legitimacy of the Israeli state, its morality, its crisis of identity, and its guilt complex towards the Arabs. These and other questions are raised allegorically in his last important novel, *The Lover*.[10] It is, however, in some of Yehoshua's lectures at Haifa University that he underlines what seems to be the profound inconsistency between political Judaism and existential Jewry. The persistence, indeed the indestructibility, of the Diaspora phenomenon, as he sees it, seems to be not just a consequence of continuous persecution, or of the attraction which the non-Jewish world always exercises for the Jews: it is the inevitable result of the dialectical tension between the inability of the Jews to live according to the élitist requirements of the *Halakha* and their equally *halakhic* desire to perpetuate these requirements as recognized constituents of the Jewish identity. Without changing its basic Jewish condition, the choice given to the Jews, religious and non-religious, princes and slaves, whether or not they are faithful to the Sinai Covenant, has always created a break of identity or a tension of which the Diaspora was at least one permanent resolution. The Diaspora allowed the Jews to remain Jewish even after they stopped being religious, different even when slaves, bound to the Covenant by the rejection of the non-Jewish environment, even when they wanted to obliterate their Jewishness through total adhesion to the environment. The Diaspora, says Yehoshua, allows the Jew to be Jewish also by default. Obviously in a State of Jews, the choice becomes inevitable and troublesome.

Finally, Bruno Zevi: for the Italian-Jewish architect and historian of art, the essence of Judaism is its conception of time. The identity of the Jew is moulded by the tension created between the temporal and the territorial dimensions in which he lives. 'The consciousness of space', says Zevi, 'promotes idolatry; the consciousness of time promotes heresy. Jews are Jewish in so far as they reject static ideas and objects, and believe in change and redemption.'[11]

In modern times the Jews have been able to express themselves more and more in the arts, something not done in the ancient past. Jewish opposition to classicism, enlightenment, and analytical cubism is not by chance: classicism is founded on the supposition of the existence of an *a priori* order; enlightenment defends universal absolute and absolutist ideas; cubism plays with forms, devoid of matter, in a process which is not moved by true dynamics but by the interplay of figures. Thus the arts of the Jews, says Zevi, from the music of Mahler, Bloch, and Schoenberg, to the paintings of Chagall, Soutine, Modigliani, Lipschitz, and Zadkine, through the Yiddish theatre and the films of Eisenstein and Chaplin, contain a Jewish message. They are relativistic and tend towards 'lawlessness and normlessness of the real'.

These are three expressions of the sense of conflict. Viewed from the outside, it is simply a shattered identity, yet Eisenstadt raises the question of normlessness in a totally different context, connecting the present crisis of Jewish identity with the heterogeneity developed in contemporary Judaism. Eisenstadt recalls that heterogeneity always existed among the Jews because of their geographical dispersion. But it was an outer, not an inner heterogeneity, since in the past Jews were kept together by their adhesion to a common set of laws and values. The *Halakha*, by a combination of religion and nationhood as well as of several other dimensions of identity, offered 'a certain type of response to the basic dilemmas of Jewish existence and self-conception which developed from the beginning of Jewish history'.[12]

The dilemmas mentioned by Eisenstadt are well known: the tension between the universal and particularist cultures; that between the concrete, given reality and eschatological orientations and hopes. There are those mentioned by A. B. Yehoshua and Zevi as well: the Diaspora and the centre, the static and the fluid, the spatial and the ahistorical. Eisenstadt also recalls the fact that prior to Emancipation the Jews, as a persecuted minority, could afford to be less tolerant of internal heterodoxy. This is a crucial aspect of Jewish tradition which has radically changed in modern times. The contemporary patterns of Jewish identity are still influenced by geographical dispersion and by variations of customs and economic activities. But in modern Jewry there is a much greater cultural heterogeneity than in the past, a complete differentiation of symbols of Jewish collective identity, as well as changes in the foci around which a new type of unity is being created. In the Western world there are Jewish religious 'congregations'– Orthodox, Reform, Conservative, and Liberal—and beyond them, for the first time, masses of Jews who do not belong to any religious Jewish grouping. Some Jews, intellectuals, liberals, atheists, rationalists, and socialists, believed and still believe that by giving up the historical, national, and primordial Jewish elements of their identity they can become better integrated in the general society while at the same time being able to give a more progressive expression to their Judaism. The rise of Zionism, as we have noted throughout this book, was based on similar assumptions on a collective level. But contemporary Jewish reality cannot be explained in terms of the new dichotomy created by the coexistence of assimilationist and nationalist trends. Its dynamic can be understood as a new type of tension and of utopia which reveal 'the deep connection which binds Jews together in a new type of institutional, cultural and symbolic framework'. It may also be taken as an indication of the great potentiality of Jewish cultural and social creativity.

The trouble with this type of creativity and with the multiple contemporary images which Judaism—in the Diaspora and in Israel—presents to the rest of the world and to the Jews themselves, is its amazing complexity which does not readily lend itself to any type of rational simplification. Even when it seems possible to fit certain patterns of Israeli behaviour and that of the Jews in the Diaspora into those of other societies, this is usually done for the wrong reasons. This is an old and recognized problem in anthropology, raising the argument about the tendency to interpret primitive societies in terms of non-indigenous concepts. The trouble with this argument is that Diaspora and Israeli Jews are never judged as a primitive society or in terms of their own explicit and implicit traditional culture. They are invariably depicted according to the standards and images of the societies to which they have, while remaining fundamentally alien, outwardly assimilated. As a result, erroneous judgements are made by people who consider themselves experts on Judaism without knowing its language, culture, customs, and history—namely, without having acquired that basic knowledge that any student of anthropology would consider the obvious precondition for expressing any view on a society. The ignorance of Judaism creates tragi-comic situations when Israeli and non-Israeli Jews, totally ignorant of their own past and culture but emotionally alert to their identity problems, set themselves up as reliable representatives or intepreters of Jewish problems in our time. The banality, superficiality, and stereotypic presentation of such ignorant interpretations is often coupled with a claim to credibility based on 'biological' affiliation which in any other situation would be rejected as absurd. The outcome is that Christian theologists, as well as Nazi ideologists, Palestinian propagandists and advocates of Jewish assimilation, all have 'their' Jews (and more recently, 'their' Israelis) as a guarantee for the existence of a Jewish reality.

Thus the problem of understanding the true nature of Jewish identity is

complicated not only by Gentile ignorance of Jewish history and civilization (an understandable ignorance, after all), but by the even greater
ignorance of 'involved' Jews and Israelis about Judaism, Zionism, and the
effects of emancipation on their society. Things are made worse by Jews
and Israelis using wrong facts about or distorted images of Judaism, absorbed from the Gentile cultures which they admire or in which they live,
as valid and authoritative proofs for their arguments in defence of Judaism.
These ignorant but well-meaning apologists for the Jewish/Israeli case
sooner or later fall victim to their own unintentional lies and to the impossible situation of remaining Jews without Judaism or—worse—Jews against
their will, because of anti-Semitism.

The position of the traditional Jew who refuses to recognize the Jewish
State may be pathetic but at least it is clear. It is no longer clear for the
average Jew, be he Zionist or anti-Zionist, religious or secular, when faced
with any aspect of Judaism about which he has superficial knowledge
only. It is worth recalling once more that this was not the case with the
Jews until the time of their Emancipation. Up to the end of the eighteenth
century for a minority of Western European Jews and up to the middle/
end of the nineteenth century for the majority of Eastern European Jews
and those living in Muslim countries, both Jews and Gentiles knew their
reciprocal and complementary places in society. They possessed distinct
and distinguishable identities based on social function, cultural identity,
and power relations. All these identities interlocked well. Certainly the
Jews were kept in a state of social, economic, and political inferiority but
both Jews and Gentiles were also offered a clear perception of their different though coherent cultures, religious communal structures, and
economic activities. These characterizing perceptions legitimized the two
groups—the majority and the minority—in their reciprocal self-esteem.
Contrary to persistent vulgar error, it was not persecution which made
Jews stick to their separate identity before the Emancipation: it was the
genuine and plain desire to remain Jews.

Paradoxically, it was easier for Jews to convert to the local religion and
to assimilate to the Gentile society when this society was dominated by
religion than it was later when it became virtually agnostic. As long as there
existed clear religious-political criteria such as those characterizing the
Christian or Islamic 'city', the Jew who accepted them could become an
integral part of the Muslim and Christian 'populi'. But as soon as these
'populi', these members of 'cities of God', became nations, and were exposed to the process of secularization, the conversion of the Jew to the
Gentile society paradoxically became impossible.

Even more of a paradox is the fact that in the old days forced conversion to local religion did not easily distort identity—as is indicated by
the communities of 'conversos' which continued to exist centuries after

the great Spanish Expulsion. Today a conversion of convenience does not work in the same direction, and for good reasons. The rediscovery of the need for individual freedom in Western society and the growing belief that ultimate happiness could not be achieved except through the abolition of all external pressure, led to the progressive breaking away from all constraints. The natural constraints went first, through science, then came the constraints of church and faith, followed by those of the hereditary powers —of the divine right of kings as well as of the heads of families—down to the absurd flight from one's own self, through ideology, drugs, sex, or any other conceivable means. This frantic need and search for ever-growing freedoms by Westernized society and the rapid social change accompanying it, made it difficult for the Jews, especially those who had lost the meaning and consciousness of their own traditional identity, to 'convert' to the new, changing, and multiple Gentile identities. An individual non-identity obviously cannot convert into a collective non-identity. The loss of Jewish identity therefore called for the development of a new individual identity. Few had—or have—the resources for this development, since the demands of the new trends are always too high. No less important is the fact that the new secular 'religions' which took the place of the traditional ones were far less tolerant and far more demanding than the old ones. National, social, or even cultural ideologies, in spite of their declared humanist universalism, soon proved to be more authoritarian and selective towards the outsider than Christianity or Islam.

The tightening selectivity and increased exclusion of Jews from Western societies was not due only to the radicalization of the secular religions. It was also a direct consequence of the fear of freedom developed by the members of the new society.

The rush towards conformism, among others the conformism of radicalism and revolution; the need to join the herd felt by the depersonalized members of modern societies, has proved both appealing and fatal to the emancipated Jew and to the Israeli. Appealing, because it permitted the Jew to find a place in any new trend or social experiment, where his marginality allowed him to move with greater ease than his Gentile compatriots; fatal, because that same marginality, the strangeness which the Jew carried with him (or which was attributed to him by the social environment in which he lived) made it more difficult for him to integrate—as an individual or, as in the case of Israel, collectively as a sovereign State—into the secularized Gentile world in which there were no longer any clear criteria for identification or emulation. The Jew inevitably met growing opposition from new, exclusive, often oppressive ideologies and institutions which, despite all their liberalism, rejected him.

The European society, and later the Westernized societies of the Third World (but not the American society), developed a uniformity of fear and suspicion towards the 'stranger' which made it almost impossible for them to accept the Jewish existential diversity. At the individual level the dilemma found its most extreme and tragic expression in Nazi Germany, the European country in which Jews, during the first three decades of the twentieth century, had reached an unprecedented level of assimilation and influence. On the collective level, Arab and Communist efforts to transform Israel into a pariah state are not very different from those of the Nazis, although the results, owing to a different balance of forces, have so far been quite different. The case of Germany, on the individual level of relations between Jews and Gentiles, was certainly not unique. The Austro-Hungarian Empire shows even better the paradox that the more the Jews assimilated, the greater was their rejection.

The Hapsburg society was more tolerant than the Prussian, because it was multinational and consequently more cosmopolitan. The recognition of the existence of multinationality led to the recognition of the existence of nationality, and thus admitted some measure of cosmopolitanism with conformism. Yet even this mixture was embarrassing for the Jew. Gustav Mahler, the Viennese composer, expressed the multiple stress imposed on Jewish identity when he voiced the feeling that he felt Bohemian among the Austrians, Austrian among the Germans, Jewish everywhere, without a home either for his music or his politics. Despite his unparalleled social and artistic success, he felt alienated and expressed his alienation and hope of emerging from it in music which Zevi defines as 'a grandiose anthology of broken pieces'.[13] The situation is no different today for many Americanized Jews in the United States—the Malamuds, the Bellows, the Salingers, and Roths—who all share the anguish of the insecurity of a people still dominated by the pre-eminence of time over space. Yet as far as Jewish–Gentile relations are concerned there is one fundamental difference between the Jews of America and those of the rest of the world. In Europe (as in Islamic countries), where the Jews could not participate in the making of local history (specifically Christian and specifically Muslim, not even specifically German or French), to be a Jew was and still is one way among many others of being different; in America, the land of immigrants, to be a Jew is one among many specific ways of being truly American.

Modern Jewish national identity, while separate from the old Jewish one, remains profoundly different from any existing identity in our time, both at the individual and at the collective level, although, as we have repeatedly stressed, similarities could be found with the identity problems of traditional societies in the developing countries. Yet the similarity in this case is not a matter of content but of external constraint: European colonization, Westernization, a strong desire to modernize following the example of the most industrialized countries, processes which cause strains and confusion and give rise to similar uncontrollable emotions and ambitions as well as to similar institutional and leadership crises.

The similarities between Israel and other nations are far less if one turns from the individual's identity problem—his ties with the collective, and his ability to switch identity by cultural conversion, emigration, and so on—to that of the collective national identity. Here the question hinges on the clear definition and signs of identification of the collective: the clearer they are, the easier is the technique of switching, and the easier the switch, the clearer the voluntary choice of staying with one's identity—for example, of staying Jewish despite persecution and enticement to assimilation.

The situation changes radically when the new collective barely exists, when it is fluid, and when it is crystallized by definitions which do not stand up to the test of human and political realities. When Stalin decided in the early twenties, as Commissar of Nationalities in the USSR, that a 'national community is inconceivable without a common language and there is no nation which at one and the same time speaks several languages',[14] he was, of course, being quite high-handed. So much so, in fact, that no one, not even an orthodox Stalinist, has ever applied the definition to any multilingual emerging nation. Yet Stalin was not the only one to try and find a workable, logical definition of what is and what is not a nation.

The simplest, widest, most correct, but tautological description of a nation is 'a body of people which feel that they are a nation'.[15] In practice such a definition can only be used for demagogic purposes, since it legitimizes situations of permanent instability which subvert all established political institutions. In fact, despite all the words and blood spilt on behalf of nationhood, nationality remains an impracticable political principle and a poor tool for legitimization. Lord Acton's belief that states might in the course of time produce nationalities, but that a nationality could not produce a state, has been proved right by events in most of the new, emerging 'national' countries of the Third World, and even in the Old World, where separatist movements such as those of Scotland and Wales, Corsica and Flanders, Croatia and Sicily, are just a few significant examples.

For Arnold Toynbee, nationalism has been 'a perversion of Industrialism and Democracy, a corruption, a poisoning of political life in Western Society'.[16] For Pastor Reinhold Niebuhr, nationalism has transformed civilization into a device for deflecting individual vice on to larger and larger communities.[17] And according to him, the theory of nationality 'is marked with material as well as with moral ruin, in order that a new invention may prevail over the work of God and the interest of mankind'.[18] Ortega y Gasset claimed that there were no Spaniards or Frenchmen before Spain and France came into being. Who can say today who is Nigerian and who is Congolese?

'The principle of self-determination has no relevance where the issue is territorial disintegration.'[19] Professor Ali Mazrui, the African political scientist, has written extensively on the problem of nationalism and nation building in the developing countries. He has noticed, correctly, that in Europe, by contrast to what happens in most new, developing countries, nationalism develops in inverse proportion to the national consciousness: the more of the one, the less of the other. As a consequence, there is in Africa, as in many other places, a visible conflict between culture, ethnicity, territory, and often religion, so that the only term of reference for defining nationhood and political legitimacy has been the principle of self-determination. But the trouble with self-determination is that however much it appeals to the hearts and minds of subjugated nations, it proves to be a non-principle the very moment that political independence is achieved. It does not stand up to the challenge of realities because before a people can decide about its self-determination, somebody has to decide who the people are.

As a result of the difficulty of defining nationality in Africa, owing to the artificiality of the new states' territorial boundaries and the multiplicity of tribal-ethnic groups, the concept of nomadic self-determination has often been raised in theoretical and diplomatic debates. This concept has its origin in the fact that in pre-colonial Africa it was a viable and often practised method (thanks to the continent's wide unpopulated spaces) for dissatisfied clans to move away from the parent tribes and establish independent collective existence. Pan-African ideologists supporting 'Back to Africa' movements, like that of the American Negro ideologist Marcus Aurelius Garvey,[20] favoured the idea of nomadic self-determination to justify the collective political expression of those American Negroes who believed in the existence of a 'nationality based on pigmentation' (here, at least, identification is clear). Pigmentation permitted the assertion of the self's identity without deciding on the identity of the self's claimed territory. And to many pan-African ideologists, Zionism seemed to lend support to the idea of the legitimacy and viability of a 'race without territory'. There is undoubtedly some similarity between the nationality problem of the American Negro desiring to return 'home' to a no longer existing 'national' Africa, and the secular Jew desiring to return 'home' to the no longer promised land. These common desires have played a role in the interest shown by some African leaders in Israel before and during the early years of their own countries' independence, and the similarities between American Negro and Jew have often been stressed by African nationalists. Yet the very fact that both American Negroes and African ideologists could look at the Jewish case when trying to define the fluid nature of their 'nationality by pigmentation' and of the principle of non-territorial self-determination, underlines the very particular character of Jewish national identity rather than that of the African one.[21]

This is not the place to deal with questions of self-determination, yet from the little that has been said up to now it seems clear that self-determination may perhaps be a useful tool in the search for self-identity, but not for its definition, and even less for building durable political institutions. In this context, the fluidity of modern individual identity can help to define the collective no less than the other way round. And here, but only here—that is, in the conceptual framework of change—the fluidity of nations is a hindrance, for Jews, for Blacks, or for any other group with a strong feeling of identity other than that linked with territory.

Jews, of course, did not have to look to Africa for ideological models: they could find theoretical justification in many Western political thinkers. For Burke, for instance, a nation does not consist merely of people linked to a given territory, but rather of a group strongly connected with the ancient order in which they were born. For Renan, a nation is a group 'who had many things in common and that had also forgotten a good many things'.[22] The combination of common memories and common forgetfulness was what transformed a nation 'in an everyday plebiscite'.

All these intellectual exercises amounted to very little when the political chips of nationalism were down. They did not stand up against the force of a movement which 'against the reason of the Enlightenment proclaims the rights of the fantasy and of the feelings; against common sense and restraint the rights of passion. Against the levelling trends of philosophy and the anti-heroic tendencies of the eighteenth century, [the movement] exalts the hero, the genius, the man who is capable of breaking the chains of day to day life, the traditional rules dear to the bourgeois philistines, and calls for adventure.'[23]

Whether the newly discovered character of the nation was seen as a product of such physical factors as geography or climate, or whether it was moulded by moral forces such as destiny or history, secular national adventures cannot be attained without at least some deformation of realities which never fit exactly into abstract conceptions, particularly when they consist—as in the case of national theories—in rational absolute ideas or confused emotional aspirations. Whatever the reason, the dichotomy thus created between the theoretical models of political thinking or values and the expediency of political interests, generates constant tension between wishes and realities, and as a result a conscious or unconscious suppression of truth which in turn causes uncontrollable aggressiveness within the community (as within the individual). This is a recognized psychological phenomenon, well understood and exploited by politically totalitarian regimes such as the Nazis, who believed they could whip up and exploit such tension to further their own ends.

Modern psychiatry has rediscovered the negative effect of the distortion of truth on both individual and masses. 'The internal judgement of truth,' writes French psychiatrist H. Baruch, 'a humble judgement which does not have any imperative character, gives man the freedom to do good or evil. Beneath this humble mien, however, there lurks a terrifying force, making peace or war within the soul of the individual as well as within the nations.[24]

Repression, psychiatrists tell us, is an active effort, and repressed people are constantly tense and tired. In the Palestine conflict the permanent distortions of truth from all parties concerned—a distortion caused not only by propaganda but also by the emotional inability of both sides to operate according to stable criteria of collective identity—is a permanent well of tension. Israel is bearing the effects of two distortions of truth: when it tries to live according to shifting norms of alien identities, to find in them an impossible legitimation, while claiming that it is sticking to its own Jewish identity; and when it generically depicts its enemies as anti-Semites. Its enemies—Arabs, Communists, Western rationalists—do likewise: they have to bear the same negative effects of truth distortion when they depict Israel as the spearhead of colonialism, racism, imperialism, social reaction— namely the source of all evil, indeed as the scapegoat for these evils, which they know they practise in their own countries on a far larger scale than Israel.[25] These accusations bear little relation to truth; they are dictated by political propaganda mingled with a strong element of magic and unconscious fear, as the pro-Arab resolution adopted by the Bandung Conference in 1955 shows well.[26] At that time the State of Israel was a shaky political entity of fewer than two million people, most of them Jewish refugees from Europe and the Arab States. True, it had conquered some 2,000 square kilometres of Arab territory beyond what was allotted to it by the UN Partition Plan; but this had been done in a war launched against Israel by five Arab states which rejected that UN resolution and which, in the course of that same war, had taken over territories in Palestine four times larger than those conquered by Israel. Furthermore, in 1955, at the time of the Bandung Conference, Jordan and Egypt enjoyed the security of a military alliance with Britain, a power still so unfriendly to Israel that it did not object to the closure of international waterways such as the Gulf of Akaba and the Suez Canal to Israeli navigation. Together with the USA, Britain, in 1954, had demanded the return of the Negev desert (half of Israel's territory) to the Arabs. In sum, Israel in 1955 was far weaker and more vulnerable—militarily, territorially, and economically—than the Israel of 1973; yet at Bandung the representatives of over two billion Third World people declared the Jewish State to be the standard-bearer of colonialism and the most dangerous enemy which the family of new nations had to face. These were not mere words: the very absurdity of the accusation indicated the inner tension and fears expressed towards a state different from all others. The tension has not been allayed with the passing of time; rather has it increased, causing three more wars and a number of world-body resolutions without precedent in international history, such as the UN resolution equating Zionism with racism, or the UNESCO decision to dissociate Israel from any regional group.[27] The ideological isolation and denunciation of Israel was the logical precondition for Israel's politicide, just as the isolation and denunciation of the Jews as enemies of the German race by the Nazis was the precondition for the subsequent Jewish genocide. Yet psychologists acknowledge that scapegoats not only serve the purpose of self-liberation; they also indicate—as Freud and Baruch have underlined in different ways in their studies—the acceptance of the conquered culture by the conqueror.

To recapitulate, individual identity is linked with national identity; both have positive as well as negative elements: firm, proven traditions on the one hand and shaky repressed truths on the other. To use another formulation, identities are made up of 'real' (biological, historical, etc.) and invented (socially constructed) elements. All these elements may contribute to the making of a stable or unstable personal or collective identity.

There are diverse possible combinations and manifestations of weak and strong individual and collective identities. What is interesting is the joining of shaky individual and collective identities. For, when a shaky individual joins a strong collective, he seeks salvation there; when strong individuals join together in a shaky collective, they become leaders and create strong collective identities. But when both individual and collective identities are shaky or fluid, a search for a source of strength naturally gets under way. One such search is through the attempt to establish criteria for a strong collective identity, like the principle of racial identity. Erich Fromm claimed that the impetus for Nazism was just this, and that Jews had a strong identity and did not need such criteria.[28] Today they do. The general label for these criteria is, of course, legitimacy. It is the magic formula for the source of strength of collective identity. And the joining of a crisis of identity with a crisis of legitimacy can become explosive.

In the Middle East conflict, both Arabs and Israelis see themselves as developing countries, materially and psychologically linked to a situation of permanent change, measured but not controlled by external standards. This common, transitional character finds its legitimation in the promise of future achievements which require a radical transformation of the very aims and ideology of the indigenous society itself. But this is a contradiction in terms.

Legitimacy, according to the Oxford Dictionary, means conforming to rule. *Identity* is the internalized sense of participation, or, as psychologists such as Laing put it, the need of ontological security.[29] For Erikson, identity can even be an expression of insecure adolescence.[30] And it is not reinforced by heterogeneity and imported innovation: change and identity, as is well known, do not go well together. Legitimacy goes with identity, therefore legitimacy does not go well with change. To put it differently, the thing you legitimize in a rapidly changing society is already out of date.

For Israel, not to conform to the rules not only means (as is claimed by the Arabs) being an international outlaw; it means having to face the challenge and burden of establishing for herself, for the Jewish people of the Diaspora, new criteria of legitimacy. Israel's legitimacy crisis is both the consequence of change, of modernization, as in any other developing country, and of the effort to revive, even if only partially, cultural traditions which, because they rest on eternal values, deny the possibility of improvement through change. In other words, Israel's crises of legitimacy and identity cannot be envisaged only in terms of relationships with the outside world, nor as one of internal consensus on which part of the national tradition should be kept and which discarded. Heavily as the relationship with the outside world and with the Diaspora weighs on the Israeli society, outside constraints are not the determining factor of the Jewish identity problem. It is a multiple problem: political, social, historical, and psychological, demarcated both by need for immediate as well as ontological security; by nonconformity to rules, and inborn necessity to create new norms. It is hard to say whether it is more unfortunate to be a static society pining for change like Saudi Arabia, or a changing society pining for tradition, like Israel.

In a sense, the largest part of the Israeli nation and of Diaspora Jewry fits the description which Disraeli gave of himself to Queen Victoria: 'A blank page between the Old and New Testaments.' No ideology can cope with such a situation. Any attempt to apply one to the Israeli case could only underline Marx's claim that ideology is a false consciousness of social and economic realities, a collective illusion shared by the members of a given class. The crisis is indeed one of lost direction.

When a man is stranded in the desert or in the mountains, one sure way not to get anywhere is to try to interpret signs which belong to an unknown context, says social anthropologist Ernst Gellner.[31] Likewise, for modern Israel there is no point in going back to the original Hebrew Covenant of Abraham through an artificial 'back to the sources' movement, discarding 3,000 years of a history which remains Jewish even if it is not that of a Jewish State. The Covenant, without the Law of Moses, can only be interpreted as an inspiration to territorial messianism, and the Land without the Law can belong to another people as well as to the Jews. When Haim Hazaz has Yudke, one of the characters in his short story 'Hadrasha', declare, 'I oppose Jewish history. We have not made our history, the Gentiles made it for us, in their own way, according to their own will, and we only accepted it—and therefore this history is definitely not ours', Yudke stands as a 'blank page' on the Land of his ancestors just as Disraeli stood as a 'blank page' between Old and New Testaments in front of Queen Victoria.[32] On the other hand, to go back to the Covenant of Moses, to the Law, without at the same time going back to the Land, is equally impossible. It would mean—as in fact Aḥad Ha'Am said—perpetuating in the Promised Land a kind of territorial Diaspora, a soul without a body. The Palestinians and many Jewish radicals demand just that: 'an Arab democratic secular state', in which the Jews would have all the rights of a religious community and none of the rights of a national one. Another often-heard request is that Israel should express its Jewishness by becoming some kind of unique 'vegetarian' state in a carnivorous political society. This demand is as impracticable as it is hypocritical. It expresses the old demand of the anti-Semite that the Jew shed his particularism and become like the others, only to legitimize a new type of persecution once it is done, claiming that he must be punished for not behaving according to stereotype and expectation.

The drama of Jewish identity and legitimacy in modern times can be likened to an imaginary theatrical piece acted by four characters. There is the traditional Jew who says to the nations of the world: 'I am different from you; I do not want to be like you. Let me live my own way, however anachronistic it may appear to you, and I shall neither mingle in your affairs nor trouble you.' This is the position taken by the small extremist groups such as the *Neturei Karta* in Jerusalem and various Hassidic 'courts' in the USA. Their trouble, of course, is that the Gentiles—at least in Europe and the Middle East—do not agree to let them live in their own anachronism, although they certainly can be anachronistic and technologically unadapted in a society like that of America. One of the reasons for this intolerance is that Jewish traditionalists cannot control their members and prevent marginal elements detaching themselves from the anachronistic groups and penetrating the Gentile society, as happened with Jews in Europe after Emancipation, creating hostile reactions through this unwanted social mobility.

The second, no less tragic, character is that of the Jewish assimilationist who says to the nations of the world: 'I am like you in every respect, therefore I have the right to mingle in your life, culture, society in every respect.' He got his answer at Auschwitz, in the Siberian Lagers, in the Liberal Clubs of the Old and the New Left, and in the authoritarian organizations which he joined at various times and in various places.

The third character, more romantic, robust, less tragic but equally trouble-making, is the Zionist. He says to the nations of the world: 'I am like you in my nationhood, and therefore I have the right to separate myself from you, nationally, by virtue of the principle of self-determination. But once I have become sovereign, I also become equal to you and I have as much right as anybody else to delve into international affairs, especially since I have solved at least one of your problems—that of the presence of the unwanted Jew in your society.' The answer to this is, of course, that of the Arabs, who, contrary to the European nations, never felt they had a Jewish problem in hand because they were late in waking to the idea of secular nationhood. They not only refused to admit any Zionist presence in the Middle East, which they consider their own exclusive domain, but denied the Jews even the right to see themselves as equal to other peoples in terms of nationhood.

Finally there is the fourth character, the Israeli, whose claim to the nations of the world is: 'I exist as a sovereign entity and as a new *status quo* which I have created through my blood and sweat. My legitimacy equals yours and I am not responsible for the problem which my existence creates for you, just as you have never felt responsible for the troubles you created for me or for many other weak nations.'[33]

No playwright would compound four characters in one, or end his play by producing a *deus ex machina* embodying the virtues of them all. Such a hero would be an angel or a devil, but in any case a caricature of reality. The Israeli Jew, as has been repeatedly pointed out, cannot be Moses and Spartacus at the same time, although this was indeed the dream of the State's founding fathers. Yet the Israeli more than anyone else can, if he remains fundamentally attached to Jewish identity, hope to help create an atmosphere and foster aspirations conducive to the realization of a society capable of educating peoples of different cultures and origins to live and work together. This can be done because of the belief that it is possible to remain human and different even in a world of dehumanized conformism.

Such a society cannot be static. It must change continuously like life and history and reject *a priori* every type of model of behaviour. This is what made the Jews of the past so different in the eyes of the classical world, which strove instead to realize ideals of static perfection. To the artistic serenity of the Greeks, the Jews proposed their burning religiosity; to contemplation they preferred action; to the search for absolute ideas they presented the search for absolute means. Jews have always tried to develop a consistent and effective way to live normally while remaining conscious of the tragedy of the human condition, making the best of the fact of being suspended, more than any other people, between time and space, between life and death, paradise and hell. Their will to remain human and sane in the midst of madness contributed in the past to their survival and may still turn out to be an essential quality for civilization in times when people have proved that it is possible to enjoy reading Goethe in the evening and accurately perform the 'patriotic' task of burning human beings at Auschwitz in the morning.

Judaism is not the only culture seeking for sanity; Hinduism and

Buddhism have the same vocation. What is peculiar to Judaism is that the search for sanity is carried out in this world, not in seclusion from it or in the hope of some other world in the future. The Jew stays with the human 'herd' without ever identifying with it. His sanity is conditioned by his ability to stand aloof and at the same time act as 'a light unto the nations'. Yet to be such a light is not the vocation of the Jew: the vocation is to live his own life, achieve what is believed to be a special destiny, to 'burn' in his own way, and as a consequence of this 'burning', but not as a motivation or cause, also to shed light upon others.

Until Emancipation, this élitist conception of the meaning and role of Judaism gave its followers the feeling of superiority which for centuries allowed them to prefer the insecurity of a persecuted minority to the security offered by joining with the 'barbarians'. This sense of absolute superiority and inner security, so conflicting with the situation of inferiority and external insecurity in which the Jews had to live, was also a source of accusations of arrogance on the part of their enemies, and a justification for the religious, social, political, and racial hatred felt towards them. Yet up to modern times this sense of inner security and superiority was also the strongest Jewish antidote to the degradation of the Exile. Like the Victorian Earl captured by savages, the Jews could be beaten, insulted, even eaten . . . never ashamed.

With the advent of Emancipation and the liberalization and secularization of the non-Jewish society—at least in the West—the Jews gradually came to feel that their cultural and moral superiority was waning. It seemed that many of their most cherished values—monotheism, human dignity, freedom of expression, fundamental civil rights—had been adopted by the Gentile society and brought to a philosophical, political, and social level of development which seemed superior. Jewish traditional culture, in turn, appeared to most as the stagnant, backward belief of a persecuted and increasingly defecting tribal minority. With their increasing admiration for the Western world and growing loss of confidence, Jews lost both their traditional cultural system and their sense of direction. Jewish élites became alienated from their own people and marginal to the outside world. Without being colonized in the same way as the tribal élites of overseas empires which were created by the European states, they turned into the assimilated and, in many senses, culturally dependent élites of the societies in which they lived. Thus they were more despised and alienated than their African counterparts because of their proximity to the centres of the alien culture.

The Jews, therefore, fitted Frantz Fanon's model of colonial alienation, well before he discovered and described the psychological illness of the colonized. The principal source of this illness—according to him— consists of a process of Westernization involving, as a *conditio sine qua non*, the detachment of the native from his own history and culture. Just as the worker, according to Marx, is alienated by the fact that he is a victim of a system based on exploitation, so, claims Fanon, the *évolué*, or the colonized intellectual, is alienated by the fact that he conceives the European culture as a means by which he can strip himself of his own race.[34]

Fanon enlarges upon Hegel's analysis of relationships between the lord and the bondsman and the theory of relationships between colonizer and colonized. But whereas, in the latter's dialectics, the reciprocal relationship between lord and bondsman is seen as a precondition of liberation, between the Negro and his colonizing master no process of liberation can exist because the black bondsman receives his freedom from his master, he does not fight for it. 'The transformation reached the Negro from without: instead of acting, he was acted upon. His change of status from slave to bondsman remained external to him. The Negro is a slave who was allowed to assume the attitude of a master.'[35] This is exactly the contention of Yudke in Hazaz's story, quoted above: the Jew is an object, not a subject of history. He got his emancipation from others as part of their conception of human society; he did not fight for it; he did not take his freedom by force. There was no dialectic 'liberating' tension. And, one could add, Zionism did not liberate the Jew either, because as an idea it was the product of an alien political culture, and as a programme of action it did not call on the Jew to fight his 'colonial' oppressors but to run away from them while continuing to imitate them. As a result, a politically independent society of Jews was created, but Jewish political and cultural independence was not. On the contrary, the more the Israelis became the masters of their destiny, the more desirous they became of continuing to assimilate collectively to the Western world.

Agnon described this situation metaphorically, particularly in two of his works already mentioned—*T'mol Shilshom* and *Shira*.[36] With the creation of the State of Israel, Jews renounced the Messiah. When the old Jewish State was destroyed by the Romans, he argues, the *Halakha* took its place, on the double assumption that there would be no state until the advent of the Messiah: with his coming the State would be progressively rebuilt, and at the same time the Jews would be exonerated from the constraints of the *Halakha* wherever it contradicted the needs of the State. Instead an historical error took place which the creators of the *Halakha* had not foreseen: the Jews reached a point at which it became impossible for them to wait for the Messiah, so they decided to create a State without him. By doing so 'they lost the Messiah', which in turn created a deep cleavage of opinion within the Jewish people. Some felt that the *Halakha* could not coexist with the State and therefore the State was a mistake and a sin; the majority, however, felt that in a case of collision between the State and the *Halakha*, the *Halakha* should give in or find a compromise through a coalition government.

Agnon knew very well that compromise could not solve the identity dilemma of the Israelis. What was not indicated in his literary work was whether or not the return of part of the Jewish people to their ancestral homeland was a precondition for the creation of a new *Halakha*, a new code of behaviour, or at least a new chapter to be added to the original ones, to reconcile the Israeli Jew with the Messiah and prepare the way for his 'return home'. In other words, the question is whether or not the existentialist problems can promote a real process of Jewish/Israeli cultural revival, a 'decolonization' which would not stop at the level of political independence but would reach the deeper layers of collective autonomy (something no former colonized society has so far been able to achieve). Here the prescription of Frantz Fanon—decolonization through violence—has little practical relevance. As Renate Zahar notes, Fanon's idea of liberation through the eruption of spontaneous emancipatory purifying violence is inadequate because 'the success of the colonial revolution depends on whether or not development of consciousness has been set in motion in the oppressed during the first phase of revolution . . . [and] whether or not their indignation has been channelled and conceptualized so that the oppressed gain an insight into the mechanism of their oppression.'[37] Zionism certainly helped to set in motion a new national consciousness among the Jews. Pre-Zionist and early Zionist thinkers such as Hess, Pinsker, Aḥad Ha'Am, Nordau, and Herzl successfully (if only marginally to the Jewish masses of Western and Eastern Europe) conceptualized and channelled Jewish indignation towards a clear purpose: the resurgence of national independence and the re-establishment of Jewish self-respect. But it was a Westernized conceptualization, not a Jewish one. In this sense, Zionism as a movement of national liberation stands in open conflict with Fanon's ideological view of the Third World liberation process. Underdeveloped countries, he says, should do their utmost to find their own particular values and methods and style, peculiar to them. 'Come, then, comrades, the European game has finally ended; we must find something different. We today can do everything as long as we do not imitate Europe, as long as we are not obsessed by the desire to catch up with Europe. . . .'[38] No wonder Israel does not fit into the scheme of contemporary anti-colonialism. Yet the Fanon theory of national liberation and decolonization of the Third World has—with the sole exception of China—proved to be inadequate to political realities as it is void of constructive content.

Where does Israel stand in all this? It has certainly developed strong aspirations to become similar to the West and nothing, or almost nothing, in the Zionist tradition has promoted a trend of cultural autonomy similar to that which achieved the political independence of the State. Yet this very independence created the premises for the need for cultural autonomy. Israel is not part of the Third World because its independence was brought about at the expense of the Arabs, who are the most powerful group of nations in the Third World. It does not belong to what Ling Piao, the dismissed heir of Mao, once defined as the 'world of rural areas, standing against the cities of the world', because of its high standards of life, technology, and industrialization. The Yom Kippur crisis underlined the extent of this isolation. It also dramatized the need to find an answer to the central question raised by the identity problem of Israel. It can be formulated as follows: if this problem is due to a special type of decolonization process and of adaptation of tradition to modernity, what would be the most appropriate path for Israel to follow? To integrate into the Communist and the Western world at a price of increased cultural dependence; or to integrate into the Third World at a price—as the Arabs demand—of political dependence; or to stay aloof despite overwhelming difficulties, both as a consequence and a condition of survival in a situation of growing solitude?

Since Jewish traditional culture was and remains élitist and to a large extent apolitical; since modernity calls for participation, and participation in turn implies politicization of all aspects of life, the answer seems to lie in the direction of the elaboration—indeed, the invention—of a system in which the opposing trends of élitism and populism, aristocracy and democracy, can coexist in a more or less integrated way.

The existential situation of Israel, constantly calling for the confrontation in the military and economic fields of quality versus quantity, has created a fertile ground for the emergence of combinations of opposite trends. Some original institutions which combine the aspirations of both have been developed, of which the kibbutz is the most representative of democratic egalitarian institutions. It was organized on the basis of the élitist principle of inequality of duties, of *noblesse oblige*. But there is more to it than new types of institution, such as the kibbutz or the Israeli Army—at least in the original, Ben-Gurionist conception of an élitist people's framework, charged with as much civic educational responsibility as military duties. Trumpeldor's *Hechalutz* (Pioneer Movement) in the days of the First World War was no different, since it included the idea of a new type of Jewish socialist, ready to fight and work as a kind of new proletarian 'knight'.

However, the contemporary Jewish and Israeli crises of identity and legitimacy are taking place at a time of a world-wide crisis in values and the expectation of a new renaissance. 'There has been a demise of other forces, of bright idols which have competed for the allegiance of the Jew. Secular humanism, rational liberalism—the cornerstones of modern progressive society—perished for us Jews at Auschwitz when the priests of humanism and reason and science and liberalism found no voice during the Holocaust. These gods died in and of silence. There was another persuasive idol, Marxism, which once beckoned. That perished in the slave camps of Siberia.' Thus the alternative to Judaism now is not another values system: it is a void. 'The option for us Jews is much reduced and very clear', says a distinguished Jewish scientist.[39] The option is the acceptance of the Covenant, which, apart from being the distinguishing factor of Jewishness, is an unbreakable link, according to the biblical statement which says: 'I will rule over you, even against your wishes; I shall be yours, whether you wish it or not.'

CHAPTER 8

Postscript

The thirty-year war between Israel and Egypt officially ended on 26 March 1979 with the signing of the peace treaty in Washington. It is too early, and in any case not relevant to our purpose, to speculate on its potential longevity or its short- and long-term effects on the life of the peoples of the Middle East. What seems clear is the fact that the peace between Israel and Egypt will depend to a very large extent on the ability of their respective governments to control and direct the powerful internal forces which up to now have been restrained by the state of emergency in which the two countries have been living for more than a generation. These forces draw their energy from ancient and modern cultural and ideological sources. In Israel, perhaps more than in Egypt, they are liable to exacerbate problems which have little to do with foreign policy: problems of leadership, of identity, of legitimacy. In this context, the peace treaty will not significantly affect the fundamental dilemmas of the Jewish State.

It may therefore not be inappropriate to add to this book, which was largely completed before the advent of Mr Begin to power, a discussion of the events which took place in Israel during the period between the defeat of the social democrats in the May 1977 elections and Mr Begin's trip to Cairo in April 1979, from the point of view of the clash between tradition and modernity which is taking place in Israel as well as in the majority of the new Third World states.

After thirty years of rule and almost as many of political, ideological and social predominance in the pre-state Jewish society of Palestine, the socialist Establishment, as already mentioned, suffered a crushing defeat in the May 1977 general elections. The transfer of power from the alliance of socialist parties (*Ma'arah*) to the nationalist-liberal parties (*Likud*) was surprisingly smooth, confirming not only the deep-rooted democratic civism of the Israeli society but also the state of decay of the Labour Party (*Mifleget ha'Avodah*)—which up to the eve of the elections still looked powerful to its opponents.

The defeat of the *Ma'arah* was not an isolated case: the socialists of Sweden, Denmark, and Australia met with the same fate, almost at the same time, while the socialists in Italy, France, Spain, and Portugal, outside the government, are faced with hard ideological and organizational choices. They are all suffering from the crumbling of that god of self-sustained economic growth to which socialist-inspired welfare states owe their contemporary legitimacy.

In the case of Israel, as in that of India, the ruling party was also the victim of its overlong stay in power. Power corrupts, and the entire Zionist Labour movement had come to be identified with the faults of the government Establishment, whether its members were socialist or not. Ideologically, Israeli social democrats were less state-oriented than the nationalists of the *Herut* party; they were more prone institutionally and ideologically than *Herut* or the liberals to absorb and share power with the masses of the oriental Jewish immigrants.[1] Nevertheless, the protracted state of emergency together with Ben-Gurion's conception of *étatisme*—a personal and rather naïve version of Jewish *étatisme* and pioneering voluntarism which he called *Mamlachtiut*—contributed to the turning of the state into a supreme value, into an exclusive fount of honours and a source of legitimation of social status. The Labour movement, thus identified with the government Establishment, had focused upon it the growing dissatisfaction of many groups in the electorate.[2] Already in the late sixties a voting trend was evident in which the ethnic socio-cultural protest of the Jews favoured the *Herut* (later *Likud*) opposition party while the nationalist, socio-cultural protest of the Arabs benefited the Communist Party (*Maki*, and later *Rakah*), irrespective of the acceptance by the voters of the nationalist, capitalist, or marxist doctrines of these parties.[3]

What is surprising is not the fact that the socialists were replaced after thirty years of rule: it is the fact that they remained in power for so long in spite of the great demographic and cultural changes which had taken place in the Israeli society. Their political longevity was due partly to the permanent war situation in which the country found itself, partly to the strong institutions which the workers' organization had established before the creation of the state, partly to the fact that time was needed for the new interest groups, mainly made up of new immigrants, to take stock of their strength. About one generation was needed before a new bourgeoisie, created by the rapid economic growth of the state, felt strong enough to object to the intervention of government and socialist bureaucracies in its financial, commercial, and industrial activities. Concurrently, it took considerable time before the locally born or trained intellectuals began to feel the need to break away from the parochial limits and ideological conformism of a socialist brand of Zionism which had lost moral and ideological content. Finally, there was a marked trend among the young people to use the ballot given to them at the age of 18 to promote the opposition parties.[4] This was not, generally speaking, an ideological choice but an expression of dissatisfaction with the Establishment, doubly resented because usually supported by their parents but also disliked for the arrogance of its unusually inept bureaucracy. It is interesting to note, in this connection, the emergence among young people of oriental extraction of activist groups like the 'Black Panthers'[5] which adopted a language of revolt (against the European (Ashkenazi) sector of the Israeli society) made up of the most stereotyped Third World, New Left, and anti-Western clichés. With the nationalist party attacking the 'bolshevism' of the social democrats from the right, the oriental Jews denouncing its 'racialism' from the left, and the intellectuals defecting from the centre, the stage was set for a coalition between the bourgeoisie, the mainly oriental low-income groups, dissatisfied youth, and the frustrated intelligentsia which would challenge the prolonged rule of Socialist Zionism in Israel. The victory of the *Likud* in the 1977 elections was thus not simply a change of government but a change of regime. One could almost say that it signalled the end of the First Israeli Republic and the conception of a Second Republic, a republic which, if it did not bring about a revolutionary or constitutional change (as in France) yet represented far more than a simple switch in government administration: it was a profound revision of political ideas, traditions, loyalties, ideological symbolism and, above all, of political style.

The fall of the social-democratic regime was due, among others, to four main 'precipitant' causes within the general preconditional factors already described: quarrels between Labour Party leaders; the practical expulsion of the Religious Party from Mr Rabin's coalition;[6] the growing disorder of the economy produced by wildcat strikes and rapid inflation; and, finally, the financial scandals connected with top personalities in the socialist Establishment. The emergence of a new political formation, the Democratic Movement for Change (DMC), is commonly believed to have been a primary reason for the defeat of Israel's social democracy. This is highly unlikely since it has been proved that the DMC drew as much support from non-socialist as from socialist voters.[7] But the sudden appearance on the political scene of the DMC (which obtained 15 seats in the 1977 elections) is interesting since it represents a new type of non-ideological reformist élite which, for the first time, successfully challenged the established power of all the old Zionist parties. The factor which turned out to be decisive both for the defeat of the *Ma'arah* and the rise to power of the *Likud* was the break-up of the 'historical alliance' between the socialists and the National Religious Party (NRP). Although the parliamentary strength of the NRP increased only moderately (from 10 to 12 seats), the transfer of its support from the Left to the Right, and its natural co-operation with other, smaller, orthodox groups,[8] made it possible for Begin to form the first right-wing coalition government in the history of the State of Israel.

The new coalition (which even with the defection of Moshe Dayan from the Labour Party originally only had a 2-seat majority in the Knesset, later to grow from 62 to 78 out of the 120 seats by the entry of the DMC into the government) was soon overshadowed by what could be called 'the Begin phenomenon', based entirely on the new premier's powerful personality and his seeming ability to fill the vacuum created in the political consciousness of the population by long-standing crises of Zionist ideology and Jewish identity. Menahem Begin's major asset was, and still is, his credibility, a credibility born of genuine Jewish culture as well as of a public thirst for a leader in whom to believe. A complementary asset is his masterly manipulation of Jewish and non-Jewish national symbols and of the mass media. His speeches, delivered with the consummate experience of thirty years in opposition, draw freely on his vast knowledge of traditional Judaism and on his rhetorical talents. He uses local and foreign radio, TV and newspaper interviews to establish with a remarkable alternation of wit and pathos (though often with untactful petulance!) a direct link with the Jewish masses in Israel and even more in the Diaspora. His sincere, even if theatrically expressed, piety has certainly made it easier for him than for the socialists to deal with the religious parties which hold the key to his parliamentary survival. Begin's coalition is certainly more vulnerable and unstable than the preceding ones, because the *Likud* does not occupy that central place in the Israeli politico-parliamentary scene which the social democrats held for so long and which Ben-Gurion so ably used to keep opponents of the Right and the Left divided. But this very weakness of the coalition makes Begin's personal position stronger since all his ministers know that he is irreplaceable as the country's national leader. Both friends and foes realize that for a people at war, which has been longing for a strong leader since the day Ben-Gurion left the political scene; for a nation of immigrants in need of a father-figure to assume responsibility for running the country after the shock of the Yom Kippur War; for a new state in search of an old identity; for a disenchanted working class and an ambitious, rising bourgeoisie, Begin is the contemporary Israeli politician who can best fulfil many contradictory expectations. He himself knows this and does not allow many opportunities to be lost. For example, on the anniversary of Ben-Gurion's death he led the entire Government to the grave of his old socialist political enemy. Later, on another occasion, he took to Cairo representatives of the various underground groups—the *Haganah*, his own *Irgun Z'va'i Le'umi*, the *Palmah*, the *Lehi*[9]—which before and during the War of Independence had ideologically fought each other, together with representatives of the war veterans, prisoners of war, bereaved families, Jewish community leaders from America, and Zionist officials, while conspicuously leaving behind all members of the Cabinet. Through these and other gestures, Begin stressed his magnanimity, his role in continuing the state-building process initiated by Ben-Gurion (which in the past he had often been accused of attempting to destroy), his exclusive

ability to soothe ancient rivalries and create a new and wider national consensus, while constantly promoting his own image as statesman, founding
father, and national mediator. He can do all this because he possesses
natural and acquired talents which no other Israeli leaders, Ben-Gurion included, ever had, namely an extensive and genuine Jewish and Western culture, and a taste for a certain quality of life which the punctilious propriety
of his dress, the politeness of his manners, and the purity of his Hebrew (a
permanent source of inspiration for satirists and caricaturists) express in an
anachronistic way which none the less appeals to many different strata of
the population of a styleless, immigrant country. His personal honesty and
his patriotism are beyond doubt; the sense of dignity which he displays
certainly has meaning for the oriental Jew, for whom formality and decorum
are important ingredients of social and political behaviour. Furthermore,
Begin's private and public life is conducted in accordance with the established forms of traditional Judaism; he continually reminds his audiences
of the duty of the State of Israel towards the Jewish people, rather than
the contrary, as did secular Jewish leaders in the past. He appears to the
masses both as a pious Jewish scholar and a national 'paterfamilias'. At the
same time he is also the prototype of Zionist hero who participated in the
dramatic events of recent Jewish history: the Holocaust, the fight against
British colonialism, the War of Independence—in sum, he has a deep
involvement in every stage of the life of the State of Israel. He behaves like
a veteran democratic parliamentarian playing the Western political game in
all its formal details, upholding the neutrality of the civil service—even if
highly politicized by the previous regime—exercising power legitimized by
election and not by tradition. He appears as a man of 'the two publics',
the imported and the indigenous, capable not only of playing one against
the other for his own political benefit, but also of bridging the gap between
the two in a way which gives him, as the only Israeli leader who can talk
with equal force in the language of traditional and secular Jewish nationalism, the authority to take unpopular decisions.

The question of how long Begin will be able to fill the implicit and explicit hopes of many Israelis and Diaspora Jews, acting as a kind of *deus ex
machina* capable of integrating two systems of norms—the traditional and
the modern, the Jewish and the Western—cannot be answered. Nor can
anyone at this stage predict whether he will eventually turn out to be like
a second de Gaulle, acting towards the Palestinians as de Gaulle acted towards the Algerians. What is certain is that Begin, by nature, education,
and in his political ideas, is neither an Israeli version of the French leader
nor, as many feared, a dictator of fascist type. He is a nineteenth-century
liberal, nurtured on a Middle European mixture of legalistic culture,
nationalism, and romanticism. Deprived for thirty years of governmental
experience, ignorant of economic and social problems in general and

unprepared to face those of Israel in particular, supported by the enthusiasm of very large sectors of the population, who saw in him a father-figure, but without a trusted and capable staff to advise him on the running of public affairs, he is constantly faced with the problem of coping with the internal and external realities of Israel on a basis of expediency dressed in outdated Zionist Revisionist formulas. In his understandable efforts to save the principles of his lifelong belief in the indivisibility of Eretz Israel, and in his genuine desire to achieve peace with the Arabs, he promised— against the advice of the military—to return the whole of Sinai to Egypt, in the hope that President Sadat would bend on the West Bank issue, accepting a long-term compromise on the Palestinian issue based on a system of autonomy applying—nobody knows how—to people and not to the territory on which they live. This hope has already proved unfounded: the Palestinian issue makes the peace treaty itself and the two leaders who signed it extremely vulnerable. There are many and often contradictory explanations of the reasons which induced the two leaders to enter into such an agreement. One reason is certainly the fact that both Sadat and Begin hope that time will change the parameters of the Arab-Israeli conflict in a manner more favourable to what each party considers vital to its own national interests.

Many Egyptians, President Sadat among them, have not, in the past, concealed their belief that, as President Bourghiba of Tunisia claimed as early as 1965, peace would be more harmful to Israel than war. According to this theory the Zionist entity, like the Crusader state of old, would disintegrate through its own insoluble contradictions.[10] Many Israelis, while not accepting such a gloomy forecast, are convinced that the signing of the peace treaty with Egypt will bring to the fore all the internal social, moral, and psychological crises of a country which had relied in the last thirty years on the state of national emergency for the solution—or at least the postponement of the solution—of its identity problems.[11]

Looked at from this particular point of view, the Begin phenomenon and the replacement of a Zionist social-democratic regime with a Zionist national-liberal one make very little difference. Both are regimes founded on imported systems of political thought and institutional content; both are 'illegitimate' as far as traditional Judaism is concerned; both are incapable of providing the fundamental solutions required by the establishment of a modern Jewish polity. After more than two years in power, the Establishment of the Right has proved to be made of the same cultural, social, and moral stuff as that of the Left: corruption is equally widespread; the economic and bureaucratic situations have not been improved; the new right-wing coalition has shown the same symptoms of political disease as the old; personal infighting, leakage of state secrets for the sake of publicity, lack of imagination and parochialism, in addition to a level of unsurpassed inefficiency due to the new ministerial team's lack of experience, and a high-handed attitude towards the public and the law,[12] are no less prevalent. Pre-election promises to change Israel's image crumbled into an inter-ministerial squabble; immigration from the West and from the communist countries did not increase, while emigration has continued to rise. The *Likud* government's increased verbal emphasis on Jewishness has so far expressed itself exclusively, as in the past, through tactical parliamentary compromises with the religious parties of the coalition (the exemption of observant girls from army service, the allocation of a budget to religious academies, a stricter definition in the legislation of 'Who is a Jew?' and an effort to change the law on abortion) but not in any visible spiritual revival or attempt to develop new institutions of greater Jewish content and character. There is, in sum, no answer in Begin's programme to the problem of how to 'normalize' the Jewish people through the establishment of a modern state without exacerbating the conflict between Jewish religious nationalism and Jewish secular nationalism. There is no answer to three fundamental problems in the relationship of Israel towards the Arabs under its control: how to keep a state 'Jewish' while still controlling the hundreds of thousands of people who are not only hostile to Zionism but are also in no position, through no fault of their own, to know what a Jewish State is or is meant to be; how to promote a healthy democracy without granting full rights to all members; how to do this while retaining Judaea and Samaria without creating a binational state. This dilemma, which troubled all the socialist governments, became more acute after the Right came to power. The old consensus which existed in a small Israel besieged by powerful enemies could not hold after the 1967 war, in a territorially extended state occupying an area three times as large as the original state, denounced for its 'colonialism' and 'imperialism' in relation to the Palestinian Arabs, and appearing aggressive and arrogant to the majority of the nations of the world.

As for foreign policy, the old national consensus generated by the need for security was weakened even more by Sadat's visit to Jerusalem, an event which, according to popular belief, seemed to have taken Begin's government by surprise, just as the 1973 war caught Mrs Meir off guard. This belief cannot be substantiated until more is known about Foreign Minister Dayan's secret meetings with Egyptian and Saudi emissaries prior to Sadat's trip to Jerusalem[13] and about Dayan's role in modifying Begin's foreign policy views, or at least adapting them to the realities of the situation. What is clear is that at the beginning, after going through the emotion and enthusiasm of the Jerusalem meeting, both Sadat and Begin came up against opposition which they found they could not overcome. No less important in causing political misunderstandings between Begin and Sadat is the dichotomy in their respective cultures and world views, the contrast of their characters, and the differences in the actual meaning of the English words they used to talk to each other—American mediation efforts notwithstanding.

What is relevant to the topic under discussion here, namely the Israeli Jewish national consensus, is the effect on the Jewish public in Israel and abroad of Begin's policy towards the Arabs and the USA. It provoked harsh debate between believers and nonbelievers in Sadat's peaceful intentions, and this changed the tone and content of the debate on Israel's policy towards the Arabs. Before 1976 there was no complete consensus, but because there was nobody with whom to talk on the Arab side, the debate was largely academic. Now, following the Sadat peace initiative, there is no consensus on what to talk about: the political debate in Israel is becoming increasingly polarized into two equally simplistic movements, one in favour of 'Peace Now' and the other in favour of 'Peace with Security'. These movements will certainly diverge even further after the evacuation of Sinai and the prolongation of the debate over the future of the West Bank.

How the situation will evolve is a matter of conjecture. Yet, independent of the impact which the external situation will have on internal developments, one of the factors which will play an increasingly important role in the shaping of the Israeli political society will be the religious factor, which hitherto has been identified with the NRP. Its importance is due less to its present electoral strength than to the fact that neither the socialists nor the right-wing liberals can compete with it in terms of Jewish legitimacy. The secular Zionist parties of the Left and of the Right are in fact marked, like their French Republican counterparts, by the 'sin' of 'regicide': a king of flesh and blood was beheaded in France; in the case of the Jewish polity a transcendental Sovereign was deposed by the Zionist Movement which established the first secular community of Jews in history.

Religious Zionism, on the other hand, never had to bother with this problem, since its nationalism aims to revive traditional Judaism, not just to revive Jewish political independence. Religious Zionism had to struggle in the past with different and more earthly types of problem: poor leadership (due to the refusal of orthodox Judaism to join the Zionist establishment—with a few notable exceptions); the physical destruction of Eastern European Jewry, still faithful, in its majority, to genuine Jewish traditional culture; the quasi-monopoly of secular socialist Zionism over the society of pre-Israel Palestine; and a prolonged feeling of inferiority caused by the fact that religious Zionism had for a long time trailed behind secular Zionism and been incapable of creating any original institutions of its own.

The 1967 victory, the deepening search for legitimacy and identity following the years of growing international isolation, the transformation of a besieged state into an occupying power, and the shock of the Yom Kippur

War which plunged the Israeli man-in-the-street once more into a situation
of insecurity which had been the characteristic mark of the Jew for centuries, all provided fertile ground for the increased popularity and credibility of the NRP. It also helped the party's Young Guard, led by Education
Minister Zevulun Hammer and American-educated Yehuda Ben-Meir, to
rise to leadership positions in the party, thanks, *inter alia*, to party infighting and to their backing of the *Gush Emunim* activist movement.

   Gush Emunim is probably one of the least orthodox Jewish political
organizations in Israel.[14] Its aim is the immediate, massive Judaization of
Judaea and Samaria through the establishment of hundreds of settlements,
promoting a revival of Zionism as an ideological and cultural movement
which would not only bring millions of Jews into an enlarged Israel but—
and above all—refurbish Jewish consciousness in Israel and the Diaspora.
It is backed chiefly by young (not exclusively religious) people mainly because it is, as already noted, the first political and ideological movement
developed by the religious establishment which does not imitate the socialist or secular nationalist example. Inspired by the outdated, European-type
geographical concepts of the octogenarian Rabbi Kook, *Gush Emunim*
bears a striking resemblance to the Italian poet d'Annunzio's romantic
political nationalism (in connection with the historical Italian lands inha-
bited by Slavs and allotted to Yugoslavia after the First World War). The
movement's appeal derives from the fact that it offers a medium of expression to a generation of locally born religious Israelis who, rightly or
wrongly, feel themselves discriminated against in a secular society. *Gush
Emunim* also has a strong appeal to those Israelis—religious or otherwise—
who feel that imported Western ideologies have lost their relevance to the
new problems faced by the state. Whatever the reasons, *Gush Emunim*'s
real strength lies in its ability to exert sentimental blackmail equally on the
Israeli Left and Right (how can a pioneering socialist party like that of Mrs
Meir really oppose the establishment of a new settlement? or how can a
nationalist party like Begin's *Herut* dissociate itself from biblical political
myths?) and in the opportunity which it has offered to the young, militant, religious establishment to advance to the forefront of Israeli and
international public opinion.

   The *Gush Emunim* extremism, the inconsistencies of their aims with
the realities of an international and national Jewish situation, the activism
of a minority which takes the law into its own hands whenever the government, Right or Left, displeases them, has been the object of intense criticism inside and outside Israel. Considering the great debate which *Gush
Emunim* has stirred up, and the very small following they have so far
elicited among the masses, it is difficult to make any forecast about the
future of the movement. Two things *Gush Emunim* has certainly achieved:
first, the movement has served as a launching-pad for the new leadership

of the NRP, and second, it has aroused a considerable backlash against its own politics within that party, which served as the cradle and political frame for the annexationist movement.

The national congress held by the NRP in 1978 showed the confident unity achieved by the party under the New Guard and the realism of the young leaders once in positions of power. The principle that the NRP cannot renounce any part of the Promised Land has been reaffirmed. At the same time, the resolution calling for NRP ministers to resign from any government renouncing any part of the Land of Israel has been officially cancelled. The justification for the latter move has been that the obligation had been made obsolete by the political and ideological stand of Begin's government. However, the satisfaction expressed by both 'hawkish' and 'doveish' members of the NRP with the decisions taken by their congress show that the new political programme approved is more than an empty formula of compromise.

The time has certainly not yet arrived for the NRP to lead Israel's foreign and military policy; the party lacks sufficient qualified personnel. But the religious party's recent national congress leaves no doubt about the direction in which it intends to move. Banking on the widespread and justified recognition of the fact that, individually, Israeli religious youth possesses a higher standard of morality than the rest of the population, the NRP intends to present itself more and more as the only sincere, ideological party promoting and defending indigenous moral and social values and opposing the corrupting influence of the Western, fundamentally anti-Jewish, ideologies held by Israeli secular political movements. The religious school systems, both private and governmental, also offer the NRP the possibility of enlarging its future electoral recruiting ground. This fact is less important than the fact that the religious schools strive to impart an élitist, selective education to their pupils and to create élitist cadres (which in the past were the monopoly of the kibbutz schools) in spite of the disproportionate share of underprivileged students whom they freely admit into their institutions.[15]

The religious groups, led by the NRP, are trying to emerge from their narrow aim of introducing more orthodox religion to the country and are becoming more concerned with social problems. Israel, like every country of immigration, has its own brand of 'root' problems. But while the geographical roots of the economically more advanced Ashkenazi Jews are—as far as the secular political parties are concerned—in Europe, and those of the underprivileged oriental Jews in Asia or Africa, the religious, moral roots of both groups are in that very tradition of which the NRP is the politically recognized standard-bearer.

The fact that the NRP is considering the possibility of joining the *Histadrut*, Israel's Labour Federation, is a sign both of the weakening of the Federation of Labour as a compact ideological force and of the NRP's desire to take a larger part in the organized life of the working classes. Yet the most revolutionary step, announced as one of the aims of the party by Education Minister Hammer, is the creation of a political framework for religious people who are not members of the NRP and for secular Israelis who favour the strengthening of Jewish values and culture. This does not yet mean the transformation of the NRP into an Israeli version of Europe's Christian Democratic parties, but it is a significant move aimed at transforming a minority political organization into a mass, centrist party, albeit tainted with a strong 'clerical' connotation, but of the type imagined by Adenauer and de Gasperi for their Christian Democratic movements in the early fifties.

Here we are once more confronted with the dilemma of the 'two publics', the traditional and the modern, which raises the fundamental question of the nature of the cultural effort required of Israel in order to graft its Western structure on to ancient traditional roots without compromising the positive values of either. The challenge of the NRP is as much of a political nature as it is one of historical, social, cultural, and moral responsibility, and it has not gone unnoticed by the other parties.

The Labour Party leader Shimon Peres admits the tragic error committed by the social democrats in letting the 'historic alliance' with the NRP break up before the elections, while Mr Begin's party has hastened to create a combined 'propaganda front' with the NRP to counter the possibility of the religious party being tempted to go back to the socialist camp.

These alliances are, for the moment, an extension of the old ones, namely the traditional parliamentary or municipal collaboration of party bureaucrats, financial group interests, or past political enemies. The idea of collaborating with a movement for the rejuvenation of political Judaism embodied in a religious Zionist party is for the time being very far from the preoccupations of Israeli leaders, of the Right as well as of the Left. The important issue here, therefore, is not if and how the religious Zionist establishment and the NRP will in future deal with secular Zionism in its various formations to the Right and Left of the Israeli parliamentary spectrum, from a position of political equality and ideological superiority: the questions to be asked are, first, whether the NRP will follow the example of the European Catholic parties (and fall into the same ideological trappings and decadence of the Israeli socialists and nationalists imitating their Western counterparts); or, second, prove itself capable of becoming a leading movement of renewal for both Zionism and Judaism; or, third, whether in the absence of any Zionist organization capable of fulfilling such an historic task, some other force from within Israel or from the Diaspora will be created to fill the vacuum. The answers to these questions depend to a large extent on the ability of the Israeli leadership to become *conscious* of the very special type of decolonization process which Israel must undergo in order to overcome, physically and spiritually, the great internal obstacles which stand in the way of the consolidation and development of the Jewish commonwealth at the end of this millennium.

These obstacles are the consequence of historical and often dramatic experiences which are bound to mark the soul of the Jewish people for a long time to come. The possibility cannot be excluded that under the impact of this trauma Israel may continue to live on the reveries of ephemeral territorial grandeur and of an heroic military and pioneering past powerful enough to justify future suicidal adventures. And yet, if there is a quality in which Jews have excelled throughout history, it is their ability to survive and make the best of the situation in which they live.

One hundred years ago, at the time Leon Pinsker wrote his *Auto-emancipation*, the Zionist adventure looked utterly utopian. It achieved its aim because it understood that the salient feature of political struggle was secular nationalism and because it was able to mobilize enough consensus among Jews and non-Jews to become the driving force around which the dispersed elements of Judaism could coalesce. Today, the national, the class, and the racial factors, although still very much present in modern Israeli society, are no longer its prime motives. In the West, as in the communist countries, the search for new content, new values, a new consensus, has emerged as the principal preoccupation of the developed societies, while in the new states of the Third World, the clash between modernization and tradition has transformed religion (institutionalized or concealed behind tribalism) into a political legitimacy and the cause of political struggle.

Israel finds itself at the centre of this new type of involvement. At a time when other peoples are struggling with the problem of how traditional—but not only traditional—societies can face the challenge of modernization without losing themselves in the process, Israel offers the probably unique experience of a society searching for a way to face the challenge of traditionalism without losing the benefits of its acquired Westernization.

The crisis of the Zionist state may lead to an Israeli version of the Lebanese 'religious' binationalism, in which the Jews might be lured into the dream of maintaining a permanent relative majority—similar to that of the Maronites—thanks to the support of their Diaspora and of the West. But history does not repeat itself: Israel is not Lebanon and Jews are not Arabized Christians. Although the success of the Israeli adventure is by no means assured, the choices for its future are not unlimited and its present crises may well turn out to be the birth pangs of a new era.

It is the consciousness of the existence of such alternatives which is a first condition, although certainly not a sufficient guarantee, of the survival and development of the second Israeli Republic and those which may follow it. History can vouch for the ability of the Jews, if they so desire, to face the challenges of the future as vigorously as they faced the challenges of the past.

Notes

Chapter 1 Zionism as a National Movement

1. Amos Elon, *Herzl* (London, 1975), p. 186 (italics in the original text).

2. Simmel sees in the history of the European Jew the classic example of the stranger who 'intrudes as a supernumerary, so to speak, into a group in which the economic positions are actually occupied' ('The Stranger', in Kurt H. Wolff, *The Sociology of Georg Simmel* (New York, 1950), p. 403). This was certainly one of the sources of nineteenth-century anti-Semitism which in turn perpetuated in Western secular society the religious hatred of Christianity for the Jew who had remained an outsider to the Verus Israel, and prepared the ground for the forceful estrangement of the Jew from the European nations and the human race well before the rise of Nazism. Paul De Lagarde (*Juden und Indogermanen* (Göttingen, 1887), p. 339) was probably the first to give a biological dimension to anti-Semitism, by comparing Jews with *Trichinae* (i.e. parasitic worms in human and animal bodies) and bacilli, with which 'one does not negotiate [since] *Trichinae* and bacilli are not subject to education. They are exterminated as quickly and as thoroughly as possible.' This idea was expressed almost verbatim by Himmler, in a speech to SS leaders in 1943 (Nuremberg Documents, PS-1919, quoted by S. Friedlander at the International Scholars' Conference on 'The Holocaust—A Generation After', New York City, 3-6 March 1975). In the Islamic world the estrangement of the Jew was of a different nature, but strongly institutionalized in the status of the 'protected' communities, the *dhimmi*, which of course was not restricted only to the Jews (*Encyclopedia Judaica*, vol. 5, pp. 1604-5). At all events, the various forms of Jewish discrimination reflected upon the Jewish people's own conception of uniqueness among the peoples through its special relationship to God, an idea which increased the feeling of estrangement in direct proportion to the aggression of the non-Jewish world, since 'the more the Jew was forced to close on himself, to withdraw into the imposed confines of the Ghetto, the more he tended to emphasize Israel's difference from the cruel Gentile without' (*Encyclopedia Judaica*, 'Chosen People', vol. 5, pp. 489-502).

3. Simon Dubnow, *Nationalism and History, Essays on Old and New Judaism*, edited with an introductory essay by Koppel S. Pinson (Philadelphia, 1958), pp. 41-60.

4. Joseph Tekoah at the UN Security Council on 21 October 1973. For a popular socialist interpretation of Zionism, see M. S. Arnoni, *Zionism as a Movement of National Liberation* (Tel Aviv, n.d.).

5. The literature on the founder of Zionism is very rich, and increasing. Alex Bein's *Biography*, first published in Vienna in 1934, remains one of the best-documented. Amos Elon's *Herzl* (n. 1) has added little new evidence to that already existing but has given a new, profound, and dramatic interpretation to Herzl's personality.

6. *Encyclopedia Judaica* (Jerusalem, 1971), vol. 16, pp. 1066-9. For further readings see the Bibliography, pp. 1160-2. The existing literature is too vast to be listed here. However, see also Leon Poliakov, *Histoire de l'Antisémitisme*, 3 vols. (Paris, 1956-68), which is the best documented and interpretative modern work on the subject.

7. C. H. Cooley, *Human Nature and the Social Order* (New York, 1902), pp. 183-4.

8. F. S. Spiers, 'Zionism and Judaism', in P. Goodman and A. D. Lewis (eds.), *Zionism: Problems and Views* (London, 1916), pp. 223 ff.

9. J. Yankelewich, *Information Juive*, Paris, 1975.

10. Hans J. Morgenthau, *Politics among Nations: The Struggle for Power and Peace* (New York, 1967), pp. 48-54.

11. Elon, *Herzl*, p. 226.

12. Raymond Leslie Buell, *The Native Problem in Africa* (New York, 1928), vol. II, p. 81, quoted by Rupert Emerson, *From Empire to Nation, The Rise to Self-Assertion of Asian and African Peoples* (Cambridge, Mass., 1960), p. 72.

13. 'The Passing of the European Order', *Encounter*, Nov. 1957, IX, 5, quoted by Emerson, op. cit., p. 84.

14. Edward A. Freeman, 'Race and Language', *Historical Essays*, 3rd series (London, 1879), p. 203, quoted by Emerson, op. cit., p. 132.

15. *Marxism and the National and Colonial Question* (Moscow, 1940), p. 6.

16. Hans Kohn, *A History of Nationalism in the East* (New York, 1929), ch. 2.

17. The idea of a separation between state and religion is included in the official platform and line of several Israeli political parties and movements, such as 'Peace and Equality Camp' (SHELI), 'Citizens' Rights Movement' (RATZ), 'The Democratic Movement for Change' (DASH), and the 'League Against Religious Coercion'.

Chapter 2 The Anguish of the Jewish Victory

1. The US Secretary of State J. F. Dulles made it clear in a speech in New York in August 1955. This same idea was expressed by the British Foreign Minister, Anthony Eden, in his Guildhall address in November 1955. Both called for a compromise between the partition borders and the *status quo*, believing that territorial concessions by Israel in the Negev would facilitate the creation of a land bridge between Egypt and Jordan.

2. Joseph Duriel, in *Ha'aretz*, 26 March 1975.

3. Letter to the Editor in *Ha'aretz*, 27 May 1975.

4. 'Does Zionism have a future?' in *Tradition* (1964), vol. 6, no. 2.

5. 'Reflections of a Historian in Jerusalem', in *Encounter*, May 1976.

6. Ezra 10:3.

7. A Talmudic legend told by Yoets Kayam Ish, 'Siah Sarkhei Kodesh', in *Rakol*, vol. 1 (Warsaw).

8. Koppel S. Pinson, in the introduction to Simon Dubnow, *Nationalism and History* (New York, 1961), pp. 43–4. For a critique of Dubnow's national theories see Ezekiel Kaufman, *Gola ve-Nekhar* ('Diaspora and Strange Land'; in Hebrew, Tel Aviv, 1929–31), vol. 3, pp. 300–18; see also Oscar I. Janowsky, *The Jews and Minority Rights, 1898–1919* (New York, 1933) and Israel Friedlaender, 'Dubnow's Theory of Jewish Nationalism', first published in 1905 and then reprinted in his *Past and Present* (Cincinnati, 1919).

9. E. R. Bevan, 'Hellenistic Judaism', in E. R. Bevan and C. Singer (eds.), *The Legacy of Israel* (Oxford, 1953), pp. 29 ff.

10. Yitzhak F. Baer, *Galut* (New York, 1947), p. 9.

11. Saul Friedlander, 'The Historical Significance of the Holocaust', in *The Jerusalem Quarterly*, Fall 1976, no. 1, pp. 36–59.

12. Baer, op. cit., p. 22.

13. Jacob Katz, *Tradition and Crisis* (New York, 1971), pp. 13–17.

14. For élite structures and the transfer of knowledge, see the author's *The High Road and the Low* (London, 1974), pp. 47–58.

15. Katz, op. cit., pp. 245–59.

16. Ibid., p. 255.

17. Walter Laqueur, *A History of Zionism* (New York, 1976), p. 16.

18. Katz, op. cit., p. 259.

19. Laqueur, op. cit., p. 8.

20. For example, Rabbi Schneur Zalman of Lyadi's (1804) famous remark: 'If Napoleon wins, so much the better for the Jews; if he loses, so much the better for Judaism.'

21. David Vital, *The Origins of Zionism* (OUP, London, 1975), pp. 25–6.

22. 'A People That Shall Dwell Alone . . .' in *The New York Review of Books*, 12 Dec. 1974.

23. Stanislas de Clermont-Tonnerre, in the National Assembly, 24 Dec. 1789. Cf. Arthur Hertzberg, *The French Enlightenment and the Jews* (New York, 1968), pp. 359–61.

24. Vital, op. cit., pp. 3–22.

25. On the transformative capacity of religion see S. N. Eisenstadt, *The Protestant Ethic and Modernization—A Comparative View* (New York, 1969), pp. 9–17.

26. See especially Lesson 7 in Nachmann Krochmal, *Moreh Nebucheh ha-Seman* ('Sive Director Errantium nostrae aetatis', etc.), ed. Dr. Leopold Zunz (Leopoli, 1851), reprinted in Simon Rawidowicz (ed.), *The Writings of Nachmann Krochmal* (London, 1961), pp. 34–9.

27. Hillel E. Levine, *Menahem Mendel Lefin: Sociological Studies of Judaism and Modernization*, an unpublished Ph.D. thesis, Harvard University, May 1974.

28. Numbers 23:9.

29. Such as Rabbi Yehuda Alkalai, Rabbi Zvi Hirsch Kalischer, Rabbi Samuel Mohilever, Yehiel Michael Pines, Rabbi Abraham Isaac Kook, and Samuel Hayyim Landau. For a brief critical assessment of their contribution, see Arthur Hertzberg (ed.), *The Zionist Idea* (New York, 1966).

30. On *Hovevei Zion* see Vital, op. cit., pp. 135–86.

31. For a concise analysis of *Auto-emancipation* see ibid., pp. 109–13. The full, original title of Pinsker's pamphlet in German was *Autoemanzipation!: Mahnruf an seine Stammesgenossen von einem russischen Juden* ('Auto-emancipation!: A warning to his kinsfolk by a Russian Jew'), Sept. 1882.

32. Vital, op. cit., p. 128.

33. Ibid., p. 127.

34. Ibid., pp. 188–200.

35. Ibid., p. 373.

36. Ibid., pp. 373–4.

37. Levi Eshkol was Prime Minister from June 1963 until his death in March 1969. Golda Meir succeeded him in this post until June 1974.

38. Arieh 'Lova' Eliav, *Israel's Ladder: The Dream and its Meaning* (Tel Aviv, 1976).

39. 'L'État de Guerre: Répercussions sur l'Individu et la Société', in *La Conscience Juive face à la Guerre* (Paris, 1976), pp. 127–41.

Chapter 3 The Two Publics: Israel and Africa

1. The historical relationships between Jews and Africa is a subject which has been studied in a very erratic way. The relationship between Jews, Palestine, and Ethiopia is, of course, well known: see Jean Doresse, *L'Empire du Prêtre-Jean* (Paris, 1957), vols. 1 and 2; Ernst Hammerschmidt, 'Jewish Elements in the Cult of the Ethiopian Church', in *The Journal of Ethiopian Studies*, July 1968, vol. III, no. 2; and Sven Rubenson, 'The Lion of the Tribe of Judah: Christian Symbol and/or Imperial Title', ibid. The links between the Jews and other parts of East Africa are less certain. There are many oral traditions and a few historical documents concerning Madagascar: see Gabriel Ferrand, 'Migration Musulmane et Juive a Madagaskar', in *Revue d'Histoire des Religions*, 1905, vol. 52, pp. 381–417; and R. P. fr. X. Razakandrainy, *Parenté des Hovas et des Hébreux* (Tananarive, 1926), as well as the more contemporary Arieh Oded, 'Ha'Bayudaya U'myasda Semei Kakungulu' (in Hebrew) in *Hamizrah HeHadash*, 1967, vol. 27, no. 1-2. Turning to West Africa, historical evidence of a Jewish presence and influence is richer and more extensive than for Northern Africa and the Sahara. First, there is a vast literature on the Kahina and the Berbers: see *Encyclopedia Judaica* (Jerusalem, 1971), vol. 10, pp. 587–8

and 685, as well as a very interesting article by Israel Levi, 'Le Lait de la Mère et le Proselytisme' in *Revue des Études Juives*, 1929, vol. 87, pp. 94-5, and H. Z. Hirschberg, 'The Problem of the Judaized Berbers', in *Journal of African History*, 1963, vol. 4, no. 3. One of the most acute studies of the ancient presence and role of the Jews in West Africa is Raymond Manny's article, 'Le Judaisme, Les Juifs et l'Afrique Occidentale', in *Bulletin de l'Institut Français d'Afrique Noire*, July–Aug. 1949, vol. XI, no. 3-4.

2. Edward W. Blyden, *The Jewish Question* (Liverpool, 1898).

3. *Crisis*, Feb. 1919.

4. Theodor Herzl, *Old-New Land* (English translation, New York, 1960), p. 1.

5. Those more relevant to this chapter are: Albert Memmi, *Portrait d'un Juif* (Paris, 1962) and Frantz Fanon, *The Wretched of the Earth* (New York, 1968). Another very pertinent book, although relating to the special experience of the Jewish Lebanese intellectuals, is Lucien Elia, *Les Ratés de la Diaspora* (Paris, 1969). I also found some illuminating evidence for the common mentality of Jewish and African intellectuals in 'Les Intellectuels Africains: Où en sont'ils?' in *Réalités Africaines* (Paris, Dec. 1963–Jan. 1964), no. 6.

6. Peter P. Ekeh, 'Colonialism and the Two Publics in Africa', in *Comparative Studies in Society and History*, 1975, no. 1, pp. 91–112.

7. Jacob Katz, *Tradition and Crisis* (New York, 1971), p. 262.

8. The very expression 'self-hater' was coined in relation to the Jewish complex of alienation by the German philosopher Theodor Lessing, who himself symbolized the tragedy of Jewish alienation. Born a Jew in 1872, he was converted to Lutheranism while a student, returned to Judaism with the rise of Zionism, and wrote his famous essay, 'Jewish Self-Hate' (1930), which led to his assassination by the Nazis in 1933. On Karl Marx regarding this subject see Edmund Silberner, 'Was Marx an Anti-Semite?' in *Historia Judaica*, April 1949, vol. XI, no. 1, pp. 3-52. Also on self-hate, see Luciano Tas, 'L'Odio Ebraico di Se', in *Gli Stati*, Oct. 1972, no. 7, pp. 3-7. The Israeli aspects of Jewish self-hate are often denounced by the Israeli press. See, as an example, Eliezer Livne's article in *Ma'ariv*, 28 May 1971. The numerous acrimonious exchanges of stereotyped 'Jewish' insults between the Prime Minister of Israel and the Chancellor of Austria renew and typify the old quarrel between self-loving and self-hating Jews.

9. Hannah Arendt, *The Origins of Totalitarianism* (New York, 1951), p. 131.

10. See the author's 'Madagascar: An Example of Indigenous Modernization of a Traditional Society in the 19th Century', in *African Affairs*, no. 3 (OUP, London, 1969), pp. 67-91.

11. David Vital, *The Origins of Zionism* (OUP, London, 1975), p. 36.

12. Speech delivered by Max Nordau to the First Zionist Congress in Basle in 1897.

13. Frantz Fanon, Congress of Black Writers and Artists, Paris, 1956.

14. Marion J. Levy, Jr., *Modernization and the Structure of Societies, a Setting for International Affairs* (Princeton, 1966), pp. 741 ff. I have made

wide use of this fundamental work on modernization here and in the chapters dealing more specifically with the crises of the Israeli society.

15. S. D. Goitein, *Jews and Arabs, Their Contacts Through the Ages*, 3rd edn. (New York, 1974), especially chapter 8, pp. 212–25, on the cultural aspects of the coinciding revivals. Although not specifically devoted to the subject, the collection of speeches and articles by Yaakov Herzog, *A People That Dwells Alone* (London, 1975), is illuminating on the multiple facets of the Jewish/Zionist, Arab/Islamic, secular/Christian ideological and political encounter. The fact that the late Yaakov Herzog was not only a top Israeli diplomat and influential adviser of Ben-Gurion and Levi Eshkol but also an observant Jew with an exceptional Jewish and Western cultural background and a famous talmudic scholar, gives a unique dimension to his posthumously published and other scattered reflections on the problem. The following are also relevant: Arthur Jeffery, 'The Political Importance of Islam', *Journal of Near East Studies*, Oct. 1942, vol. 1, no. 4; Francesco Gabrieli, *Il Risorgimento Arabo, Grandezza, Decadenza e Rinascita dei Popoli Arabi* (Novara, 1958); Albert Hourani, *Arabic Thought in the Liberal Age, 1798–1939* (OUP, London, 1970).

16. Albert Hourani, 'The Decline of the West in the Middle East', I and II, *International Affairs*, Jan. and April 1953.

17. Clifford Geertz, 'Ideology as a Cultural System', in David E. Apter (ed.), *Ideology and Discontent* (New York, 1964), pp. 47–76.

18. Ibid. Geertz correctly notes that social theory has been deeply influenced by almost every major intellectual movement of the last century and a half—Marxism, Darwinism, Utilitarianism, Idealism, Freudianism, Behaviourism, Positivism, Operationalism—but has been virtually untouched by what Kenneth Burke called 'symbolic action' in his *The Philosophy of Literary Form, Studies in Symbolic Action* (1941), and has found expression neither in the works of philosophers such as Peirce, Cassirer, Wittgenstein, Langer Phyle, nor in those of literary critics such as Coleridge, Eliot, Burke, and Empson. This lack of attention by social and political scientists in the field of politics is particularly felt in the study of conflict among nations of different cultural backgrounds, where symbols are not only extremely important elements of political language but often impossible to translate into appropriate Western concepts. Think, for instance, of the multiple symbolic meanings of the Western Wall of Jerusalem: it is a Jewish Arc de Triomphe-cum-Lourdes-cum-War Memorial. But it is also a kind of political and religious Speakers' Corner, on top of being a sacred place and an archaeological curiosity, physically dominated by the El Aksa Mosque which, in turn, was a Crusader bastion and a Byzantine church.

19. For an impressionistic but forceful description of the quick rise and fall of the military in Israeli public opinion see Amos Elon in *Ha'aretz*, Sept. 1978.

20. Baruch Nadel, 'Black Money', in *The Jerusalem Post*, Jan. 1977, and 'Black Controls White' in *The Jerusalem Post*, Feb. 1977.

21. See, *inter alia*, David Krivine, 'Rebuttal on Black Money', *The Jerusalem Post*, 4 March 1977. The rise to power of the *Likud* did not change the trend towards increased criminality, the extent of which was underlined by the discovery at the end of 1978 of an organization called *MAAZ*, the Hebrew initials of the words 'Underground of Army Deserters'. Its

members perpetrated a series of major crimes—murder, arson, robbery, and sabotage—and planned their operations in military fashion. Columnist Amos Keinan wrote in *Yediot Aharonot* (8 Sept. 1978): 'The Hebrew society, before the State came into being, created the Haganah, the Irgun and the Lehi—underground organizations to oppose the British. The State of Israel has created *MAAZ*, the underground which fights the State. This is the true change at the end of this decade—a revolt of the underworld. Israel has become the major supplier for the underworlds of the free world. Anyone disbelieving this should go to Amsterdam, Frankfurt and New York. The Israel of Borochov and Trumpeldor . . . is selling heroin, prostitution and crime incorporated.'

22. Yitzhak Rabin, a speech delivered on Mount Scopus after receiving a doctorate *honoris causa* from the Hebrew University, July 1967.

23. *A Year Later*, pamphlet published by Hashomer Hatzair, quoted in *Ha'aretz*, 22 Nov. 1968.

24. Albert Memmi, 'Negritude and Jewishness', in *Dominated Man* (Boston, 1971), pp. 27–39.

25. Ibid., Introduction, pp. 3–15.

26. Ibid., pp.

27. Ibid., pp. 93–109.

28. Jean-Paul Sartre, *Anti-Semite and Jew* (New York, 1965).

Chapter 4 Traditional Jewish Political Thought

1. See Joseph de Maistre, as quoted by Jacob L. Talmon, 'Reflections of an Historian in Jerusalem', *Encounter*, May 1976.

2. The Science of Judaism Movement is linked with the name of a great Jewish scholar, Leopold Zunz (1886–1974), who coined the expression 'Wissenschaft des Judentums', meaning the understanding of Jewish antiquity in all its parts, as far as expressed in literary movements. This very 'objective' approach to Judaism was one of the most powerful intellectual justifications for Jewish 'self-colonization' and it is significant that Eduard Gans, the President of the Centre for Jewish Culture and Study founded by Zunz, was also the first member of the movement to embrace Christianity for the sake of a university career (1825), followed by Heinrich Heine, the poet. This was the inevitable consequence—even with a pious Jew like Zunz himself—of the two competing tendencies within the Science of Judaism Movement, one of them set upon the liquidation of Judaism as a living organism, the other directed towards its transfiguration.

3. For the origin of the legitimacy conflict between Judaism and Christianity over the 'true Israel' see Marcel Simon, *Verus Israel* (Paris, 1964), especially the first part dealing with the religious and political framework of the conflict.

4. Sir Reginald Coupland quoted by Basil Davidson, *The African Past* (London, 1964), p. 32. The European cultural egocentrism did not, of course, limit itself to ignorance of African history and culture. It extended to most fields of non-European learning. James Lorimer, the Scottish jurist, could still write, as late as 1880, in perfectly good faith that mankind was

divided into civilized and savage nations, including in the latter category countries like Persia, Japan, and China. See his *The Institutes of the Law of Nations* (Edinburgh, 1883), vol. 1, pp. 101–3. Africa remained at the bottom of the scale till after the First World War. A serious revision of its history did not begin till after the Second World War. See Roland Oliver and J. D. Fage, *A Short History of Africa* (London, 1966), and Roland Oliver (ed.), *The Dawn of African History* (London, 1961).

5. Quoted by Laqueur, *A History of Zionism* (New York, 1976), p. 12.

6. Ibid., p. 22.

7. Ibid., p. 31.

8. Erich Fromm, 'Individual and Social Origins of Neurosis', in *American Sociological Review* (1944), no. 9, pp. 380–4, quoted by P. Ekeh, *Social Exchange Theories* (London, 1974), p. 29.

9. Jacques Maritain, *Antisemitism* (London, 1939), pp. 20–1.

10. Jacques Maritain, *Le Mystère d'Israel* (Paris, 1965).

11. Jacques Maritain, *The Degrees of Knowledge.* Translated from *Les Degrés du Savoir* by B. Wall and M. R. Adamson (London, 1937).

12. Marcel Dubois, *Paradoxes et Mystères d'Israel* (Jerusalem, 1977), pp. 43, 53.

13. Ibid., p. 54.

14. Joseph Agassi, 'Conventions in Knowledge in Talmudic Law', in *Journal of Jewish Studies*, Feb. 1974, X X V, no. 1, pp. 16–34.

15. Robert A. Nisbet, *Social Change and History* (New York, 1969), pp. 4 ff.

16. Sir Herbert Read, *English Prose Style* (rev. edn., New York, 1952), p. 23.

17. There were 310 *Yeshivot* (Rabbinical Academies) with over 19,000 students in 1973.

18. Adin Steinsaltz, *The Essential Talmud* (London, 1976), p. 3.

19. Ben-Ami Scharfstein, *The Mind of China* (New York, 1974), pp. 131–59.

20. Tacitus, *History*, V, 2:5.

21. Hayyim Ze'ev Hirschberg, *Yisrael be'Arav* ('Jews in Arabia'; Jerusalem, 1946) and *Toledot ha'Yehudim be'Africa ha'Zefonit* ('History of the Jews in North Africa'; 2 vols., Jerusalem, 1965).

22. For the communal structure in Eastern Europe see Louis Finkelstein, *Jewish Self-Government in the Middle Ages* (New York, 1964) and Jacob Katz, *Tradition and Crisis* (New York, 1971).

23. Josef Salvador (*Histoire des Institutions de Moise*, 3rd edn., 1862), is the major, and little-known, exception. Although much of his work is pervaded by strong Jewish–Christian apologetic syncretism, his interpretation of Moses as a political rather than a religious prophet is original. Nahum Sokolow rightly included Salvador among the significant pro-Zionist thinkers. As for this century, the only book known to the author on this

subject is Hans Kohn, *Die Politische Idee des Judentums* ('The Political Idea of Judaism', Munich, 1924).

24. On Jewish autonomy see S. Morell, 'The Constitutional Limits of Communal Government in Rabbinic Law', in *Jewish Social Studies*, April–July 1971, vol. xxxiii, nos. 2–3, pp. 87–119; also Louis Finkelstein, op. cit., and H. H. Ben-Sasson, *Toledot Am-Yisrael* ('The History of the Jewish People', 3 vols., Jerusalem, 1969–70), pp. 260–86.

25. See Daniel Elazar's article, 'Government, Biblical and Second Temple Periods', in *Encyclopedia Judaica Year Book*, 1973, pp. 210–15.

26. Ibid.

27. See Joshua 24:12–13. The Jewish propensity towards a system of national autonomy rather than a centralized state is clearly demonstrated in the period of the Judges, when Joshua, the first Judge, voluntarily put an end to the well-knit military-political organization through which the conquest of a large part of the Land of Canaan was carried out, and instituted a loose federation of autonomous tribes. The Messianic vision of the Jewish state presented by the prophet Ezekiel (Ezekiel 47:32, 48) is also based on the idea of autonomy rather than of state, with severe limitations on the power of the King, who, incidentally, is called *Nassi* (President). Throughout every manifestation of Jewish statehood the anarchical, autonomist trend is present and often quite prominent. The ancient states of Israel and Judaea both ended in similarly dramatic fashion (the former conquered by the Assyrians in 722 BCE and the latter by the Babylonians in 586 BCE) and developed similar social tensions. Once the strong nationalist consciousness based on military power was broken, there was nothing to hold the people of the Israeli Kingdom together. The ten tribes that formed it disappeared into the night of exile.

The fate of the two tribes—Judah and Benjamin—that composed the Kingdom of Judaea was quite different. Their political independence lasted longer, despite their inferior numbers and military might; their exile to Babylon was a stepping-stone to their return to the ancestral land, to the re-creation of a national state and the establishment of a powerful diaspora which lasted, as an autonomous, self-governing country in Babylon, until the tenth century CE. Among the factors behind this survival were the centrality of Temple life in Jerusalem and the legitimacy and strength of the royal House of David, which succeeded in checking the rise of the land-owning class. With the economic power of their estates, this class turned into a decisive factor in the political life of the Kingdom of Israel but does not seem to have played the same role in Judaea where, from the middle of the ninth century BCE on, the section of the population described as 'the people of the land' (*am ha-aretz*) became increasingly prominent. Little is known about this group, which played a very active part in revolutions and regicides (2 Kings 11:14; 2 Chron. 33:25, *et al.*). According to the *Encyclopedia Judaica* (vol. 8, p. 613) it may be inferred from the sparse biblical references that the 'people of the land' were a broadly representative class in Judaea and that their power rested on land ownership, although it seems unlikely that they included major landowners. Apparently the 'people of the land' replaced the ancient, 'democratic' congregation (*edah*), which had more or less vanished shortly after the establishment of the monarchy.

28. *Babylonian Talmud*, pp. 105b–106a.

29. After the fall of Jerusalem the Sanhedrin was reconstituted at Jabneh under Rabbi Johanan ben Zakkai. Between 70 and 132 CE Jabneh was the city of scholars and rabbis.

30. The supreme court organized at Jabneh by Johanan ben Zakkai not only gradually dealt with the whole range of legislative problems formerly invested in Jerusalem, but kept the chairmanship open until a scion of the royal House of David—Rabban Gamliel—could once again come into the open and become the *Nassi* (President) of the Academy. While descent from the royal house was a condition for becoming Ethnarch in Babylon, and possibly elsewhere, Palestine remained the 'Eternal Centre' of Judaism. The practical affirmation of the pre-eminence of the Land of Israel over all other Jewish centres of the Diaspora lasted until the middle of the fourth century CE. It was in the wake of the crushing of the Jewish Revolt against Emperor Gallus (351–2) and the consequent destruction of many Jewish communities in Palestine, that Patriarch Hillel II agreed to limit his functions as *Nassi* in connection with the proclamation of the New Moon, and published the *Sod ha-Ibbur* ('The Secret of the Intercalation') and *Keviuta de-Yarha* ('Fixing of the New Moon') in 358, on which the Jewish calendar is based.

31. Elazar, op. cit.

32. Bar Kokhba (died 135 CE). Acting as a single commander-in-chief in the revolt in Judaea against Rome (132–5 CE), he united the nation under his leadership. Moreover, the Messianic hopes which were cherished by the nation centred around him. Even in later generations, despite the disappointment engendered by the defeat, Bar Kokhba's image persisted as the embodiment of Messianic hopes. See Maimonides, *Yad Melakhim* ('Hand of Kings'), 11:3.

33. Isaiah 2:4: '. . . and they shall beat their swords into plowshares, and their spears into pruning hooks: nation shall not lift up sword against nation, neither shall they learn war any more.'

34. Gershom Scholem, *Les Grands Courants de la Mystique Juive* ('The Main Trends in Jewish Mysticism', Paris, 1950), chapters 1 and 2 (pp. 13–93) and 'Toward an Understanding of the Messianic Idea in Judaism', in his *The Messianic Idea in Judaism* (New York, 1974), pp. 1–36.

35. Gershom Scholem, *Sabbatai Sevi, The Mystical Messiah, 1626–1676* (New Jersey, 1973).

36. See Gershom Scholem's article, 'Jacob Frank and the Frankists', in the *Encyclopedia Judaica*, vol. 7, pp. 55–72; also the article 'The Crypto-Jewish Sect of the Dönmeh (Sabbaticans) in Turkey', in his book, *The Messianic Idea in Judaism*, pp. 142–66. (It is interesting to note that even today many people in Turkey believe that Kemal Ataturk was a member of this sect.)

37. Some preliminary work has been carried out in this direction at Haifa University. It consists of the collection of passages with obvious political significance from the Bible and the Babylonian Talmud, followed by their classification according to standard political questions. Although it is still too early to draw any definite conclusions, this simple preliminary work has clearly underlined the strong consistency of many political ideas in

biblical and talmudic literature. One should also note that no comprehensive study has ever been made of Jewish diplomacy, although extensive records exist of diplomatic activities carried out by Jewish leaders on behalf of their own countries (communities) or of Gentile states.

38. A notable contribution in this field has been made by Professor Daniel Elazar, through the Institute for Judaism and Contemporary Thought at Bar Ilan University, and the International Seminar held yearly on Jewish Political Problems. See forthcoming volume of Proceedings, *The Jewish Political Tradition and its Contemporary Uses*, Ohio State University Press.

39. For instance, Rabbi Ovadia Sforno (1475–1550), who saw the covenants with the Patriarchs as a prelude to the time when Jews would be 'a large enough people to make a political group'; *Kavvanot Hatorah* ('The Intentions of the Law'), Introduction; and relevant biblical passages: Genesis 8:17; 17:1–4; 19:22; 28:13–15; Exodus 3:17; Numbers 33:50–6; 31:1-15.

40. Joshua 24:12–13; 2 Samuel 7:12–13; 1 Chronicles 17:14.

41. 2 Kings 17:21–3.

42. Ibid. 23:1–3.

43. Nehemiah 10:1–3.

44. Elazar, op. cit., pp. 210–15.

45. 2 Chronicles 34:31–3.

46. Nehemiah 9:38: 'And because of all this we make a sure *covenant*, and write *it*, and our princes, Levites, and priests, seal *into it*.'

47. Jerusalem Talmud, *Rosh Hashanah*, ch. 1; *Halakhah* 3, p. 57b.

48. Babylonian Talmud, *Baba Metzia*, p. 59b.

49. Benedetto de Spinosa, *Trattato Teologico Politico* ('Theological-Political Treatise', Italian translation by C. Sarchi), 1875, p. 303.

50. Daniel Elazar, 'Jewish Political Studies as a Field of Inquiry' in *Jewish Social Studies*, July 1974, vol. 36, nos. 3–4, pp. 220–33.

51. Leviticus 19:17.

52. Ezekiel 33:8.

53. Babylonian Talmud, *Sanhedrin*, p. 101b.

54. Babylonian Talmud, *Sanhedrin*, p. 17a.

55. 2 Samuel 12:1–14.

56. Babylonian Talmud, *Sanhedrin*, p. 42a.

57. Elazar, 'Government, Biblical and Second Temple Periods', loc. cit., p. 214.

58. Arthur Koestler, *Promise and Fulfilment, Palestine 1917–1949* (London, 1949).

59. Yehezkel Kaufmann, *Toledot ha-Emunah ha-Yisre'elit* ('History of the Jewish Faith'), 8 vols. (Tel Aviv, 1937–57).

60. *Mishnah Zera'im*, tractate *Kilayim*. The tractate deals with the six kinds of mixed species: mixed seeds, grating trees, seeds in one vineyard,

cross-breeding of animals, the pulling or leading of cattle, and the mixing of fibres in the same cloth (*sha'atnez*—'mixed cloths').

61. A very interesting attempt to analyse the significance of the dietary laws according to structuralist theories has been made by Jean Soler in 'Sémiotique de la Nourriture dans la Bible' ('Semiology of Food in the Bible') in *Annales*, July–Aug. 1973, no. 4.

62. Yishayahn Leibowitz, 'The World and the Jews', in *Forum*, Spring 1959, vol. 4, pp. 83–90.

63. In an unpublished lecture to youth leaders at Shoresh on 12 December 1975 the late Hebrew University historian, H. H. Ben-Sasson, drew an interesting parallel between modern Israeli emancipation from Judaism and a Freudian collective type of revolt against a nation's own origins. The Jews, who are members of one of the oldest civilizations, are being forced by the world—and yielding to this pressure—to become modern barbarians and to divest themselves of their culture in order to imitate others, rather than doing it the other way around.

Chapter 5 The Crisis of the Israeli Élites

1. Marion J. Levy, Jr., *Modernization and the Structure of Societies: A Setting for International Affairs* (Princeton, 1966), pp. 72, 357–8.

2. 'A Note on the Trickle Effect', *Public Opinion Quarterly*, 1954, vol. 18, no. 3, pp. 314–21.

3. Mordecai Roshwald, 'Democratic Elitism: The Ideological Framework of Jewish Community', *Judaism: A Quarterly Journal of Jewish Life and Thought*, Winter 1978, vol. 27, no. 1, p. 50.

4. Talmudic commentary on Deuteronomy, chapters 31–3, relates, 'And God said, the religions of those is fire, and if the Torah had not been given to Israel, no tongue or nation could stand before them' (Tractate *Be'etza*, 25b).

5. Babylonian Talmud, tractate *Shevuot*, p. 5a.

6. The close interweaving of family ties and political power is a permanent feature of Jewish-Israeli politics within as well as without the religious establishment. Moreover, such family clusters can be found in the banking system, the army, the diplomatic corps, the academic community, the kibbutz movement, and the Jewish organizations. It is interesting to note that such clusters of power have hardly ever been the target for charges of nepotism, contrary to charges brought against other non-family clusters of power in the political parties, the bureaucracies, etc. See Yuval Elizur and Eliahu Salpeter, *Who Rules Israel?* (New York, 1973).

7. The Alliance Israélite Universelle was the organization of Jewish solidarity established in the wake of the Damascus blood libel in 1844, mainly under the impulse of French Jewry, which at the time undertook an active role of protection over Christian communities in the Ottoman Empire.

8. *Kest* literally means chest-of-drawers, or a large box containing the bride's dowry.

9. C. Wright Mills, *The Power Elite* (New York, 1957).

10. Milovan Djilas, *The New Class; An Analysis of the Communist System* (London, 1958).

11. S. N. Eisenstadt, *Israel Society* (New York, 1967).

12. Carl Deutsch, *The Nerves of Government* (New York, 1969).

13. Yuval Elizur and Eliahu Salpeter, op. cit.

14. Alex Weingrad and Michael Gurewitch, 'Who are the Israeli Elites?', *The Jewish Journal of Sociology*, June 1977, vol. XIX, no. 1, pp. 67–77. See also their article 'Who Knows Whom? Acquaintanceship and Contacts in the Israeli National Elite', *Human Relations*, March 1978, vol. 31, no. 3, pp. 195–214.

15. Aaron Antonovsky and Alan Arian, *Hopes and Fears of Israelis* (Jerusalem, 1972), pp. 69, 109 ff.

16. Eisenstadt, op. cit., p. 388.

17. Zvi Yaron, *Mishnato shel Ha-Rav Kook* ('Rabbi Kook's Doctrine', Jerusalem, 1974).

18. Ehud Ben-Ezer (ed.), *Unease in Zion* (Jerusalem, 1974), p. 72.

19. Harold Fish, *The Zionist Revolution: A New Perspective* (London, 1978), p. 107.

20. Shlomo Avineri, interview in Ben-Ezer, op. cit., p. 52.

21. Ibid., p. 59.

22. Haim Hazaz, 'Hadrasha' ('The Lecture', a story in Hebrew), in *Selected Stories* (Tel Aviv, 1954), pp. 184–202.

23. M. Y. Berdichevsky, 'Shinui Arachim' ('A Change of Values'), in *Collected Articles of Micha Yosef Bin-Gorion (Berdichevsky)* (Tel Aviv, 1952), p. 53.

24. See the author's *Israel: A Society in Transition* (London, 1971), p. 35.

25. This is the position held by the extreme orthodox group known as 'Neturei Carta' ('Defenders of the City').

26. S. Y. Agnon, *Shira* (Jerusalem, 1971), p. 342 (in Hebrew).

27. Published in 1888 in *Ha-Melitz*, the influential Hebrew journal in Odessa.

28. *Hibbat Zion* ('Love of Zion') was a Jewish national movement active in nineteenth-century Eastern Europe, and to a more limited extent in Western Europe and the United States. This mass movement flourished before Herzl and the First Zionist Congress of 1897 and constituted Herzl's main popular support. The movement arose at a time when adherents of the Enlightenment had been disillusioned in their hopes of obtaining equal rights and in their belief in assimilation. The main aims of the movement, which stemmed from its national aspirations, were the revival of the Jewish people and the return to the Land of Israel.

29. *B'nei Moshe* ('Sons of Moses'), 1889–97: a secret order founded in Russia to ensure personal dedication to the spiritual renaissance of the Jewish people and the return to the Land of Israel. The leader and the spiritual guide of the order was Ahad Ha'Am. In his article 'Derekh ha-

Hayyim' ('Way of Life', 1889) and its supplements, Aḥad Ha'Am outlined the aim of the association: the return of the Jews to their historic homeland, but with prior spiritual preparation.

30. Ben-Ezer, op. cit., p. 68.

31. Speech at the Jerusalem Ideological Conference, 1958, published in *Forum for the Problems of Zionism, Jewry and the State of Israel*, Spring 1959, no. 4, p. 121.

32. Ibid., pp. 84–5.

33. Rabbi Adin Steinsaltz, in a symposium which took place in Geneva in 1972 on the attitudes of Jewish intellectuals and college youth to Jewish life.

Chapter 6 The Crisis of Institutionalization

1. Robert K. Merton, *Social Theory and Social Structure: Towards the Codification of Theory and Research* (Glencoe, Ill., 1949), pp. 43 ff.

2. The consciousness of this loss was equally underlined by the stress which the Israeli establishment and the Israeli public laid on the fact that the field commander of the Entebbe raid, Colonel Jonathan Natanyahu, who was killed in that operation, was a rare combination of able soldier, scientist, and Jewish scholar, reared in a family belonging to the traditional cultural Jewish élite.

3. Robert K. Merton and Robert A. Nisbet (eds.), *Contemporary Social Problems: An Introduction to the Sociology of Deviant Behavior and Social Disorganization* (New York, 1961).

4. Jacob Katz, *Tradition and Crisis* (New York, 1971), pp. 9–10. Peter Gay's *The Enlightenment—An Interpretation: The Rise of Modern Paganism* (New York, 1966) is most provocative for the understanding of the moral, cultural, and ideological dilemma which Zionist and Israeli élites inherited from the Enlightenment. They experienced—at least in part and of course in totally different times and environment—the philosophers' 'dialectic struggle for autonomy as an attempt to assimilate two pasts they had inherited' (p. xi). In the case of the philosophers, the pasts were Christian and pagan, and in the case of the Jews, Western and Jewish traditions. Gay points out that 'in the first half of the 18th century, the leading Philosophes had been deists and had used the vocabulary of natural Law; in the second half, the leaders were atheists and used the vocabulary of religion' (p. 18). In the case of the Zionists, most of the socialists were people brought up in a religious tradition who adopted a vocabulary of natural law and of Western ideology. Later even the atheists returned to a vocabulary of Jewish traditionalism to justify a situation of national utility. In any case, both the Enlightenment people and the Socialist Zionists shared 'the peculiar pleasure of being able to kill one's father and choose another' (p. 38).

5. S. N. Eisenstadt, 'Patterns of Contemporary Jewish Identity', Lecture in a symposium in Jerusalem, 11–14 January 1977.

6. Another relevant thought by Montesquieu is that 'the Romans had made a religion for the state while the others had made the state for

religion'. It has remained a permanent problem for Zionism to build a modern state which would fit the requirements of religion or at least of tradition, which remained the primary legitimacy of the Jewish national state itself.

7. I have used the summary of Gordis's article originally published in *Congress Monthly*, translated into French by Y. Levy and published by *Information Juive* (Nov. 1976), a publication of the World Jewish Congress in France.

8. Lecture to the Student Association (March 1976), at the Hebrew University, Jerusalem.

9. Talmud, tractate *Berakhot* 28.

10. According to Jewish tradition the First Temple was destroyed not as a consequence of the Assyrian conquest (553 BCE) but because of internal violence, idolatry, and adultery; the Second Temple not by the Romans (70 CE) but because of the groundless hatred of Jews toward Jews.

11. Louis I. Rabinowitz, 'How Jewish is the Jewish State?', *Conservative Judaism*, Winter 1972, XXVI, no. 2, p. 113.

12. Ibid.

13. Ibid.

14. Eisenstadt quotes Professor Baron's observation that contemporary donations by Jews to Israeli funds are the nearest thing to the old custom of taking offerings to the Temple.

15. 'Israel in Danger', *Jerusalem Post*, Independence Day Supplement, 20 April 1977.

16. Arieh 'Lova' Eliav, *Sulam Yisrael ve-Shivro* ('Israel's Ladder and its Collapse'; in Hebrew, Tel Aviv, 1977). Eliav is a former Secretary-General of the Labour Party, a pioneer in the field of agricultural development, and former Deputy Minister in charge of Immigration and Social Integration.

17. Yosef Goell, 'Kibbutz Jubilee', *Jerusalem Post*, 20 April 1977.

18. Ibid.

19. Daniel Bell, *The Cultural Contradictions of Capitalism* (New York, 1975).

20. 'L'État de Guerre: Répercussions sur l'Individu et la Société', in *La Conscience Juive Face à la Guerre* (Paris, 1976), pp. 127–41.

21. Jean-Paul Sartre, *Anti-Semite and Jew* (New York, 1965).

Chapter 7 The Crises of Identity and Legitimacy

1. *Congress Weekly*, 5 Jan. 1959, vol. 26, no. 1.

2. Baruch Litvin, *Jewish Identity, Modern Responsa and Opinions on the Registration of Children of Mixed Marriages, David Ben-Gurion's Queries to Leaders of World Jewry*, a documentary compilation edited by Sidney B. Hoenig (New York–Jerusalem, 5730/1970).

3. The two major cases brought before Israeli courts and which deeply shocked public opinion were those of Mrs Rina Eitany and Brother Daniel. Mrs Eitany, a town councillor for Upper Nazareth, daughter of a Jewish father and a non-Jewish mother and a victim of Nazi persecution, was married in Israel but was later refused recognition of her status as a Jewess by the Ministry of the Interior in 1964. Brother Daniel, a Polish Jew who conducted himself in exemplary manner under Nazi occupation in Europe but was converted to Christianity and became a Carmelite monk in Haifa, was denied the right to become an Israeli citizen under the Law of the Return, although both his parents were Jewish.

4. Litvin, op. cit., p. 5.

5. Ibid., pp. 142, 147.

6. Ibid., p. 230.

7. Ibid., p. 113.

8. Ibid., p. 172.

9. Gershon Weiler, *Theokratia Yehudit* ('Jewish Theocracy', Tel Aviv, 1976).

10. A. B. Yehoshua, *Ha-Me'ahev* ('The Lover', Tel Aviv, 1977).

11. Bruno Zevi, 'Ebraismo e Concezione Spazio-Temporale Nell'Arte', *La Rassegna Mensile di Israel* (Rome), June 1974, p. 118.

12. S. N. Eisenstadt, lecture in a symposium in Jerusalem, 11–14 January 1977.

13. Zevi, op. cit.

14. Joseph Stalin, *Marxism and the National and Cultural Question* (Moscow, 1940), pp. 5–6.

15. Rupert Emerson, *From Empire to Nation, The Rise to Self-Assertion of Asian and African Peoples* (Cambridge, Mass., 1960), p. 12.

16. Quoted by Emerson, op. cit., p. 378.

17. Ibid., p. 384.

18. Lord Acton, 'Nationality', in *The History of Freedom and Other Essays* (London, 1909), p. 292.

19. Stated by the delegation of Kenyatta to the Conference of African Unity in Addis Ababa in 1963: Obafemi Owolowo, *Path to Nigerian Freedom*, pp. 47–8, as quoted by Emerson, op. cit., p. 129.

20. On Garvey see, *inter alia*, Edmund David Cronon, *Black Moses, the History of Marcus Garvey and the Universal Negro Improvement* (U. of Wisconsin Press, 1955), especially pp. 199–200, in which Garvey's strange anti-Jewish prejudice is correctly assessed.

21. Annie Kriegel, 'Jews and Blacks', I and II, *The Jerusalem Quarterly*, Spring 1978, no. 1, pp. 22–33, and Summer 1978, no. 8, pp. 94–109.

22. Ernest Renan, 'Qu'est-ce-qu'une nation?', *Discours et Conférences* (Paris, 1887), p. 286.

23. Federico Chabod, *L'Idea di Nazione* (Bari, 1972), p. 17.

24. H. Baruch, in Litvin, op. cit., p. 176.

25. Henri Atlan, 'Bouc émissaire?', *Le Monde*, 19 Oct. 1974.

26. The Bandung Resolution '. . . declared its support of the rights of the Arab people of Palestine and called for the implementation of the United Nations resolution on Palestine and of the peaceful settlement of the Palestine Question' (*New York Times*, 24 April 1955).

27. The UNESCO decision of 22 November 1974 barred Israel from all regional activities of the organization. It passed by a vote of 48–33 with 31 abstentions, but after world-wide intellectual protest it was reversed.

28. Erich Fromm, *Escape from Freedom* (New York, 1941).

29. R. D. Laing, *The Divided Self: An Existential Study in Sanity and Madness* (London, 1969).

30. Erik H. Erikson, *Young Man Luther* (New York, 1962).

31. Ernst Gellner, *Legitimation of Belief* (Cambridge, Mass., 1974), p. 12.

32. Haim Hazaz is one of the best interpreters of the mood of Israeli society on the eve of Independence.

33. From a conversation between the author and the novelist Amos Oz.

34. Frantz Fanon, *Black Skin, White Mask* (London, 1968), p. 232.

35. Ibid., pp. 216–22.

36. S. Y. Agnon, *T'mol Shilshom* (Tel Aviv, 1959), p. 386, and *Shira* (Jerusalem, 1971), p. 342 (in Hebrew).

37. Renate Zahar, *Frantz Fanon: Colonization and Alienation*, translated from German by Willfried F. Feuser (New York, 1974), pp. 93–4.

38. Frantz Fanon, *The Wretched of the Earth* (New York, 1968), p. 251.

39. Dr David W. Weiss, lecture on 11 May 1976 to the Convention of the American Friends of Boys' Town, Jerusalem. Dr Weiss is the Director of the Lautenberg Centre for General and Tumour Immunology at the Hebrew University of Jerusalem.

Chapter 8 Postscript

1. The number of Knesset Members of oriental origin is the same (8) in both the *Likud* and the *Ma'arah*, but the *Likud* has 45 MKs as against the *Ma'arah's* 32. The discrepancy is greater in the lower echelons of institutions such as town councils, workers' organizations, etc.

2. E. Etzioni-Halevi and R. Shapira, *Political Culture in Israel* (New York, 1977), pp. 88–134.

3. A. Arian (ed.), *The Election in Israel—1969* (Jerusalem, 1972), pp. 264 ff.

4. A. Arian (ed.), *The Election in Israel—1973* (Jerusalem, 1975), pp. 299 ff.

5. E. Cohen, 'The Black Panthers and Israeli Society', *Jewish Journal of Sociology*, 1972, no. 14, pp. 93–109. M. Iris and A. Shama, 'Black Panthers: The Movement', *Society*, 1972, no. 9, pp. 37–44. E. Etzioni-Halevi, 'Patterns of Conflict Generation and Conflict Absorption: The Cases of Israeli Labor and Ethnic Conflicts', *Journal of Conflict Resolution*, 1975,

no. 19, pp. 286–309. See also irregular publications at *PASHIS*, 'Ha-Panterim Ha-Shehorim—Israel ha-Sheni'ah' (The Black Panthers—The Second Israel), P.O.B. 6676, Jerusalem.

6. The circumstances of the break-up of the 'historic alliance' between the Socialists and the National Religious Party are curious and symbolic. Although tension had been mounting steadily between the two, mainly due to the support by the NRP of the *Gush Emunim* Movement, the straw which broke the camel's back was the arrival in Israel of the first F-15 fighter planes from the USA. The occasion was to have been a festive one, and meant to strengthen the image of Rabin's government in the approaching general elections. But the two planes, which were due to reach Israel on a Friday morning, were delayed for several hours for technical reasons, with the result that they arrived after the beginning of the Sabbath (which starts an hour before sunset on Friday), thus desecrating the day of rest. In the ensuing squabbles, the NRP voted against the Government and technically brought it down, although in fact they were obliged by Israeli constitutional law to continue to serve in the Caretaker Government because of the approaching elections.

7. The rise and fall of DASH is typical of many Israeli political organizations. DASH started with the unification of an existing protest movement —SHINUI ('Change')—and the new party set up by Professor Yigael Yadin, plus the subsequent adhesion of two former Knesset Members from the Ben-Gurionist break-away group. In the 1976 elections DASH won 15 seats in the Knesset; in August 1978 it split up into three groups: one retained the name DASH (with 7 MKs); the second went back to the old name, SHINUI (5 MKs), and the third consisted of 2 MKs who joined with SHINUI one month later. Ovadia Shapiro, 'Il recente mutamento nel Sistemo Partitico Israeliano', *Rivista Italiana di Scienze Politiche*, Dec. 1978, no. 3, pp. 415–38.

8. Such as the *Agudat Israel*, with 3 MKs, which was not allowed by the religious authorities who control the Party to enter the government, but supports it in exchange for important parliamentary functions—such as the chairmanship of the powerful Commission for Economic Affairs—and for very substantial promises in the fields most important to the orthodox voters, such as the military service of girls, the revision of the liberal abortion legislation, etc. See G. S. Schiff, *Tradition and Politics: The Religious Politics of Israel*, Ph.D. thesis, Faculty of Political Science, Columbia University, 1973; Yael Yishai, 'Party Factionalism and Foreign Policy: Demand and Response', *The Jerusalem Journal of International Relations*, 1974, vol. 3, no. 1, pp. 53–71; E. Don-Yehiya, *Cooperation and Conflict between Political Camps—The Religious Camp and the Labour Movement and the Education Crisis in Israel*, Ph.D. thesis, The Hebrew University, 1977 (in Hebrew, 3 volumes).

9. The *Haganah* ('Defence') was the underground military organization of the *Yishuv* in Palestine from 1920 to 1948, controlled by the Labour Establishment since its establishment at the *Histadrut* (General Federation of Labour) in 1920, and later by the Executive of the Jewish Agency. It collaborated with the British Mandatory authorities in fighting the dissident organizations, *Ezel* and *Lehi*, in 1944, when these two military groups began attacking the British, in opposition to the established policy

of the Jewish Agency. *Ezel* (*Irgun Z'va'i Le'umi*, 'National Military Organization') was founded in Jerusalem in 1931 by a group of *Haganah* commanders who left the *Haganah* in protest against its defensive character. Joining forces with a clandestine armed group of *Betar*—the Revisionist Party's youth movement—it formed a parallel, more activist organization under various commanders, the last of whom was Menahem Begin, from 1943 until its disbandment in 1948. *Palmah*, the initials of *P'lugot Mahatz* ('Assault Companies'), was established by the *Haganah* in 1941 with volunteers recruited mainly from Collective and Co-operative Settlements. From among its commanders came some of the top military and political leadership of the State—people such as Yigal Allon, Moshe Dayan, Yitzhak Rabin, and Haim Bar-Lev. *Lehi* (*Lohamei Herut Israel*, 'Fighters for the Freedom of Israel', or 'Stern Gang', after its founder, Abraham Stern), broke away from *Ezel* in 1940 as a result of the truce declared by the latter organization with the British during the Second World War. Responsible for many terrorist operations, it was disbanded after the killing of Count Bernadotte, the UN Mediator, in Jerusalem in May 1948.

10. Y. Harkabi, *Arab Strategies and Israel's Response* (New York, 1977).

11. Among the most outspoken is Professor Y. Leibowitz, the Hebrew University professor and talmudic scholar, who believes that the peace treaty is worthless because it allows Israel to maintain her control over 1.5 million Arabs, thus prolonging a situation which will be disastrous for the moral fibre of the State (*Ha'aretz*, 30 March 1979).

12. For the first time in the history of the State, the Government has been accused by the Supreme Court of 'contempt for the judiciary' in connection with the expropriation of Beduin lands in the Negev.

13. Eric Rouleau, 'La Paix Américaine', *Le Monde*, 25, 26, 27 March 1979, partially confirmed by Mr Begin's interview with the *Jerusalem Post*, 11 April 1979.

14. Yigal Elam, 'Gush Emunim—A False Messianism', *The Jerusalem Quarterly*, Fall 1976, no. 1, pp. 60-9.

15. For a study of religious and secular school systems in Israel see C. A. Adler, 'Social Stratification and Education in Israel', *Comparative Education Review*, Feb. 1974, vol. 18, no. 1, pp. 10-23.

Index

Abraham, 18, 26, 68
Africa, Africans, comparisons with, 1, 8-9, 13, 23, 34-49, 52, 59, 117, 134; links with, 34, 35-6, 162; history, 38, 41; 'Negritude', 48-50
Alexander Yannai, 19
Alexandria, 20
Alienation, 22, 33, 132; cultural, 7-9, 16; see also Self-colonization
Aloni, Mrs S., 111
America (USA), 84, 118, 139, 153; black uprisings in, 35; equality, 72; slavery, 107; Jews of, 114, 132
Anti-Semitism, 7-8, 20, 42, 43, 53, 90, 130, 159; positive response to, 29
Arabia, statelets in, 58
Arabs, 6, 14, 30, 31, 32, 92, 101, 121, 127, 132, 140, 144, 147, 151, 153; refugees, 15; conception of Jews, 44, 136; Palestinian, 46, 151, 152; Israeli, 112, 124, 152
Aristocracy, popular, 77, 78, 80, 82, 119; rabbinical, 83; see also Élites
Aristotle, 107
Army, 92, 101, 144; exemption of girls, 114, 152
Arts, Jews and the, 128
Ashkenazim, 25, 81, 148, 155
Assimilation, 5, 7, 8-9, 10, 18, 23, 69; collective, 42, 72; of élites, 88, 108; clash with tradition, 13, 21, 26, 118; clash with nationalism, 129
Auschwitz, 74, 139, 140, 144
Austro-Hungarian Empire, 132
Autonomy, 59, 143, 167

Babylon, 5, 58; see also Exile
Bandung Conference, 136, 175
Bar Kokhba, 63, 168
Bauer, Bruno, 52
Begin, Menahem, 48, 146, 148-53, 177; personality of, 149-50
Ben Gamla, Joshua, 80
Ben-Gurion, D., 30, 31, 39, 46, 90, 91, 92, 111, 149, 150; Judaism of, 89, 93-5, 109, 147; on Jewish identity, 123-5
ben Hananiah, Joshua, 108
ben Ḥisdai, Daniel, 81
Ben-Meir, Yehuda, 154
Ben Shetah, Simon, 80
ben Zakkai, Johanan, 61
Ben-Zvi, President, 39
Bible, as basis of state, 94-5
Black Panthers, 148
Blyden, E. W., 34-5
B'nei Moshe, 93
Bourghiba, President, 151
British Mandatory Government, 117
Bureaucracy, 75, 100-1, 148; a suspension of, 116

Canaan, 17, 65, 69, 76
China, 143
Christian Church, 79
Christianity, Christians, 20, 52, 61, 72, 95, 125, 131; conversion to, 21, 23, 24, 130
Colonization, 41-2, 141; cultural, 73, 77, 90, 96; see also Self-colonization
Communism, Communists, 6, 14, 108, 121, 132, 136, 147
Conversion, religious, 130-1
Covenant, 65, 67-8, 77, 103, 106, 126, 127, 138-9, 145
Crime, 47, 99, 164-5